S·E·A L·E·G·S

HITCH-HIKING THE
IRISH COAST ALONE

Rosita Boland

N E W
ISLAND
BOOKS
Dublin

Sea Legs
is first published by
New Island Books
2 Brookside,
Dundrum Road,
Dublin14.

© Rosita Boland, 1992

ISBN 1 874597 00 6

A catalogue record for this book is available from the
British Library.

New Island Books receives financial support from
The Arts Council (An Chomhairle Ealaíon),Dublin, Ireland

Front Cover Photograph by Derek Speirs.
Back Cover Photograph by John Westley.
Cover design by Rapid Productions.
Printed in Ireland by Colour Books Ltd., Baldoyle.

Rosita Boland was born in Ennis, Co. Clare in 1965.
Her first collection of poems, *Muscle Creek*, was
published by Raven Arts Press in 1991.

For everyone who gave me lifts

CONTENTS

ACKNOWLEDGEMENTS

Acknowledgements and thanks are due to the following: all those friends and relations who welcomed my unexpected arrivals during the journey so warmly; Bernard and Mary Loughlin and staff at the Tyrone Guthrie Centre at Annaghmakerrig, where the opening chapters of this book were written; Caitríona and Tony, and Máine and Gerry, who provided me with space to work; Dermot Bolger for his encouragement; Colm Tóibín who read the manuscript; my friends on both sides of the Irish Sea, who supported me throughout, especially Elaine, Laura and Arthur.

Extract from *Coasting*, by Jonathan Raban, by permission from Picador Books.

Extracts from *Ireland: The Rough Guide*, by Sean Doran, Margaret Greenwood and Hildi Hawkins, by permission from Rough Guides Ltd.

Extracts from Tim Robinson's Burren map and *Connemara: Introduction and Gazetteer* by permission from Folding Landscapes.

Home is always the hardest place to get into sharp focus. If only it could be *encompassed*... by a slow, stopping, circular voyage.

Jonathan Raban,
Coasting

The life of the Wandering Jew agreed with me so well that, although I was wet to the skin nearly every day, and often much fatigued, I grew visibly fairer and fatter. If I met with good or ill, I knew how to enjoy the one without becoming desperate over the other. Allowing myself to be guided by a good Providence, I put the whole of the cares and anxieties of this world aside. My whole baggage slung over my shoulder, or in my pocket, I walked, I ran, I searched; nature appeared to me in many guises, new scenes occupied my attention and gave me instruction.

Le Chevalier de La Tocnayne,
A Frenchman's Walk Through Ireland, 1796-97

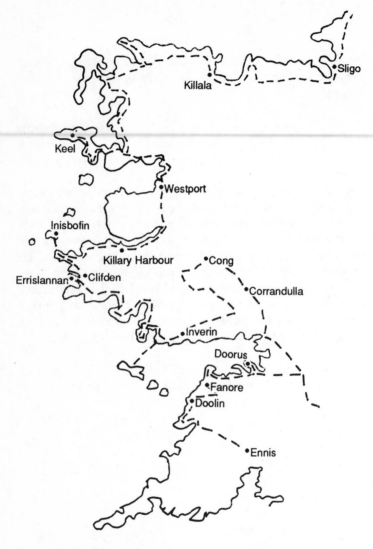

• overnights
--- route followed

Map 1   Ennis to Sligo

INTRODUCTION

Travelling across the Nullarbor in southern Australia in 1988, a distance of almost three thousand kilometres through a landscape of nothingness, I couldn't help being reminded of the Burren in County Clare, at the other side of the world.

Both the Nullarbor Plain and the Burren are karst landscapes; areas of porous rock with an intricate, unmapped landscape of caves on their undersides. The Nullarbor – bad Latin for "no trees" – has a very thin layer of soil on its surface. The Burren – anglicised Irish for "rocky place" – is bare limestone. General Ludlow, one of Cromwell's men, had said of the Burren that "It has not enough timber to hang a man, water enough to drown a man, or earth enough to bury him"; an enduring description of the Burren and one which is equally applicable to the Nullarbor Plain.

It took three days to cross the Nullarbor from Adelaide to Coolgardie. From Ceduna on, the names of settlements on the map turned out to be nothing more than solitary roadhouses, where water was so scarce that the showers were saltwater; buildings that were only there to service the people who drove the road.

The landscape was utterly flat and utterly empty. The blue sky was a huge unbroken bowl. There was no horizon. The road was arrow-straight; the longest stretch of straight road in the world.

"It's God's own country," the man at Nullarbor Roadhouse quipped. "Only God would want to live here."

When he found out where I was from, he leaned his arms on the counter of the bar and sang, *It's a Long, Long Way from Clare to Here* .

I spent a year travelling around Australia; hitch-hiking, camping, hostelling, taking odd-jobs here and there. In a year, I only lightly skimmed the continent, but I came back to Europe with an enduring restlessness and a new curiosity about Ireland. Except I didn't come back to Ireland; I spent the next two years working in London.

A favourite haunt of mine in London was Stanford's Travel Bookshop on Long Acre. Stanford's claim to stock the largest selection of maps, guide-books and books of travel literature in the world. To cross the threshold of Stanford's was to feel that the entire world was within my grasp, if only I had the time and money to explore it.

I bought several maps and books in Stanford's. One day, I bought a Michelin map of Ireland, for the simple reason that I didn't have a map of Ireland.

The Michelin map is the most detailed map available of Ireland. When I spread it out on the floor, I was amazed by the dense network of tiny roads and villages that cobwebbed out from the major roads and towns. Ireland suddenly looked enormous. It swelled with the names of places unknown to me. I found myself wanting to go back and explore my own country.

It was several months before I was able to set out. With some qualms, I gave up my job and shipped my possessions over to Ireland, telling myself that I could always come back to England again. I now had time, but I'd never had much money. I decided to stay in youth hostels and the occasional bed and breakfast. It wouldn't be luxurious accommodation by any stretch of the imagination, but it meant that I would be able to travel for three months.

Hitch-hiking seemed to be the obvious way to travel on such a budget, and a sensible way to travel in winter, when public transport to rural areas is greatly reduced.

The *Concise Oxford Dictionary* has a rather disapproving definition of hitch-hiking. *Hitch-hike: travel, obtain (transport), by begging free rides in passing motor vehicles.* It makes it sound slightly seedy and desperate. But I knew that hitching was an accepted form of local transport in Ireland, especially among young people. A hitch-hiker doesn't pay money for a lift, but he repays in kind by talking to the driver, who will often pick someone up precisely for that reason. And a hitch-hiker can choose whether or not to get into a car, just as a driver can decide whether or not to stop.

So I didn't think of myself as begging free rides, but as using a form of transport which was unscheduled and unreliable, and also sociable, informative, and rewarding.

Previous to this journey, I had already done a lot of hitching alone. Provided a hitch-hiker exercises some basic commonsense, Ireland remains one of the safest countries in the world to hitch around. During the years I had hitched, I discovered that the temporary intimacy within the cocoon of a car which is going five, ten, fifteen miles down the road, loosens tongues; reveals scraps of lives in both driver and hitch-hiker. As a way of meeting local people and casting a plumb-line down into the area through which you are travelling, hitching is unbeatable.

The thing that took me longest to decide on was the route. I kept staring at the map until it occured to me that I was looking at a ready-made route. Here was a serrated, rambling coastline, tongued by bays and loughs and harbours. I would simply drift along by the sea and let myself be washed up on a new shore each night.

And my starting-point would be the town of Ennis in my birthplace of Clare. It had been a long, long way from the Nullarbor Plain back to Clare.

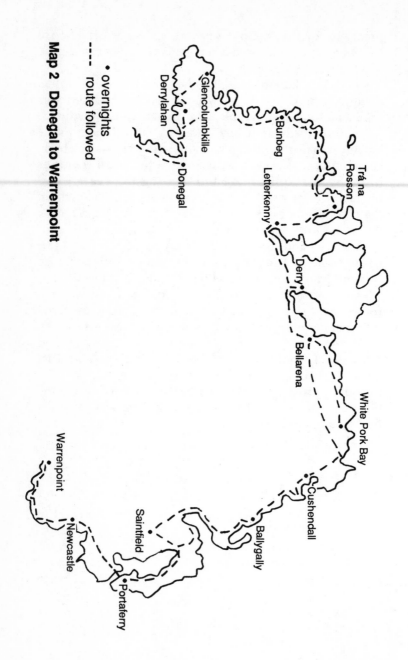

● overnights
---- route followed

Map 2 Donegal to Warrenpoint

Trá na
Rosson
Bunbeg
Glencolumbkille
Derrylahan
Donegal
Letterkenny
Derry
Bellarena
White Pork Bay
Cushendall
Ballygally
Saintfield
Warrenpoint
Newcastle
Portaferry

12

1
THE NAME'S TOM
Ennis to Aranmore

Before leaving London, I had done some shopping in the
Outdoor and Adventure Shop in Covent Garden, a place
as heady with possibilities as Stanford's. The Outdoor and
Adventure Shop was crammed with tents, sleeping bags,
camping gas, rucksacks, waterproofs and boots. For an
afternoon, I wandered among the rails, choosing the things
I thought I'd need on my journey. I tried on Gore-Tex
jackets and shouldered several rucksacks, glancing around
at the other people in the shop who were also busy with
trying on jackets and rucksacks and boots. *I'm going to hitch
around Ireland*, I felt like shouting out loud. *Where are your
jackets and rucksacks going?*

In the end, I bought a pillarbox-red Gore-Tex jacket and
trousers and a 45 litre capacity Berghaus rucksack in
purple and jade. I also bought a waterproof map-case,
thermal gloves, a survival blanket and a block of Kendal
Mint Cake.

Back in Ireland, I rummaged through some of the boxes
and took out my compass, Swiss Army knife, torch, pocket
radio, sheetbag, and walking boots. To these, I added
leggings, a pair of jeans, two jerseys, a couple of t-shirts,
several pairs of woollen socks, a scarf and a spare pair of
shoes. I completed the packing with my washbag, a towel,
a tin of Nik-Wax (waterproofing wax for leather), a
thermos flask, *The Rough Guide To Ireland*, various maps
and my diary.

I set out from Ennis on the first of October; a bleak and
wet Monday morning, passing by the gaunt cathedral as
the bells were striking eleven.

Browsing in a secondhand bookshop the previous year,
I'd come across a great green tome with the title *Lovely*

Britain stamped in gold across its spine. It proved to be a Victorian volume full of grainy photographs and a rambling text.

The text filled a tremendous number of pages about lovely locations in lovely Britain, but the author's vocabulary and powers of description were limited so that each place I read about sounded exactly like the last.

There was a section on Ireland at the back of the book and in this, there was a short piece about Ennis. Here, *Lovely Britain* departed from its predictable ramblings and stated quite firmly that "the streets of Ennis were full of queer, foreign-looking folk." I read it again. Ennis? Full of queer, foreign-looking folk?

The anonymous author gave no reason or explanation for this description, which jolted me into a fascinated respect for a town I had grown up in, yet taken very little notice of. This Victorian author hinted at having discovered something romantic and mysterious in his wanderings through the narrow streets of the town with which I was so familiar.

The Ennis streets were shiny with rain that October morning. I remembered what I'd read in *Lovely Britain*. The only folk abroad were a handful of middle-aged women, pushing shopping bags on wheels along the pavements of O'Connell St. I peered searchingly at their faces until I caught a glance of my reflection in a shop window and discovered that if anyone was foreign-looking that morning in Ennis, it was me, rucksack on pillarbox-red back.

I passed the O'Connell Monument, went down Abbey St, crossed the Club Bridge, walked beyond the outskirts of the town to the start of the Lahinch Road, and started hitching. Having chosen a coastal route, I wanted to be within sight of the sea as soon as possible.

The third car that I hitched, stopped. It was a white Panda van, going as far as Fountain Cross, a few miles away. The driver was a cheery Dutchman named Jan, with startlingly blue eyes, who was over in Ireland for three months to work for the Forestry Commission. He asked me where I was going. "Around Ireland!" I said extravagantly, and he laughed.

"Where did you start from?"

"Ennis."

"So this is your first lift?" He sounded the horn, laughed again, and wished me luck as I clambered out at the Cross.

A silent farmer brought me to Ennistymon, one of those old Irish villages whose shopfronts missed out on the age of neon and plastic, and which now finds itself remarkable, simply for continuing to look the way it has looked for generations.

Two men were discussing the price of cattle outside O'Dwyer's Medical Hall. Inside the windows, neatly piled on glass shelves, were bottles of Old Spice and Blue Stratos aftershave and containers of talcum powder. And among the aftershave and the talcum powder and the perfume, were packets of Endorat poison ("Kills Rats Fast"), tins of Argo louse powder and Panacur worm drench for cattle. *I'll have a bottle of Blue Stratos and a tin of louse powder, please.*

The rain was continuing to drizzle down. I crossed the road to Blake's pub and shop; a low, dark-blue building which I had to step down into. Once inside, I felt aware that my bright red and purple and jade, which had seemed perfectly ordinary colours on the rails of the Outdoor and Adventure shop, were intrusive in this dim interior.

The shop side of Blake's sold mostly tinned food and rows of sweets. On the bar side, there were just two beers on draught; Guinness and the now seldom-seen Double Diamond.

A woman with grey hair scraped back in a bun, pulled me a glass of Guinness with quick movements, her lips tightly set. I asked how old the pub was.

"Three generations!" she said, folded her arms into her body and watched me drink.

It was lunchtime, and some of the local schoolchildren cascaded in to buy sweets. Mrs Blake eyed them. "Aha! You cut your hair!" she shot out to a girl with shoulder-length fair hair, who looked embarrassed and muttered she had.

Mrs Blake cackled good humouredly. She fairly cackled at the idiocy of it all. "And you after going to all that trouble to grow it!"

I looked at the old framed posters for Seven Up and

O'Connell's Ale, and drank up, feeling that Mrs Blake would not be at all above giving me a friendly clip behind the ear and telling me to hurry up with my Guinness. But when she heard I was a Clarewoman, she warmed visibly.

"And are ye travelling around alone?"

I said yes. "Hitching," I offered.

She pondered this. Then, after a silence, she slapped the counter, gave me a wicked grin and hooted, "And would ye take a lift from a Motor-Cycle then?"

I was certain that she had an image in her mind at that moment of me, heading off to the Cliffs of Moher on the back of a motor bike, all flapping reds and purples and jade and screeching like a crazed bird of paradise. The two of us laughed raucously at each other, until I gathered the soggy feathers about me, and went on my way.

The red Mini that brought me to the Cliffs of Moher was possessed. Something bounced and rattled and growled at the back of the car with all the fury of a trapped beast. The driver and I conducted our conversation in yells, to make ourselves heard over the beast.

At Lahinch, the sea moodily slapped itself in and out of the deserted beach. The curtains were all drawn in the holiday houses; deckchairs and sun-lounges hibernated in conservatories and front porches.

Around Liscannor, the careful, neat walls of Liscannor flag began to line the road. Many of the local houses were roofed with these flat, thin flags, and looked as old and tightly knit as clochans, but when I asked if people still used the stone as slates, the driver was derisive.

"They're only fit for sheds," he shouted grumpily, "they let in the damp."

At the Cliffs of Moher, the fog and mist had surged in from the Atlantic and hugged the coastline into invisibility. There were two coaches in the carpark, and scores of disappointed Americans wandering about.

"What a darned nuisance! No photographs of the Cliffs of Mo-hair!" The man's voice boomed out of the mist and I heard the faint reply of a female voice: "You can always buy postcards."

I knew from experience once the fog came down in this

16

area, that it would stay for the rest of the day, and thought it ironic that on the first day of my journey, the landscape seemed to be hiding from me. Not quite fifty yards away, I knew that the land sliced away suddenly and that the Atlantic battered away at the base of the cliff walls, over six hundred feet deep. The fog muffled the sound of the sea, but could not shut it out entirely. There was a distant rhythmic roar as the unseen waves lunged themselves tirelessly at the rock beneath.

In the Visitor Centre, an American man was paying for a book at the counter, and repeating, with a mixture of incredulity and bafflement, "Lis-doon *what?*"

"Lisdoonvarna," the assistant replied.

"God!" he said. "God! What a name! Lis-doon –" and then he got stuck again, or else overcome by the sound of it.

"Lisdoonvarna," the assistant repeated icily, and turned to the next customer.

"God!" He shook his head slowly. "God!"

I had coffee and wrote postcards, hoping that it would have stopped raining by the time I re-emerged.

It hadn't. It was bucketing down. I sheltered in the porch and pulled on the Gore-Tex trousers. The Doolin road was fast turning into a river. After I had been walking for only a short time, my right shoe began to squelch. I had buried my boots at the bottom of the rucksack, not thinking they'd be needed so soon. Minutes later, symmetry was restored. Squelch, squelch, left shoe. I slooshed along, passing fields full of cows, who munched on peacefully, unperturbed by the downpour.

No cars. I continued walking, as the land began to melt away on all sides under the mist and rain, and even the placid cows drifted from sight. Every now and then, I stopped to listen for cars, my torch casting a weird yellow light through the gloaming.

At last, I heard the approaching purr of an engine, put my arm out, and waited. A station wagon lurched uneasily into view, and came to a cautious halt, the torchlight swallowed up in its fog-lamps. Four upturned faces stared out at me through the rain. One of the occupants rolled down a window.

17

"You want to go somewhere?" he inquired politely.

They were a party of four: three Parisian men and a Spanish woman, all understandably dismayed by the wall of weather between themselves and the scenery. Was there anywhere, *anywhere* interesting they could go that was out of the rain, they asked. I arranged myself in a grateful, sodden heap on the back seat, and told them yes, Doolin was a great place for the music, and was in fact where *I* wanted to go – so I could direct them there.

Doolin is a tiny village, perched above an inlet of the sea, at the edge of the Burren, and has what's called "the name". It's a placename synonymous with traditional Irish music, and although there are scores of places in Ireland where you can find good music, Doolin is the one everyone seems to know. It makes the boast that there is music to be found in either O'Connor's or McGann's (or both) every night of the year. There are three independent hostels at Doolin, a sure yardstick for the volume of people constantly passing through.

Three hostels there were, but in that rain, I simply made a dash for the one closest to the car. The independent Doolin Hostel, a large modern house across the way from O'Connor's, had opened that year, and everything was new and still fresh-looking. It was almost too clean and bare, holding nothing of the resonance of the many people who had already stayed there. But it was warm.

The Independent Hostels of Ireland are, as the name suggests, independently owned and often family run. All hostels provide dormitories. They are also supposed to offer fully-equipped kitchens and hot showers. The overnight charge in an independent hostel in 1990, regardless of age, ranged from £3.50 to £4.50. The Independent Hostel Owners of Ireland started up in 1983, with 16 hostels. By 1990, there were 76 hostels listed in my "I.H.O. Hostels Guide".

An Óige, the official Irish Youth Hostel Association, was founded in 1931 and in some of their hostels, there is a feeling of the hostel being run in an outdated manner. However, being such an established network, An Óige has acquired some lovely buildings over the years, which are

18

now used as hostels; a shooting lodge at Cahir, a castle in Kilkenny, a former coastguard station in Donegal. Although they can be annoyingly regimented, with allocations of chores and even a "lights out" rule in some hostels, An Óige hostels are almost always unfailingly clean.

The overnight charge in 1990 in an An Óige hostel for someone over eighteen, depending on whether the hostel was Grade A, B, or C, was £4.90, £4.30 and £3.50 respectively for the peak months between June and September, with a reduction of 50p for the remaining months.

The two biggest advantages that the independent hostels have over An Óige are that there are no curfews and they are open all day. In some of the An Óige hostels, you are required to leave the building between ten in the morning and five in the afternoon – hard luck if it's raining and the hostel is miles from anywhere else – and there are strict curfews. Some An Óige hostels do provide day-rooms where you can shelter, store your rucksack and make hot drinks; but by no means all.

I signed into the Doolin Hostel, and set about drying my shoes and investigating the rucksack – which had a liner inside – to see if it had leaked. It hadn't, and I felt very relieved. If it could survive being out that long in such a downpour, then I thought it would stay watertight all the journey long.

In the evening, I headed for O'Connor's, which had a somewhat urban facade with a lot of black, and gold lettering. O'Connor's was about half full. Two men were warbling a drunken version of *My Darling Girl from Clare*, slapping each other on the back at the end of every line.

A thin woman from Ohio, at the start of a three-week trip to Ireland, was sitting up at the counter, valiantly trying to eat her way through an enormous plate of Irish Stew. "The rain is standing on the roads!" she exclaimed, jabbing her fork uneasily into a piece of meat.

As the place started to fill up, four men came to sit around the table where I had ensconced myself with a newspaper. Ivan, Chris, Dave and Andy were members of a caving group in Yorkshire and had been coming over to Doolin for years, to go pot-holing and caving. Doolin is located on the fringe of the Burren; a hundred square miles of porous limestone rock, which the rainwater has fissured with grykes, swallow-holes, passages and caves.

They asked me if I would like to come caving with them the next day. This invitation, however, was based on the hope that the rain would have abated by then and that the caves would not be flooded. There was a pint glass on the seat beside me, catching the raindrops from a leak which plinked steadily into it all evening. At intervals, I watched the glass, and could see the opportunity for exploring the underside of this limestone county slowly dissolving.

All this time, music had been emanating rather self-consciously from the opposite side of the pub; fiddle, accordion, concertina and spoons. One of the Parisians came over and gripped my hand. He waved an arm in the direction of the musicians. "Thank you for all this music," he said fervently.

More cavers arrived.

"We can only ever afford to come over for the one week," Dave said, "because of the price of drink over here."

We arranged that I should walk up to their cottage the next morning, when they would have decided whether or not the conditions were suitable for caving. I said my goodbyes, braved the rain once more, and fell into bed at the hostel where I was asleep almost at once.

The rain was still sluicing down the following morning. I opened the Velux window and looked out. The mist had temporarily risen, and beyond a tangle of houses with shining roofs, beyond the zig-zag of a river which cut through shockingly green fields, was the grey and sour-looking sea.

After breakfast, I wrote up my diary in the common room, where the electric lights were still burning. The entry was obsessed with rain.

The land is drowning. Rivers pour themselves over the side of the cliffs. The roads are running. The sea is a dull grey, foam-

flecked: the white-edged waves remake themselves furiously. If I could put a giant ear to the limestone, I would hear the water roaring in the caves. The sky bellies low, breathing rain. The grass is sodden. Only very close by is there colour – after a hundred yards or so, everything fades to grey; is swathed in mist.

At midday, I walked down towards the quay, where the cavers had their cottage. They were in the middle of eating breakfast and staring mournfully out the window.

"It's the show cave for us today," Chris said. "We're going to be guided around a cave instead of doing our own thing." He was referring to Aillwee Cave, which opened to the public in 1976. He speared a sausage gloomily. "D'you want to come?"

But I didn't. I hated the thought of being driven somewhere and then being driven back again. I had decided that any exploring I did would, as much as possible, all be part of a continual, onward journey. It was difficult enough to feel like a traveller when I was in my own country, but a day-trip to the Aillwee Caves would have made it impossible. So I left them clearing up the breakfast things and looking at maps, and went for a walk.

Doolin pier projects about twenty feet into the sea. It looks strangely out of place among the limestone pavements and the huge slabs of stone hurled about the foreshore. Pools of stone in the grass looked like ice – the bits of ice on a lawn that are last to melt. Crab Island, with it's ruined coastguard hut, crouched in the bay and I could just make out the thin grey line of the Aran Islands on the horizon.

I remembered General Ludlow's saying about the Burren; "not enough water to drown a man..." Perhaps he had never been there when the rain was falling and the turloughs were full; those temporary lakes which fill up with water overnight when the underground caverns become flooded, and which vanish just as suddenly as they appeared, leaving behind a rich green sward. You could have drowned an army in the Burren on that sodden October day, which was all water and stone, and all the

21

subtle, complex colours of water and stone – greys and sheen and black and silver.

I had with me Tim Robinson's extraordinary map of the Burren. Tim Robinson's work is difficult to describe. He has made maps of the Aran Islands, the Burren and Connemara. He has compiled a detailed gazetteer to Connemara. He has written a classic book, *Stones of Aran: Pilgrimage*, about a journey around the edge of Árainn – a contemplative journey through a palimpsest of geology, history, folklore, legend, topography and the evolution of placenames. *Stones of Aran* is indefinable, because it is so many things. It is a Chinese box of a book.

The maps are the visual equivalent of this book. They are in monotone; a variety of delicate, tiny pen-strokes depicting the different types of relief. The more I looked at the Burren map, the more layers it began to yield up – historical, mythological, religious, geological. I began to read it like a book.

deserted village. mass rock. Tobar Cholmáin arched stone for headache cure. site of ancient racecourse. carved hand. Caves of the Wild Horses. hoofmarks of Glas Ghaibneach cow. site of MacClancy law school, 16th C. Blessed Bush and marks of St. Brigid's knees. track of Sir Donat's Road. legend of the Hag of Loch Rasca. 12th C parish ch. and market stone. mark of saint's fingers in stone. cottage built by Land League. Cnocán an Chrochaire Armada men hanged 1588.

I went in search of earth forts, or raths, which were marked on the map by the symbol of a circle within a circle. Four of them nestled close together on the map; located on the curve of the Aille River, to the west of Roadford, just north of Doolin. *Cnocán an Chrochaire*, where the Spanish sailors had been hanged, swelled gently and innocuously a few fields away.

It is not always easy to decide if you have actually come across a rath or not, since they are often well grassed over and can look like part of the natural landscape of small hills. I was probably walking right over them, but I couldn't tell for certain exactly where they were. Several

22

cows left off grazing and stared curiously at my efforts with map and compass in the soggy fields.

Before diverting into the fields, I had passed McGann's pub on the road. It was still pouring and I decided the best exploration I could do for the rest of the day would be to find the interior of a dry space.

The only other customers in McGann's were three men, propped against the counter. I ordered coffee and set about pulling off the waterproof trousers. Roars of laughter from the counter. I unzipped the jacket. The men clutched their fists to their chests and swayed backwards and forwards.

One of them lurched over and gave me a beery leer. "And will ye be taking off many more of yer clothes, now?" he spluttered, while the other two chortled into their pints and slapped their thighs.

"You wear these things in the rain," I said coldly. "It's not raining in here, is it?"

It was no good. They weren't going to let their source of entertainment dissipate so easily.

Beery Leer poked me in the ribs. "And do ye often take off yer trousers like that?"

I ignored them, took the Robinson map out of the case and spread it on the counter.

One of the Thigh Slappers sidled up and squinted over my shoulder. "A map!" he cried. "Sure, would ye ever come over here and this man will read the map for ye. He's a grand man for the maps."

Beery Leer, the grand man for the maps, gave me a toothy grin, adjusted his tweed cap and ordered another Smithwicks. The second Thigh Slapper guffawed loudly and spat into a corner.

I drank my coffee and continued to ignore them. They drifted back into their original huddle and stared sullenly over at me, muttering "trousers" and "stranger" at intervals.

By evening, Doolin was fairly gurgling with water. The drying-room in the hostel was a steamy tangle of wet jeans, socks, jerseys, boots, shoes, jackets, hats, gloves and scarves. It had now been raining for two days and a night.

23

I let my boots dry off and then rubbed them with the waterproofing wax.

Above the bar in O'Connor's, where I had a bony mackerel salad for supper, was a wooden panel with the letters 'WYBMADIITY' carved on it. In between removing the pin-like bones from my mouth, I asked the barman what it meant.

"Would-you-buy-me-a-drink-if-I-told-you?" he rattled off.

There was a new crowd of musicians by the fire. The barman told me they were a group of friends from Dublin, who came down at the same time every year. One of the group, a man about fifty, stood up to great encouragement and did a series of impressions of The Way Men Sing In Public. There was the Man Who Pretends To Be Shy, yet goes on and on. There was the Tone-Deaf Man who bellows out *Danny Boy* on emotional occasions. There was the Man Who Fancies His Chances at the Feis. There was the Drunken Man called on to sing at a wedding.

This man did all the impressions with such wicked brilliance that several people in the pub shifted uncomfortably in their seats. When he had finished, there were no further volunteers to continue the singing. People stared at their pints, or looked into their pockets, or engaged in sudden bursts of conversation with each other.

Someone tapped me on the shoulder.

"You mind if we join you?"

Damien and Denis were in their late twenties, and halfway through a two-week holiday. They had come over from Strasbourg and were travelling around in a hired car.

"But we have had trouble with it," Damien said.

"What sort of trouble?"

It emerged that when they had been driving up the narrow, winding road off the Ring of Kerry that leads from Castle Cove to Staigue Fort, a man with a donkey and cart had backed out of a field without looking and dented the side of their car. They had got out and tried to get his name and address for insurance purposes.

"But he spoke only Gaelic," Damien said. "So we ended up paying for it ourselves."

Clever bastard, I thought, half-amused and half-angry at

24

the quickness of the man with the donkey and cart. I had spent two months in a cottage close to Staigue Fort, and I knew most of the people who lived on that particular road. They could all probably speak Irish as well as anyone, but there wasn't a soul who couldn't also speak English.

Denis was already rather drunk. "I work in the air-force," he told me. "But what I really want to do is paint. That is all I have ever really wanted to do."

Damien smiled. I had the impression that he had heard this many times before.

"And what do you really want to do?" I asked him.

He shrugged his shoulders and smiled again. "Me, I am happy the way I am."

They wanted to know if I had ever been to France.

"Only to Paris."

"But you must come to Strasbourg for the New Year!" they said, and now it was my turn to shrug my shoulders and smile.

There was a rectangle of bright blue in the Velux window next morning. I packed up and headed out past Roadford, to the turnoff for Lisdoonvarna, where I got a lift from four young Scotsmen.

The annual matchmaking festival in September, a month-long series of events, from the raucous (mud-wrestling), to the prim (tea dances), had just panted out of town for another year.

Lisdoonvarna was like a ghost town. I noticed an unusually large number of public benches. Perhaps for courting couples? But they were all empty that morning. There was nobody on the streets. The hotels and guesthouses looked absolutely still; not a flicker of a curtain, or a smell of a fried breakfast anywhere.

I walked down the hill towards the Spa Wells, and passed the Imperial Hotel.

The Matchmaker's Bar was tacked onto the end of the Imperial Hotel. Painted on the front wall of the bar was a vicious-looking cupid and the words: "Matches may be made in Heaven but most couples meet at The Matchmaker's Bar". No wonder the cupid looked so angry. The Matchmaker's Bar was doing him out of a job.

25

The bar window was all etched glass. At the bottom half of the window, several naked couples snogged in what was a brave attempt at the missionary position. Above them were representations of the local sights; high crosses and the Poulnabrone Dolmen. Perhaps the idea was to meet in The Matchmaker's Bar and then go screwing your way around the sights. The whole thing was breathtakingly tasteless, and yet, was etched out with a considerable measure of craftsmanship.

The Spa Wells Health Centre consisted of a square, white-painted Victorian-looking Bath House and Pump Room. There was also a modern restaurant, which overlooked a noisy river. The sulphur spring, for which the Spa is famous, was discovered in the early 1700s by a man who was hunting across the Gowlauns.

I wandered into the Bath House, with the vague idea of taking a bath. Sulphur baths were £6.00. But you could have an "Electric Sulphur", whatever that was, for £7.00. "Infra-Red Treatment with Massage to Affected Areas" would set you back £9.00. I found myself wondering what your areas would have to be affected with to cause you to have infra-red treatment.

At the reception desk, a woman in a housecoat looked me up and down and told me that sulphur baths were really only of benefit to those with rheumatism or arthritis. I hesitated. The Bath House was a lovely old building and I wanted to see more of it. But I'd had my share of being soaked in the last couple of days, so I thanked her and went over to look at the Pump Room.

The Pump Room was a high, empty place, with a tall Victorian metal turnstile in front of one of the closed doors. The sulphur well itself was in a corner of the room; glassed over and illuminated. It looked like a vertical porthole, dropping down far beneath the surface of the floor. On a semicircular counter, there was an enormous copper boiler, in which the sulphur water bubbled. You could buy a glass of water (hot or cold) for 30p. The only other things to buy in this cavernous space were postcards and a selection of cookbooks.

Another woman in a housecoat stood behind the

26

counter. She looked completely bored. There couldn't have been too much trade in glasses of sulphur water and postcards that morning. There was one other customer; an old man who called me over to sample his glass of sulphur water. As soon as I lifted the glass and got a whiff of the contents, I was most heartily glad that I had not gone for a bath in what smelt to me like centuries-old eggs.

He chuckled. "And to think I paid money for that!"

Five miles from Lisdoonvarna is the Burren Heritage Centre at Kilfenora; an audio-visual exhibition which explains some of the history and geology of the area. I thought that it would be a useful thing to see before going deeper into the Burren, and so turned left when coming out of the Spa Wells, and started hitching towards Kilfenora.

An Antrim man stopped for me. He was down on holiday for a week and had caught the back-end of the Festival. "It's gone queer quiet since the weekend. There was great dancing all last week. Every sort of dancing you could imagine – waltzing, foxtrot, jiving. I did the whole lot of them. You missed a great time."

When he heard I'd been born in Ennis, he said, "I went with a girl from Ennis once who worked in a confectioners. But I can't remember her name." He frowned, and went silent. I looked out the window. "Josephine! It was Josephine her name was." He looked very pleased. "It's not far more into Ennis. Do you know, but I think I'll go and try to look her up!"

He dropped me at Kilfenora, waved, and continued on in the direction of Ennis, in search of the confectioners and Josephine.

Under a grey sky, Kilfenora looked drab. The houses were painted pale shades of emptiness; beige, lightest blue, grey, white. The only splashes of colour were the huge blue gentian flowers painted on the walls of the Burren Heritage Centre, which was closed for lunch.

I took out the Robinson map again. In a field to the north-west of the village were printed the mysterious words "carved hand". *Carved hand*. Carved out of what?

I set off down the road in search of this carved hand.

The scraps of blue sky had long since vanished and the

rain began to spit down again. I followed the road out of the village and found what appeared to be the right field. If it was the right field, then according to the map, the hand should be in a corner. I left my rucksack in the ditch and began to pace the walls, peering carefully at the stones and kicking the long grass at the base of the walls.

But there was no sign of anything that resembled a carving of any sort, let alone a hand. Twice, I paced the walls. Nothing.

The three houses near the field were all either closed up, or the owners were out. At the fourth house I tried, a white bungalow, a suspicious-looking woman opened the door a couple of inches.

Carved hand? Yes, she'd heard of it all right. Where was it? Oh, in that field over there somewhere, and she waved a hand in the direction of the field where I had just been searching. Had she ever seen it herself?

"Oh no. I have no interest in that sort of thing at all." With that, she shut the door in my face.

I tried looking one more time, but the mysterious words retained their mystery. The rain was belting down again. I collected my rucksack from the ditch and walked back into the village. The Burren Heritage Centre was still closed for lunch. *Sod this*, I thought, and started heading back towards the coast.

The quickest way there was back through Lisdoonvarna. A white Peugeot, which was more red than white since it had rusted so much, stopped to give me a lift. The driver, a middle-aged man, banged straw off the passenger seat and grinned widely at me from a mouth of broken teeth.

"Ah, ye have no need of that yoke!" he said, when I sat in and reached for the seat-belt.

I was to come across this over and over again. Very few of the people whom I got lifts from in the Republic wore a seat-belt. Across the border, it was completely the opposite. Usually, I had scarcely shut the door when I was asked if I would mind putting the belt on, as there was a £50.00 on-the-spot fine for not wearing one. In the Republic, it is also illegal not to wear a seat-belt in the front of a car. But most people ignored this with baffling consistency. They either took great offence or were extremely puzzled when I insisted on wearing a seat-belt. They said things like: "First time that's ever been used!" "I didn't know that even worked." "But you're safe in my car." "There are never any guards on this bit of road."

In my position, as a hitch-hiker, it would have been tactless to point out that, apart from being the law to wear a seat-belt, it was a proven safety measure in a car. I grew desperate. The last thing I wanted to do was insult anyone and thus sour the conversation just as I'd got into their car, when they'd been decent enough to give me a lift. But I was absolutely determined to wear a belt. So I invented a cousin who had been tragically killed in a car crash as a teenager because he wasn't wearing a belt.

"So I just put it on out of habit now," I explained.

Usually there was a gruff, respectful silence for the mythical dead cousin and no more would be said about my offensive wearing of a seat-belt.

Broken Teeth was a Doolin man, who kept telling me that I should go there to visit it.

"But I've just been there."

"You weren't!"

"I was."

"When?"

"Last night. And the night before that."

"You weren't! Was it in O'Connor's you were?"

"It was."

"I missed you so. It was McGann's I was in."

He too told me that I'd missed all the crack at Lisdoonvarna. I asked him if he'd ever taken the baths.

"Them things?" he said scornfully. "They're for the tourists."

He looked sideways at me and cleared his throat. "I have a grand bed and breakfast in Doolin, and I need a good woman to help me run it. Would you be interested?"

I couldn't help laughing out loud. "But didn't you meet anyone at the Festival?" I asked eventually. "Isn't that what it's supposed to be all about?"

He snorted. "Strangers! Sure they come here from the four corners of Ireland; from the Six Counties and all. You

29

wouldn't know what sort of woman you'd be getting at all. You'd only have them a couple of months and they'd be gone off on you again."

He spat this out so bitterly that I wondered if he was speaking from experience. Being a woman from his own county apparently was the necessary requirement; hence the invitation to me.

We arrived in Lisdoonvarna.

"Where are you heading tonight?"

"Ballyvaughan," I said, before I realised what he was getting at.

"Ballyvaughan," he said, puzzled. "I didn't think there was a hostel there."

I was sure I'd seen one mentioned in the *Rough Guide* .

"Ballyvaughan," he repeated. "I was thinking of heading over that way myself tonight. I'll probably see you in the pub later on. Goodbye to you now, but I'll be seeing you later on."

"Goodbye to you," I said firmly.

I fell into step with a man who had just come from the Spa Wells. He had neatly combed white hair and carried a coat over his arm. He told me that he was from Enniscrone and had come to Lisdoonvarna for the baths.

"I have arthritis," he said. "But divil a bit of good the baths are doing me. Still, you have to go somewhere on your holidays and I suppose Lisdoonvarna is as good a place as anywhere."

"Do you enjoy the baths?"

He looked surprised. "I don't think about whether I enjoy them or not. And to tell you the truth, the smell is a bit unpleasant."

In the town square, I met the man who had offered me the sulphur drink. He asked me if I knew where he could get a taxi. "How long have you been here?" he said. "I've been here since Monday and it's gone fierce quiet." He wandered off gloomily in search of transport out of the ghost town.

The man with the grand bed and breakfast in Doolin had been right. There wasn't a hostel at Ballyvaughan. But there was one at Fanore, and so I decided to spend the night there instead.

Mike and Tom gave me a lift outside Lisdoonvarna. Mike was from Doonbeg and Tom from Ennis. We talked about that evening's National Lottery prize, which was one and a half million pounds.

"Did you ever win anything?" I asked.

Mike laughed. "No, I did not." Then he considered. "But we were reconstructing a house once in Kilrush and when we put in a new fireplace, didn't I find a box with twenty golden guineas in it!"

The landscape began to swell with stone. The further north we drove, the more it seemed as if stone was growing in the fields: a living crop. In the afternoon light, the distant terraces of stone looked white. The bushes were warped by the wind; the roadside walls were knitted together by lichen and brambles. Lines of stone walls carefully marked out fields of stone.

Tom stopped the car outside the Bridge Hostel, which was a couple of hundred yards off the main road. "Would you like to come out with us tonight? We're going into the Spa Hotel in Lisdoon. We could collect you and bring you back."

No shortage of offers for the evening's entertainment. But I declined this one also.

Fanore seemed to be a scattered townland, rather than a village cluster. It was going on for evening meal time and I wondered where I could buy some food. There were half a dozen Germans and an American clattering about the kitchen. Hadn't I known? The nearest shop was two miles away. And it was having a half day. Five minutes before, I had been mildly interested in the idea of eating. Now, knowing there was no way of buying any food, I was ravenous. There was the heel of a two-day-old cake of brown bread in my rucksack. This was dinner.

I wrote my diary in the tiny common-room cum dining room and tried to ignore my fellow hostellers tucking into their various meals.

When they'd finished eating, the bearded American, whose name was Chris, took out a guitar and began playing.

"*Where is the truth I look for...*" he sang softly, with his eyes closed. "*Yesterday's gone and it won't come back. Life's for real, if you know what I mean...*"

He opened his eyes and saw me looking at him. "You've been writing in that notebook for ages," he said. "Wouldn't you like to join in the chorus of this song?" Hunger had made me bad-tempered. I growled a rude refusal.

"Life's a challenging dream, life's a balancing scheme. Yesterday's gone and it won't come back. Life's for real, if you know what I mean," he crooned on. The Germans had got the words and now joined in loudly.

I finished writing and went to bed. The women's dormitory was directly over the common room. I pulled the pillow over my head and tried to drown out the balancing scheme of life, which was seeping up through the cracks in the wooden floorboards.

By eight o'clock the next morning, I was walking eastwards, further down the road on which the hostel was located, and which had the extraordinary name of "Khyber Pass". I was looking for the deserted village which was marked on the Robinson map as being a couple of miles from Fanore.

Apart from the Caher River, which the road followed, there was complete silence. There were no trees for the wind to pass through. There were no cars; nobody else abroad. I listened carefully, but could not hear even a single bird.

I walked the couple of miles, then turned left, and followed a green road which ziz-zagged steeply up a hill. The tangle of stone walls became more knotted. In the grey early morning, the strangest atmosphere was exhuding from this landscape of stone. Suddenly, as I climbed higher, I could see a cluster of stone gables huddled together.

In the accompanying text to Tim Robinson's Burren map are these words:

Let me mention here what is omitted, for this map is haunted by the hundreds of roofless cottages I have crossed off my copies of the old survey. Famine half emptied the land in the last century; the hazel scrub has spread and swallowed up whole villages as well as great stone cahers.

32

In the early 1840s, the population of Ireland was 8,200,000. By 1911, through a combination of famine deaths and emigration, it had dropped to 4,400,000. The Famine was the single biggest cause of the drop in population, and the most heartbreaking. It is generally accepted that over one million people died through famine and disease in the years 1846-51. And after the famine, people emigrated in their millions.

I had always known about the Famine. It is a part of history which every Irish child absorbs early on at school; something that I could never remember not knowing. And for years, I had listened wryly as the politicians continued to promise that emigration and unemployment were the two things they would tackle when in government. My own friends were now scattered through America and England. For years, I had seen ruined cottages all over Ireland. But the full impact of the Famine and of the centuries of emigration had never slammed into my awareness as keenly as it did that day, wandering about the deserted village in the Burren. It was a cruel irony that I was hungry that morning.

In John Mitchel's *Jail Journal*, he recalls a journey to the west of Ireland in the summer of 1847. Two years previously, at a "little cluster of seven or eight cabins" he had "supped sumptuously on potatoes and salt with the decent man who lives there, and the black-eyed woman and five small children". On his return to this place, he finds that:

We are here in the midst of those thousand Golgoths that border our island with a ring of death from Cork Harbour all round to Lough Foyle. Yet we go forward, with sick hearts and swimming eyes, to examine the Place of Skulls nearer. There is a horrible silence; grass grows before the doors; we fear to look into any door, but our footfalls rouse two lean dogs, that run from us with doleful howling, and we know by the felon-gleam in their wolfish eyes how they lived after their masters died. We walk amidst the houses of the dead, and out at the other side of the cluster, and there is not one where we dare to enter. We stop before the threshold of our host of two years ago, and put our head, with eyes shut, inside the door-jamb, and say with shaking voice, "God save all here!" No answer – ghastly silence, and a mouldly stench, as from the mouth of burial-vaults…

We know the whole story – the father was on a 'public work' and earned the sixth part of what would have maintained his family, which was not always paid him; but still it kept them alive for three months, and so instead of dying in December they died in March. And the agonies of those three months who can tell?

Walking to the village, I had passed four, possibly five occupied houses on the road. In the village, I counted the remains of eleven cottages. Here was the visual equivalent of all the statistics and figures given to me in history lessons.

And the agonies of those three months who can tell?

Something shivered through me as I walked around the village. This was where people from my own county had lived and either died in or been forced to desert. I saw the village and believed. I felt among ghosts, but it was not a frightening experience; it was more an awareness of a sadness seeping quietly out of that village space.

I was struck by how close together the cottages were. In that huge, empty place, some of the cottages were literally an armspan away from each other. Even in that small village, there was a variety of building styles. Some of the buildings were so small that I wondered if they had been shelters for animals. Other cottages were one-roomed or had two small rooms. The largest one had three rooms and an enormous fireplace. The gable wall was unusually high, and when I looked, I could see that over the lintel in the middle of the cottage, had been another doorway, which had been filled in at some stage. This cottage would also have had an upstairs, probably reached by ladder.

On average, the walls were two feet thick and were still remarkably intact. There was something between the stones in the walls which looked like modern-day cement. I took a piece in my fingers and it crumbled easily into white dust. I was later told that this would have been mud, or cowdung, mixed with small stones and used as a type of binding paste.

The lintel over the doorway in one of the cottages had fallen to the ground; still a whole, unbroken piece of stone. When I set my foot against it and pushed, it didn't stir. Moss and ferns were gathering it back to the ground. Perhaps, when the last stones of all the ruined cottages crumble down, the Burren will have the least traces of a missing people. Being a place of stone, the Burren will absorb into itself those stones which people lifted out of it to build their cottages with.

Back at the hostel, I picked up my rucksack and walked out towards Black Head. It was raining again. Had it always rained this much, I wondered, or had I just never noticed it before?

A silent couple brought me to Ballyvaughan. Coming into the village, I saw two men with pitchforks gathering seaweed on the shore. When asked, the driver told me that some people still used it as fertilizer on their land.

By this time, I was extremely hungry. There were several places to eat at, but most of them seemed to be shut. The Ballyvaughan Inn was shut. So was Greene's. Claire's Restaurant was only doing evening meals. I pushed the door of Hyland's Hotel, and it opened. A turf fire burned in the lounge. I sank into a chair, read the newspaper, and ate my fill.

When I'd finished, I went into the Mace supermarket and stocked up. I didn't intend arriving at any more hostels in the future without having basic supplies and the makings of at least one good meal. And in case it was Sunday or I'd been walking all day, unable to get a lift and make it to a shop, I added emergency rations of McDonnell's Wholegrain Mixed Veg Savoury Rice to the Kendal Mint Cake in the flotsam and jetsam jumble at the bottom of my rucksack.

For the next couple of hours, I walked, passing Bell Harbour, and heading out towards Kinvarra. It was peaceful, walking in the light rain, with the fields of stone on one side and the small, calm waves of the sea on the other.

There were upturned curraghs on the quay at Kinvarra, and swans gliding sedately in the water by Dunguaire

Castle. The post office had geraniums in the window. Many of the shops and pubs were painted vivid colours.

I stopped outside C. St George's. It was painted lime-green and orange; a glorious clot of colour in a grey day. A bell jangled loudly when I pushed the door in. There was a long wooden counter, running the length of the room, and a warren of shelves on the back wall.

The counter was bare of pumps and glasses.

There were no goods stacked among the shelves.

A white-haired woman limped awkwardly out of a back room and stood smiling at me. The bell was still jangling. It echoed off the bare surfaces and then melted away. I felt I'd blundered onto a half-built stage set and disturbed the designers.

"Oh, you'll not get a drink here," she laughed. "My little shop has been closed for five years."

Mary Ann St George had sold basic groceries, "tea, butter, sugar" from the shelves, and served up drinks from the counter.

"People would come and do their shopping, and then have a drink before they went on their way. But then the supermarket came and I wasn't able to compete with it. And I lost my health. So with one thing and another, I decided to close it down. And it was a *pity*. Because people liked coming here, and I liked being here, and hearing all the bits of chat." She smiled again. "You're five years too late for a drink, dear."

As I said goodbye and walked out onto the street again, I wondered why she had left the door open. Perhaps she continued to leave the door open and the bell in its old place, so that she might still get the odd person passing through, and go out to tell them what her grocery and bar had been like before the supermarket came and she lost her health.

At the other end of the street was Tully's Select Bar. At the front of the shop, there were the same warren of wooden shelves as in C. St George's. But these shelves were neatly piled with all sorts of groceries – tins and jars, bottles and packets.

At the back of the shop was a bar, with a high, curved

counter and mirror-backed shelves in whose reflection the glasses twinkled brightly and the amber liquid in the whiskey bottles glowed. In a corner of the bar was an old-fashioned black telephone of the "press button B" type. The wooden chairs looked like they had come out of a ballroom of romance. An old stove fire radiated heat. It could have been twenty years earlier.

Mrs Kathleen Tully poured Guinness and sang *The Mountains of Mourne* to the three men and myself at the counter, and to the two schoolgirls who drank minerals and sat waiting to be collected.

Was I travelling around? Wasn't that grand! So where had I been in the last few days?

"Doolin," she said thoughtfully. "And are there still people there at this time of year?"

I explained about the music being a permanent attraction.

Without a trace of irony, she settled a glass on the counter of her splendid old bar and said: "Isn't it great that they have something going for them when it's such a *backward* sort of place."

It was beginning to get dark. I reluctantly left Tully's Select Bar and hitched to Doorus peninsula, and then walked the last mile or so over a causeway to the hostel.

The hostel, now owned by An Óige, was once the home of Count Floribund de Basterot. Lady Gregory, Edward Martyn and W.B. Yeats had all been among his house guests. In 1898, when Lady Gregory was staying at Doorus House, Edward Martyn, who lived nearby at Tullira Castle, brought Yeats over to lunch. At that time, neither Lady Gregory nor Yeats knew each other very well. In Lady Gregory's *Our Irish Theatre*, she writes: "They had lunch with us, but it was a wet day and we could not go out." She and Yeats "sat there through that wet afternoon, and though I had never been at all interested in theatre, our talk turned to plays."

That wet afternoon, the idea was formed which led to the 1904 foundation of the Abbey Theatre.

Tony, the warden, lit a huge fire in the common room and told me that he thought it was this room in which that after-lunch discussion had gone on. The rain trickled down the windows. Hammocks were strung between trees in the garden. Lady Gregory had noted that "apple trees – and many plums – ripened on the walls". I could see no sign of any plums, but the apple trees were still bearing fruit.

"Help yourself," Tony said.

Next morning, the wind had joined the rain.

The local parish priest drove me back down the penin-sula and into Kinvarra. That day, I was heading for Oranmore, to meet up with my sister Caitríona, whose family I was going to stay with in Corrandulla for a couple of days.

The first car I hitched stopped. The driver had a goatee beard and wore horn-rimmed spectacles. *His* brand-new jacket was canary-yellow. He was on his way to Yeats' Tower, at Thoor Ballylee. Where did I want to go? He'd be heading on to Connemara after that and would be going through Oranmore. I hadn't planned on revisiting Thoor but I had plenty of time, so I said that this arrangement was fine. He removed a zippered case from the passenger seat and I got in.

"The name's Tom."

"Rosita."

Tom had an Australian accent. Since he seemed to be interested in Yeats, I told him the story of Doorus House. To my surprise, he knew all about the Abbey Theatre, which I thought was an unusual thing for an Australian traveller to be familiar with.

Tom had also just come through the Burren. "It was a tough place. A tough place. All those people farming those little plots of rock."

He talked about the people of Ballyvaughan and how they were reputedly the last Stone Age people in Europe. "Those faces," he said, "those *faces*." I couldn't help wondering if he had voiced this theory to the Ballyvaughan people but didn't have the nerve to ask.

I remembered the "queer, foreign-looking folk" of Ennis that had so struck the Victorian author of *Lovely Britain*. Was there really something particularly unusual and distinctive about Clare faces? *Stone Age people. Foreign-looking faces.*

Tom explained that his grandparents had been Irish and that he had been to visit the graves of his great-grandparents in Newmarket, Cork. He'd found the graves overgrown and untended.

"There was nobody left to look after them. Everyone in the family had emigrated. Wasn't that sad?"

He told me that being second-generation Irish in Australia, there had been a tremendous amount of patriotic sentiment handed down to him.

"Ireland is portrayed as a sort of Northern Hemisphere heaven," he said wryly. "And then, at the Christian Brothers in Sydney of all places, we were taught about hedge schools and of all the suffering that our ancestors had had to endure. We ended up with a mixture of facts and a whole lot of romantic sentimentality. It makes it very difficult now for me to see Ireland as it really is."

I was listening hard to all this. Tom talked very fast and the conversation was densely textured with names and dates, which slipped away from me, even as he spoke. I looked out at the grey road and the grey sky and found myself wondering about this friendly, effusive Australian, who spoke with such genuine interest and concern about things Irish.

"Are you a historian?" I asked curiously.

"No, I'm a writer. I'm doing a short text of forty thousand words, for David Ryan in England and Nortons in America. It's to accompany a book of photographs by Paddy Prendergast, the *Irish Times* photographer."

It couldn't be.

"Can I ask you what your surname is?" I said carefully.

"Keneally. I-won-the-Booker-Prize-in-1982," he rattled off straight away. "As a matter of fact, I'm taking one night off from the travel book and flying over to London with my daughter for this year's ceremony."

"I know," I said. "I've heard of you."

My head swam with the water on the road. *Say something, Rosita. This is what they call a fortuitous encounter, a lucky break, a chance meeting, a... What am I supposed to be asking this man? What should I be saying? Say something.* "You won't believe this," I said weakly, "but I'm writing a travel book too."

Tom was going to be in Ireland for five weeks. He had

set up meetings along the way, had certain people he wanted to talk to, certain places he wanted to see. He was travelling that day to meet a garda at Letterfrack to talk about poteen making. He planned on going up to the Ballinasloe Horse Fair after that, and finding the Bare Knuckle Champion Fighter. Tom had seen him on *The Late Late Show* and was fascinated by the whole idea of it.

"There's something very eighteenth-century about it, don't you think?"

The zippered case he had removed from the passenger seat turned out to be a dictaphone. He told me that he'd used one in Erithrea to record his impressions.

"I'd hoped to do the same thing this time, but it's not working. I'm not being *shocked* enough."

We came out onto a main road and I had to look at my map to see what direction Thoor and Gort were in, as there were no road-signs at all.

"This is the spiritual element of being in Ireland. Guessing one's way along," he laughed tolerantly.

While I looked at the map, Tom looked through my copy of the *Rough Guide*. I'd choosen that particular book because it seemed to contain the most practical information and was geared towards my budget. Also, it was a paperback. And what the blurb on the back cover promised – "The image of green and rural Ireland is familiar to everyone. The *Rough Guide*, though, is not like other guides: it looks beyond the blarney to explore the real charms of a vital European nation" – it tried to make a fair go of delivering inside.

"Hey, this looks like a good book," he said. He picked up *The Shell Guide to Ireland* from the floor. "I've got this and it's good, but I find it very cold and impersonal."

I agreed that *The Shell Guide* was good for basic information. "But I didn't bring it," I explained, "because it would have weighed too much."

Tom asked me lots of questions about my journey.

I explained that I'd only just started and was finding it somewhat difficult to take in the part of Ireland I'd been through in the last few days, because this was an area that had been very familiar to me as a child.

He listened to this and nodded his head. Again, he said that he was finding it difficult to separate the sense of history and mythology from his impressions of Ireland as he was seeing it. His publishers had wanted someone with a fresh, new interpretation of Ireland: "and Australia is just about as far away from Ireland as you can get."

Was it possible, we wondered, or even desirable, to baldly record Ireland in 1990? How was it possible not to be aware of the past?

A couple of weeks later, on 20 October, I read in the *Irish Times* the coverage of the *Irish Times*-Aer Lingus Literature Prizes. Tom Keneally had attended the prize-giving ceremony. Talking about John McGahern's *Amongst Women*, which had been published that year, he had said: "As for John McGahern, that's a great novel, a great Irish novel. He has combined all that history, the story of those fellows who shot the Black and Tans along with the story of present-day Ireland."

And there we were, driving to Thoor to see Yeats' Tower, which was itself a landmark of historical interest.

Thoor Ballylee was closed. We got out and walked around three sides of the grey, square tower squatting by the tea-coloured river. Tom had visited Thoor on his first journey to Ireland, some years before, and then as now, it had been closed and the day rainy.

"I'll probably never see Yeats' Tower in sunshine now," he said regretfully, as we got back into the car.

I laughed and said that it probably would have been raining most of the time Yeats had been there, so that what he was seeing today could be the reality rather than the myth.

We passed a couple of hitch-hikers outside Clarinbridge, on the way to Oranmore. They both looked chilled. It was raining and they were in t-shirts.

"Gee, don't they look miserable!" Tom exclaimed. He pulled in and they clambered gratefully into the back.

I got out at Oranmore, a few miles further on. Tom shook hands warmly with me and we wished each other good journeying.

"I might see you again on the road up the west coast," he called, and waved energetically out the window.

Thomas Keneally's fine and thoughtful book, *Now and in Time to Be: Ireland and the Irish*, was published the following winter. When I read it, I discovered that he had included a long account of our meeting in the book, although he did not mention anywhere the reason why I had been hitching with a rucksack on a "penitentially narrow, stone-fringed road in Galway" that wet October day.

2
ISLANDED ON THE ISLAND
Corrandulla to Árainn

The big news in Corrandulla was that the recently-released hostage, Brian Keenan, had been staying locally with the poet Gerald Dawe. After a couple of days in a real bed again instead of a bunk, during which I re-established friendly relations with my initially suspicious niece Sarah, was fed wonderful meals by my sister, and given lots of interesting information about Connemara by my brother-in-law Tony, it was time to move on.

Rather than go back into Galway city and continue out west, I decided to go round by Lough Corrib.

I got a lift to Headford with a woman who was on her way to work at the Headford Health Centre. She told me that she now worked mainly with elderly people who lived in country areas, but that she had previously worked in Galway city.

"I hated it. You never felt you were getting anywhere at all. People didn't even know their next-door neighbours. At least out here, everyone knows everyone else. But it's still nothing like it used to be, when everyone looked after their own."

There was a subdued, Monday-morning feel in the small market town of Headford. I wandered about the empty streets and came across The Thatch Pub.

As the name suggests, the roof of The Thatch Pub was thatched, with still-bright straw. But projecting from the thatch, in a position near the chimney, was a satellite dish. Even on the most modern of houses, satellite dishes often look like strange, space age insects. On the roof of The Thatch Pub, the satellite dish was laughably incongruous. Why go to all the trouble and expense of thatching a roof, only to negate its "traditional" look by adding something

43

so extraordinarily out of place as this dish?

A morose man in a Hiace van brought me to Cong. Cong was also quiet. An old stone cross leaned sideways in the middle of the street. Although it was thirty-nine years since *The Quiet Man* had been filmed, Cong did not let you forget that it had once been a Hollywood village.

There was *The Quiet Man* Coffee Shop at one end of the village, and at the other, a painted notice advertising tours of *The Quiet Man* countryside. Pat Cohen's Bar still looked the same from the outside as it had in the film. But when I peered in the windows, I saw a strange collection of kitsch souvenirs and ordinary hardware items, all jumbled among bottles of soft drinks and racks of sweets.

There was Phil the Fluter, Paddy Reilly of BallyJamesDuff and Paddy McGinty – all of them little china representations of stage-Irish musicians, firmly glued to slabs of Connemara marble. There was brake-fluid and paintstripper and golf balls. There were shillelaghs with the inscription 'From *The Quiet Man* Bar' painted on them. There was a giant gilt replica of a pocket-watch, complete with winder, but where the hands and figures usually are, the face of Pope John Paul II smiled benevolently instead.

On the surface, Cong still looked pretty and unspoilt by the undercurrent of kitsch. The surrounding countryside was lush and glittering with lakes. The old stone buildings in the village were genuinely quaint and there was a peaceful, mellow atmosphere in the streets. In the pink post office, where I went to buy stamps, a handwritten notice was pinned above the counter.

Service to Bougainville Island, Papua New Guinea suspended.

I was intrigued. Had the people of Cong been writing to the Bougainville Islanders?

The only building which appeared to be unashamedly cashing in on the thirty-nine-year-old film was Danagher's Bar, opposite the slanting stone cross. It was painted leprechaun-green and had red cartwheels hanging on the front walls. Over the entrance, there was a balcony with a cartload of turf on display. Engraved in the panel of glass above the front door were the words "Est 1990". *1990?* This was someone's idea of a public house in 1990?

Inside, I sat at the bar in Mary-Kate's Kitchen and drank a glass of Guinness. There were shillelaghs on the wall and shamrocks superimposed on green, white and gold bunting. Sugán chairs stood before an old fireplace in which an empty black skillet hung forlornly.

"It was our first summer with a licence – this used to be a guesthouse," the moustached proprietor told me, staring fixedly at a Sky pop concert on a television which seemed to be part of the furniture in Mary-Kate's Kitchen. "Great business. Terrific summer."

I walked out the Lisloughrey Road, left my rucksack at the Cong Hostel, and walked back to the Ashford Castle entrance, with the intention of wandering about the grounds and having a gin and tonic in the bar of one of Ireland's best-known hotels.

A boy in a grey uniform with primrose-coloured braid stopped me. "Two pounds admission," he said apologetically. I paid, with bad grace.

The grounds were what house and garden magazines describe as "well kept". The flowerbeds were orderly; the driveway bare of any fallen leaves; the lawns green and rolling. There were signs in Celtic lettering at intervals along the driveway. *Please drive slowly. Dangerous bends.*

The curves of the immaculately tarmacadamed driveway must have seemed like child's play to any hotel guest in a hired car, who would have already been rudely introduced to the narrow, pot-holed Irish country roads.

But not even my annoyance at having been fleeced could spoil the view for me, when I had wound my way around several dangerous bends and come in sight of the lakeside castle hotel. The towers and turrets were silhouetted dramatically against a rose-pink sky, the lake was dazzlingly silver, the mountains blue, the lawns verdant green. I cheered up.

There was a firm notice guarding the entrance to the hotel. *Residents Only.* I looked at it. So I'd paid two pounds to manoeuver dangerous bends and I wasn't even going to

45

be able to have a drink at the end of it. A porter hovered about, eyeing my jeans, which needed washing, and my loud jacket.

I went for a walk around the lake instead. What was I doing there anyway, lurking about the poshest hotel in Ireland? This had no place in my journey. I stomped angrily along a muddy lakeside track. There were some ruined out buildings alongside the track. I went round the back of one of them.

Scattered on the ground were eleven cider flagons, several bottles of Heineken, a bottle of gin and a litre bottle of tonic water. Obviously, the locals didn't pay two pounds to get into the grounds, and had the foresight to bring their own gin and tonic with them.

The Cong Hostel had a promotional leaflet. "Cong – the location of the classic movie *The Quiet Man* and also *Taxi Mauve*. There is a nightly showing of both films in the Hostel Cinema." Translated, this meant that I watched a video of *The Quiet Man* on the common room television that evening. Seán Thornton (John Wayne), Irish-American made good, returns to Innisfree, alias Cong, and buys the old family thatched cottage. Along the way, he marries the fiery local beauty, Mary-Kate Danagher (Maureen O'Hara).

Apart from Cong masquerading as Innisfree, the other placenames mentioned in the film were real ones: Ballinrobe and Maam. I wondered why they had changed the name of Cong to Innisfree, and how they had come upon the name of Innisfree. Perhaps they thought an American audience would be familiar with one of Yeats' best-known poems, "The Lake Isle of Innisfree", and thereby associate Seán Thornton's return to his Irish roots with the words "I shall arise and go now, and go to Innisfree". My dreams that night were full of blarney: shillelaghs and jaunting carts and beautifully thatched cottages.

I woke up to the usual beating of rain at the window and set off in the direction of Maam. Fleets of cars swooped past without stopping. Every hitch-hiker will be familiar with the signals which drivers communicate – indicating they're turning left, or right, are full up, or are turning around shortly. Sometimes – infuriating if you are hitching in the rain – drivers will wave cheerily at you. I got lots of waves that morning. And I was introduced to a new signal. One driver pointed his hand in the direction of the road. He could only have been indicating that he was going straight on, and I wondered where he thought *I* was going. Backwards, perhaps.

I had passed Clonbur and was halfway to Cornamona before I got a lift. Bruce and Margaret were from Adelaide. It had taken me a week into the journey before I had hit on a way of finding out people's names. I simply got into a car and said "I'm Rosita", and people then usually responded with their own names.

Bruce and Margaret asked me if it rained every day in Ireland. I struggled to be fair. "It's been raining a lot lately. But there are times when it doesn't rain for a couple of weeks."

They looked politely and disbelievingly at me.

The road wound along by the shores of Lough Corrib, and then through expanses of bog and bracken, with the dark shapes of the mountains on the horizon. Apart from an abandoned Bus Éireann coach, there was no sign of anything intruding upon the landscape: no houses, no cars, no animals. *Unspoilt*, I found myself thinking.

Once, it stopped raining briefly and the sun shone out.

"It's like someone's put the light on!" Margaret exclaimed, and Bruce stopped the car to have a proper look. The sunlight licked the orange-brown bracken to fiery life, the mountains glowed, the lakewater blazed, and the bog holes gleamed like gold coins. Five minutes of breathtaking alchemy. Then the sky clouded over and everything became shadowy again; brooding, complex, secretive.

At Maam Bridge, Bruce stopped the car again. "We're looking for *The Quiet Man* cottage," Margaret explained. "It's supposed to be somewhere around here. Do you know where it is?"

But I didn't. My experience of Connemara was limited to a couple of weeks in the Carraroe Gaeltacht, several years previously.

"Never mind, Margaret," Bruce said. "We can see the replica cottage at Maam Cross. It'll be much handier." He restarted the car.

There was a sign outside Peacocke's at Maam Cross. "Peacocke's. Something for everyone." The sprawling complex of Peacocke's consisted of a craft shop, garage, bar and restaurant, and *The Quiet Man* replica cottage. Outside the craft shop, there was a wooden cart of the same type displayed on the balcony of Danagher's Bar. The Peacocke's cart had a plaster donkey sandwiched between the wooden shafts. There was a jaunting cart outside the replica cottage and another plaster donkey.

On the bathroom door of the Cong Hostel, there had been a sign: "No cloth's to be washed between 9 and 12". The sign in the replica cottage informed me that: "Lifters will be proscuted".

The replica cottage was furnished with a weird and wonderful assortment of junk, most of it accompanied by ambiguous little notices. In the bedroom off the main area, there was a note on a chest of drawers which informed me that: "This very old chest of drawers is made from Irish pine". On a dresser in the main area was a piece of paper saying: "Very old dinner knives". The lifters must have been at the very old dinner knives, as they were nowhere to be seen.

There were wooden benches, jugs, harnesses, china, two plastic garden gnomes, a couple of lovely old chairs and a framed letter from Mike Tosh of Glasgow BBC, dated 19 June 1985, confirming the filming of *The Quiet Man* cottage at Maam Cross for inclusion in a television series called *The Celts*. What the replica of a cottage used in a Hollywood film thirty-nine years previously had to do with the Celts, the letter did not explain.

There was a party of Americans queuing to buy lunch in the restaurant. The very tall man in front of me announced to his companion, "Whenever I walk into a room in Ireland, I always have to check where the chandelier is, or I bang my head."

They were all wearing little plastic badges. I turned to the woman behind me, on pretext of asking the time, and looked at her badge. "Castles and Manor Houses of Ireland". The woman introduced herself as Eileen King and told me that the entire party were staff from the University of Michigan. They had only been in Ireland a few days and had so far stayed at Dromoland Castle and Ashford Castle. It emerged that they had set out that morning to tour western Connemara in the Bus Éireann coach which I had earlier seen abandoned. The coach had broken down and they had had to wait an hour for another to come.

"Luckily we had a historian among us and he filled in the time by giving us a lecture on the history of Ireland."

I was charmed by the impression of Ireland this group of Americans were getting – banging heads off chandeliers in the grandest hotels around the country and listening to an Irish history lecture while stranded in an expanse of Connemara bog.

Tacked up at the back of a white-painted dresser in the craft shop was a dog-eared letter, headed simply "The White House", dated 27 June 1985, from Nancy Reagan, thanking Mrs Keogh for the "cozy sweaters" she had sent on as a gift. Someone had added up a straggly column of figures in the margin.

I bought a John Hinde postcard of two small red-haired children, a boy and a girl, with a donkey which had creels of turf on its back. For as long as I could remember, reproductions of this particular postcard had been on sale. The same John Hinde postcards that were shot and touched up decades ago – burningly blue skies, pea-green fields, impossibly Californian-coloured waves, pristine thatched cottages – are still on nationwide sale today. They represent if not quite a fictitious landscape, a grossly exaggerated one. Where is the Ireland these images portray?

Some years ago, a couple of new series of postcards were launched. They called themselves things like "Real Ireland"and "Insight Ireland" and made offbeat and honest challenges to John Hinde Studios. In an article entitled "Not-Quite-Real-Ireland" in No. 78 of *The Honest Ulsterman*, Ciarán Carson makes the following observation:

49

When they (Liam Blake's "Real Ireland" postcard series) *first appeared in 1979, they caused a minor revolution in our perception of the tourist image: now, one did not send home a picture of wherever one was staying; one sent, instead, a picture of a parish pump, or of four plastic supermarket bags stacked on a windowsill. These images were not tied to a definite locality; the frame, in fact, excluded topographical references. They depended not so much on a view as on a point of view... the images revealed to us a world we had always known but had never really noticed.*

The images captured by "Real Ireland" and "Insight Ireland" photographers are kaleidoscopic, fragmentary observations of Ireland. They invite you to look at details and thereby explore a cross-section of Irish life. Like any photographs, they are selected images, but at least they are devoid of the rambling prose to be found on the reverse of John Hinde postcards.

Collecting Turf, Connemara. In Ireland to-day there are still vast stretches of this ancient romantic land where the old ways are still the best. In Connemara, the patient donkey brings home the turf sods which have been skillfully cut and which will warm the thatched cottage of the fisher-farmer during the Winter ahead. Cartwheels would sink in the soft bog, but the donkey's dainty feet pick their way daintily and efficently.

The only other building in the vicinity of Peacocke's at Maam Cross was an odd little place out the Oughterard Road. It was painted a mottled-salmon colour and had a stone plaque above the door: "Scoil Muire A.D. 1930". It didn't seem to be used as a school any longer and would not have made me curious, except that on either gable wall were crosses, picked out with white bulbs. Even on a dull afternoon, the crosses looked strange. To be driving along through the unlit, empty landscape of mountain and bog in darkness and come upon an illuminated cross, several feet high and seemingly floating out of nowhere, must be a surreal experience.

I asked the dour man who brought me to Oughterard if

he knew what the building was. "I don't know what it is. I don't care what it is. Like any normal driver I just look at the road when I'm driving."

At Oughterard, I went into McDonagh's shop to buy a newspaper. The woman in front of me was sounding off at great length about the Lottery Scratch Cards. I gathered she bought them regularly, but had never won anything. The man at the cash register read the paper peacefully and let her have her say. She eventually gathered up her bags and made to go.

"Scratch, scratch, scratch, the country's gone mad," she hissed angrily from the door. "I may as well be scratching my backside as scratching these Lottery tickets, for all the money I ever won on them."

The prosperity of Oughterard, a small and pretty town, largely depends on the income generated by the excellent fishing to be had on Lough Corrib. The names above the pubs and hotels read: Anglers Rest, Mayfly Inn, Boat Inn, Grand Lake Hotel. The rod-licence controversy (when the government tried to introduce a licence fee to fish) was now resolved, but the bitterness remained just beneath the surface, as it was all still in the very recent past.

There were framed newspaper articles about the controversy on the walls of the Anglers Rest, and an anonymous ballad, entitled "Fishy Notice". The last two lines read: "So here's a solution to end all the fuss/Abandon the licence, put Charles on the bus."

Stuck over the bar was a printed poster. "People of Ireland, do not pay rod-licence" it proclaimed. Under a series of sub-headings was one entitled "Penal Law".

It is a law that will make criminals out of decent people in pursuit of peace and relaxation on our River Banks and Lake Shores and subject them to fines of up to £2,000 and/or 2 years in jail. Do Hurlers, Footballers, Golfers etc. need a licence to pursue their pastimes?

At the bottom of the poster was a drawing of a fishing rod, laid sideways in the illusion of a pointed gun.

Jean, a French geology student at UCG, gave me a lift to

Moycullen. "You could come to Galway with me," he said. But I had a route to follow and miles to go before I slept.

From Moycullen, I hitched to Spiddal and got a lift in a specially-converted Mitsubishi Space Wagon. Martin was disabled. The car almost seemed to drive itself, issuing a series of high-tech clicking sounds. It was like being in the cockpit of a plane, gliding smoothly over the narrow road that wound its way through bogland and small fields. Sturdy-looking Connemara ponies grazed on calmly, unperturbed by the Space Wagon swooping past, a few fields away.

At Spiddal, I did some shopping and then headed on out west. I was going to spend that night in the Indreabhán Hostel and was anxious to get there before dark. The rain was spitting down in moody bursts and the light was rapidly draining from the sky. I walked in between hitching lifts.

At last, a car pulled in ahead. The driver was a fierce-looking woman enveloped in an overcoat, who asked me if I was a student. "I was once," I said, sensing trouble.

"I wouldn't have stopped for you unless I thought you were a student!" she said sharply.

It was now almost dark. I had no intention of walking the remaining eight miles or so, just because I was no longer a student. I smiled at her, threw my rucksack into the back seat, and sat in. "Well, I suppose you're all right," she said grumpily.

We conducted a prickly conversation. She disagreed with everything I said, yet rounded on me for not opening my mouth when I fell silent, thinking she would prefer that.

Where had I been that day anyway? When I mentioned Oughterard, she wound down the window and spat out.

"Oughterard! That crowd!" She went on to explain that she had a friend who owned a holiday cottage in Oughterard. "He paid his rod-licence fee, because he liked fishing and he was only there for a few weeks of the year. He had a big picture window in his front room and after he bought a licence, it was smashed every week."

"Every *week*?"

"Well," she amended, "every time it was replaced."

For the rest of the time it took to get to the hostel, she told me similar stories of people who had paid up and had vegetable gardens dug up in the middle of the night, flowerbeds trampled, new shrubs destroyed.

Criminals out of decent people.

There was a picture of a thatched cottage in the kitchen of the Indreabhán Hostel, two tweed collages of thatched cottages in the common room, where there was also a John Hinde thatched cottage postcard in the shape of a tray. Although I had continued to notice scores of ruined houses, so far, I had seen very few thatched cottages still in occupation.

I inquired at the office about boats to the Aran Islands. There was a sailing from Rossaveel to Cill Rónáin on Árainn at 10.30 next morning. I bought a return ticket on the *Queen of Aran* for £10.00.

"Just stand at the side of the road at ten tomorrow and the coach from Galway will pick you up," the warden told me. "The forecast is terrible," she warned. "Maybe you should wait a few days."

That night, I waxed my boots extra thoroughly. So far, I was managing to stay reasonably dry, although I was finding the Gore-Tex claim of "guaranteed to keep you dry" to be somewhat optimistic. In heavy rain, water soaked through sleeve seams, through the zippered pockets and occasionally, through the front zip seams. I soon learned to keep my pocket notebook in a sealed plastic bag, after the rain had dissolved a couple of pages into an indecipherable blur during a downpour.

The *Queen of Aran* coach from Galway duly collected me next morning. The sky was a dull shade of metallic grey and it was still very dark. As for the rain, I felt a grudging admiration at the way tremendous quantities of it were drumming down so tirelessly.

The *Queen of Aran* and the *Rose of Aran* ferries were both very full. I looked around at all the rucksacks and decided to give the hostel a miss that night. There had been a coachload of very young French schoolchildren staying at Indreabhán the previous night and I was in no mood for a bunkbed again that night.

A German man scorned the gangplank linking the two ferries and leapt instead from one to the other. The distance was further than he had expected. His arms flailed in mid-air, he let go a bulging plastic bag he had been carrying, and fell onto the deck of the *Queen of Aran*, to a wave of laughter from everyone on board.

"My tobacco!" he roared. "My film for my camera! My food!" He peered over the rail, but the sea had already claimed the bag.

The crossing took about forty minutes. From the water, the islands looked grey and bare. In places, the land tilted sharply upwards, indicating cliffs beyond.

There were jarveys waiting on the pier at Cill Rónáin. The man who had lost his bag elbowed his way off the ferry, settled himself under a rug in a jaunting cart and looked on as the driver loaded his remaining bags.

"I want to see the sights!" he said.

The rest of us watched him being driven along the curve of Cill Rónáin pier. "I wish he'd fallen in with the bag," someone said sourly, to a general growl of agreement.

I walked up past the hostel and the American Bar and through the village of Cill Rónáin. The minibuses had already passed me by, presumably on their way to Dún Aonghasa. Everyone with rucksacks had gone into the pierside hostel. The islanders were inside, out of the rain. I didn't have any clear idea of where I wanted to go, but decided that lunch and shelter were a priority.

Tigh Joe Watty's lay at the far end of Cill Rónáin; a simple, slated building with a stone floor. There was nobody else there. I warmed myself by the fire and waited for Rhoda, the bean an tí, to finish making the day's supply of soup.

"Are you Mrs Watty?" I asked.

She laughed. "I'm nobody's wife. Joe Watty is dead for years. But why change the name of the place?" She shrugged her shoulders.

Rhoda was American and had come to live on Árainn several years before. "The usual story. A man. It didn't work out, but I liked the place and decided to stay on. It's mad here in summer – full of people expecting pigs to be leaping out of doorways and thatched cottages everywhere. Winter is the best time of year, although sometimes we drive each other mad. You can do nothing without everyone knowing. But that's what happens on an island."

Rhoda smoked and mused.

I went to the door, looked outside and shut the door again. "The forecast is for worse weather," she said.

I spent the afternoon in Tigh Joe Watty's bar, talking to Rhoda and another customer, Keith Anderson; a Scotsman over on holiday for a few days. There was a set of beautifully-shot postcards pinned up behind the bar; cormorants on an Árainn cliff-top; the silver incoming tide at Poll na Marbh; an ancient stone cross against a rain-filled sky. I admired them and bought some.

A small world. The name of the photographer on the back was Keith Anderson. "There were no decent postcards of the islands, so I decided to do some myself," he explained. "I've been coming here every year for years."

We drank and talked until darkness fell.

Rhoda rang around the guesthouses to find out which ones were still open. "Gilbert Cottage is open," she told me. "You'll be fine and comfortable there. Stephen Dirrane keeps a warm house."

Gilbert Cottage was in the townland of Fearann an Choirce, a couple of miles away. I walked along by torchlight, shining the light at intervals over the warren of stone walls in the small fields that seeped up to the road.

Gilbert Cottage was like a warm wooden cave. There had been so many additional rooms built onto and over the original cottage that the living room and dining room, at the interior of the house, were almost completely windowless.

Most of the light bulbs were red or orange, and those that were not had heavy, coloured shades. There were mirrors on all the walls, reflecting this peculiar dim glow. On every available shelf and table top, there were pieces of old china and glass, winking and glinting in the firelight and mirror-light – glass bouys, bottles, gleaming candlesticks, shining copper kettles, white china plates edged with gold, wine glasses, crystal lamps.

The central heating and the stove fire combined to make the room positively tropical. I sank down into a couch, and with the heat and the afternoon's drinking and the coloured lamplight, felt vaguely hallucinatory.

Stiofán Ó Direáin had shoes tied with blue baler twine. He made endless cups of tea and talked to me for hours in a low, soft voice. I guessed him to be in his sixties. He had been born on Árainn and had returned home some years previously, after working in America for twenty years.

It was a cold, wet October, but there were swarms of flies buzzing in the heat of Gilbert Cottage. I swatted them languidly and watched the big black dog, Ollie, snapping his teeth and methodically catching any that came near him.

Whenever our conversation lulled, Stiofán crooned to his dog. Although we talked for hours, later, I could remember nothing of what we had spoken about, retaining only the sensation of heat and the image of flies disappearing into the snapping jaws of the dog.

Next morning, I set off with the intention of walking around the western end of the island.

The road which goes from Iaráirne, at the eastern end of the island, to Bun Gabhla at the western end (with a short southerly diversion to Gort na gCapall) is purely functional. It was built for carts and cars. It is the only "road" on Árainn. The real lifelines in the palm of Árainn are the scores of narrow boreens that wind off the pot-holed tarmac road and mould themselves along the myriad boundaries of small fields mosaiced together.

These fields were so small, that whenever I stood on a bit of high ground and looked down, all the tops of the walls merged together in the illusion of a stone sea, surging out towards the grey waves of the Atlantic. Some of the fields enclosed only fin-like slivers of stones; in others, the greenness lapped like water. After all the rain of the last few days, some fields were under inches of water, so that I started to feel confused about where the water began or ended and where the stone lay beneath it.

The boreen walls were shoulder high. I lost all sense of time and walked for hours in the rain and gale-force wind. For hours, I saw neither man nor beast nor any living thing, only the sea-birds, flinging themselves into the high wind along the clifftops.

There was no path along by the clifftops. The walls went almost to the edge. I scrambled my way along, climbing over the endless walls that seemed to get higher and higher. It was difficult, with the wind determined to push me off balance and onto the knife-edges of stone in the fields below, so that I leaped clumsily and dangerously between the persistent hands of the wind.

Several times, I had to lie down between the seams of stone and wait for the wind to abate a little. There were windbreaks made of stone in the middle of many fields, and I sheltered behind one of these and ate my lunch.

The mist came in from the sea and I had to wait for it to lift before it was safe to continue on. *Islanded on the Island.* I began to feel slightly bewitched. The shocking straight edges of the cliffs were hypnotic. I couldn't help clinging to walls that ran right to the end of the land and leaning over them to look down at the roaring sea far beneath.

After what seemed like many days, I saw the half-loops of Dún Aonghasa tilting blackly on the horizon.

The fort of Dún Aonghasa is reputedly over two thousand years old. There are three walls, each curving around the other, still in very good repair. There was also another wall, enclosing eleven acres of land beyond the central walls, but this is now very ruined. The three main walls become gradually thicker. The innermost wall is eighteen feet at its base. This innermost wall is an amphitheatre of the Atlantic; it faces out over the sheer cliffs, and on that stormy day, made me feel as if I was standing at the edge of some ancient world.

I climbed onto the ramparts of the inner wall, and the wind hated me. Unable to breathe properly, I looked out dizzily over the island.

From a height, the outline of the walls looked like a tangled fishing net. The island looked scraped; beaten clean of trees by the centuries of wind. The occasional green field seemed startlingly unnatural-looking among the landscape of stone. When set against the complex mosaic of tiny fields, the huge area of land enclosed by

Dún Aonghasa began to swell with meaning. More than anything, the size of Dún Aonghasa marked it out as a place of importance and great age.

Between the second and third walls, there was an expanse of stone *chevaux-de-Frise* – which takes its name from wooden beams set with spikes which were first used as a type of defence in a sixteenth-century Friesland siege. The Árainn *chevaux-de-Frise* was in existence long before it was named as such. The beams here were slabs of stone and between them, ferociously sharp thin stones bristled like the upheld sword-blades of a bygone army.

After I had come down from the ramparts and found my way out through the narrow entrances in the concentric walls, I came upon more strange stones.

There were dozens of pairs of tall, thin stones wedged into the grikes, with a third flat stone placed, lintel-like between them. They resembled mysterious miniature doorways. Some had collapsed, leaving only a finger of stone pointing skywards. Others had a heap of small stones on top of the lintel-like stone. What did they mean? I walked about them, baffled and curious.

When I eventually arrived back at Gilbert Cottage, I was amazed to discover that it was almost 6 o'clock. I asked Stiofán about the doorways of stone, but he didn't know what they were either, and told me he had not been to the fort for many years. Exhausted, I sank down into the couch for a second night, with not even the energy to feel hungry.

The next morning, it was still raining. I had hoped to walk around the eastern part of the island, but was beginning to feel suffocated by the grey skies and incessant rain, the overheated house and the ceaseless buzzing of the flies.

There was a boat at 11.30. I said goodbye to Stiofán, and walked back towards Cill Rónáin to catch the boat back to the mainland.

At Rossaveel that afternoon, I looked across at Árainn and the last few days already seemed an experience as distant and strange as the outline of the grey island, hunched down in the ocean.

3
POOLS OF DARKNESS
Rossaveel to Westport

I walked out to the main road from Rossaveel harbour and got a lift straight away from two American women, Sue and Annette, who were spending their first holiday in Ireland.

"We had no idea it would be so *pretty*," they chorused.

I asked them what they had been expecting.

"We knew it was supposed to be very green and that the people would be friendly and there'd be lots of those cute little cottages with thatch."

I waited. That was it; their combined expectations of Ireland. It was their sixth day in the country.

"Have you seen many thatched cottages yet?"

"No-oh," they admitted. "Not very many."

Neither woman was of Irish ancestry. Where had they got this impression of Ireland, I asked them. American television seemed to have been the main source of their information. Had they seen *The Quiet Man*? Yes they had. Perhaps if a person who had never been to Ireland watched *The Quiet Man* as a preview of what he might experience in Ireland, he might expect to see some of the blarney it offered.

The latest Irish film on release that autumn was *The Field*. I had gone to see it the week before starting my journey. In its way, *The Field* was not altogether dissimilar to *The Quiet Man*. The Irish-American man made good still wishes to buy property in the Old Country, although in *The Field*, the power of his dollar does not automatically entitle him to buy his way back into being a part of Ireland again. The title "The American" is used in the film credits, as if this character is symbolic; universal and manifold in its anonymity.

59

This was the most modern Irish film on offer. I wondered if Sue and Annette would have much reason to change their ready-made impressions of Ireland if they went to see it. *The Field* boasted a superb performance of Bull McCabe by Richard Harris, but it also boasted a red-haired tinker wench, gypsy caravans, rainbows, thatched cottages and turf fires; the standard clichés.

Equally, never having been to America myself, what did I know about Sue and Annette's country? My knowledge of America had also been filtered down to me through movies and television programmes. I had scores of images of America in my head.

The Statue of Liberty in New York Harbour. The infamous street crime in NY City. Skyscrapers. The white Hollywood sign. Stars and stripes. Fast food. The White House.

Perhaps anyone who has not been to America would compose a similar list: all of these things are icons; touchstones of part of what America is. But I knew them to be no more or less than single parts of the composite whole of America. You only had to look at a map to see how huge America was. There had to be more in it than burgers and the Statue of Liberty.

One of the problems with Ireland seemed to be that it was physically so *small* on a map of the world that it might seem reasonable to assume, if you were a foreigner, that the thatched cottages and green fields of your expectations could swell sufficently to cover the entire country.

"And you can drive around it so *fast*," Sue said. "We're only here for a week, but we reckon we're going to *do* a lot of Ireland."

We drove around the Carna peninsula, through miles of bracken and gorse and heather, with the rucked and crumpled-looking Twelve Pins furrowing the horizon. Once, Sue stopped the car. "Look!" she said. "Look Annette! No cars, no houses, no people. I've never been anywhere where I've seen that before."

Annette agreed.

It was my turn to be amazed. Both women were about thirty. Was it possible in all this time, they had never travelled out beyond the cities and surburbia of their own immense country?

We all stared out the windows.

"No houses!" Sue repeated.

"It'd be a bit difficult to build on a bog," I observed wryly. But I knew what they meant, and was recently enough returned from London to be marvelling myself at the complete lack of evidence of man upon the landscape.

Sue and Annette were cutting across to Clifden. I got out at the turnoff for Cashel and waved them off.

Karl, a vet on call to a sick pony, gave me a lift to Cashel. From Cashel, I walked a mile or so until a French woman, whose husband worked as a chef in the Cashel House Hotel, stopped and brought me to Toombeolo.

I had managed to climb countless stone walls on Árainn without any further casualties than a pair of boots that would never look their old selves again. Getting out of the car at Toombeolo, I managed to bang my knee very awkwardly off the side of the door. Consequently, the walk towards Roundstone was not so much a walk as a stagger. Muttering curses, I hobbled along like a foul-mouthed old woman of the roads.

Roundstone was a pleasant village with a single pier-side street. I was asked if I was looking for Tim Robinson and had the house pointed out to me. Unfortunately, I knew it to be empty, as I had written some time before to try and arrange a meeting, and had received a reply saying that he would be away all of October.

I dithered a bit in Roundstone, unsure of whether to quell hunger pangs now, or to continue on towards Clifden while there was still daylight. There had been very few cars on the road that day and I had done a lot of walking. There was no guarantee I'd even get to Clifden that evening, but the longer hitching time I gave myself, the better the chances were. Eventually, I decided to keep going and to cook up an enormous meal that evening.

I was lucky. Eamonn, who was driving an ESB van, stopped about five minutes later. He was on his way home and going all the way to Clifden. It was late-afternoon Friday. Eamonn was in a good mood. He sang and whistled and bantered. I was in a good mood too. It had stopped raining, the landscape was spectacular, and I was shortly going to have my first fly-free meal in days.

"Do you know anyone around here at all?" Eamonn asked.

We were just passing through the tiny village of Ballyconneely. I waved an arm towards Keogh's pub and shop.

"I went to school with Deirdre Keogh, but I haven't seen her for years. The last I heard of her, she was nursing in Vincent's."

"Well, if I'm thinking of the same person," Eamonn said, "Deirdre Keogh is now running the Alcock and Brown Hotel in Clifden."

From a distance, Clifden resembled an eagle's eyrie; a line of tall houses with their angular backs to the Roundstone road, perched high up above an inlet of the sea, and the two church spires spiking the skyline like pointed beaks.

Deirdre Keogh was indeed running the Alcock and Brown. She was in the lobby, discussing new carpet with a member of staff and looked up, slightly disapprovingly, at the very unlikely hotel prospect who had just thumped through the swing doors in a pair of muddy boots.

Deirdre may have been running the hotel for a mere five weeks, but she was already displaying a talent for dealing with members of the public, even those old schoolfriends who turned up unexpectedly on the evening of a twenty-first birthday party; her first major function.

"You must be a bit hungry after coming that distance today," she said tactfully. "Would you like to come up for dinner this evening?"

Leo's Hostel, where, in honour of dinner, I tried to find the cleanest clothes in my rucksack, was a curious and wonderful place.

It was an old white Georgian house; one of those buildings which backed onto the Roundstone road. Originally, it had been a guesthouse or small hotel and still retained some of the furniture from those days.

In the common room, which had been the dining room,

62

there was a dumb-waiter in one corner of the room; a magnificent old leather sofa; a huge old fireplace with coloured tiles. There was also some very ugly formica tables, a terrible picture of a thatched cottage and two really hideous armchairs. There was a beautiful red and cobalt-blue glass fanlight over the front door; there were high ceilings with cornices; there were plaster roses around the lights. My room had a panoramic view over the inlet of the sea, damp patches on the ceiling and a dubious-looking carpet.

The wardens at Leo's Hostel were very keen on cleaning. The hostel shut from noon to two each day while they scrubbed and hoovered. None of it seemed to make any lasting impact against the tattered, run-down aura that was seeping through the hostel. On the day I was there bulbs were missing from some light fittings, the plaster roses were festooned with cobwebs, carpets were torn and there were damp patches.

In the dining room of the Alcock and Brown, I feasted. Baked camenbert with cranberry sauce, noisettes of lamb, strawberry cheesecake. The wine was poured, the talk of years flowed.

Eventually, Deirdre confessed to having to make last-minute preparations for the twenty-first.

"Come back in an hour or so and join the party. In the meantime, have a drink in Mannion's or Vaughan's. They're good pubs for meeting the locals."

I went first to Mannion's. A couple of months later, on the eleventh of December, the *Sunday Independent* ran an article by Frank Khan entitled "Men still hog the bar". The article opened with the words: "The Irish pub is still very much a male preserve – particularly outside Dublin – a new survey has confirmed." It observed: "in more than 95 per cent of places men make up more than half the customers and in more than 50 per cent of premises they represented 75 per cent." The article also notes: "The strong prevalence of male customers, however, is confined to the smaller premises."

In Mannion's that Friday evening, the men represented 100 per cent of the customers.

I found myself in this situation many, many times. As a single woman, I had two choices. I could either sit quietly and read a book or newspaper while having a drink, or I could talk to people. Mostly, I chose to talk. There was absolutely no point in making this journey unless I talked to people in the places I went through. In pubs, I ended up speaking almost exclusively to men, since they were nearly always the only other customers. Sometimes I started the conversation, sometimes they did.

I ordered a Guinness in Mannion's and sat down. The barman looked like a sort of Celtic Woody Allen, with flaming red hair and thick-lensed spectacles, the frames of which were sellotaped together. A poker session was going on in one corner of the room, with plenty of ten and twenty pound notes on the table. A game of pool in another corner was being watched intently by a dozen or so people.

A very, very drunk man lurched over to me. His eyes had gone so far back in his head that they were practically slits. His face was paper-white. He was enormous.

"I'm a bogman and I'm a tramp!" he said, slapping me on the back with a hand the size of a steak. "Would a woman like yourself be interested in a bed with a man like myself?"

I was not, to be mild about it.

The bogman and tramp introduced himself as being from Ballyconneely. My name provided him with great difficulty. He couldn't get his tongue around it.

"Are ye going to be long in Clifden, Movita? Is it Movita that's yer name?"

I nodded. His face was centimetres from mine. His arm was firmly around my shoulders. I was not enjoying my Guinness.

"You wouldn't think of changing your mind at all about my offer, Movita?"

The steak was applied once more to my back. Sick of this, I drank up and went down the street in search of Vaughan's.

Vaughan's was much more subdued. There were only a handful of customers, all of them engrossed in watching

64

The Late Late Show. I talked to the barman about fish farms.

At closing time, I went to find the party at the Alcock and Brown. It was the twenty-first birthday of a local girl called Mercedes. There was no mistaking Mercedes, as she was resplendent in black ankle boots and a black cocktail mini.

"Do you know Mercedes well?" a few people inquired politely.

"Not *terribly* well."

I was asked to dance by a drunk boy. He worked in the fishing, but was currently unemployed. He fixed his arms around me and wheeled me furiously about the floor, under the impression that he was waltzing with me. We bashed into the real waltzing couples. We tripped over flexes. We trod on sandwiches. I could see Mercedes' mother looking at us with a concerned expression on her face. All this time, I was desperately trying to extract myself from his arms.

When the music stopped, I tore myself away and fled to a dark corner. I took the opportunity to sample the birthday cake, which was very good.

The music started again. Someone was planting kisses on my neck. It was the drunk boy, who had appeared out of nowhere and who was loudly declaring that he loved me. People began to stare.

I pleaded a need to go to the loo, and bolted. There was an unlocked door in the kitchen and I let myself out into the street. The curtains in the ground floor function room had not yet been drawn. I could see Mercedes making a speech at the microphone; and my admirer, who was still prowling around; and Deirdre, still looking cool and unruffled, collecting up the trays of food.

I left them to it and went to bed.

If there were fireworks going off in my head next morning, I consoled myself with the thought that there must have been cannons in the heads of others in the town. I armed myself with the newspaper and went to have a quiet coffee in My Teashop while I was waiting for the firework display to burn itself out.

The Clifden shops had some wonderful names.

Humanity Dick, Destry Rides Again, Fire and Fleece, An Spailpín Fanac. There were several craft shops, coffee shops, old-fashioned pubs; many of them with beautifully-kept shop fronts. I could well imagine it being crammed with people in the summer months, as everyone told me it was. It was clear that Clifden survived mainly on income from the holiday influx of people, and that the charming, carefully-painted shop fronts were tended and cultivated with the same care as prize garden produce, but the town itself remained vital. It did not seem to me to have traded its soul to the tourists and become spoilt, as has happened elsewhere.

The fireworks were now damp squibs. I put my boots on and started walking out the small peninsula west of Clifden, which has a name straight from a child's storybook; Bothár na Spéire, or, the Sky Road.

The road was built high up on a peninsula, so that at times, it seemed to be literally disappearing into the sky. And for once, the sky was a wide and miraculous shade of blue, making it possible to see for great distances. Peninsulas unfolded themselves on the horizon; each new turn in the road revealed another bright-rimmed beach, another cove or island.

And tacked to every second tree were signs; some hand-painted, some commercially produced. All carried the message: "No Fin Fish Farming Here". All the way through Connemara, I had been noticing these signs; tacked to gable walls, to trees, gates and telegraph poles. About halfway around the Sky Road, I saw a hand-painted sign nailed to a tree; "The West Awake/No Fish Farms/Nuvan Kills"; with a black skull and crossbones daubed underneath it. The salmon cages were clearly visible in the bay beneath me.

So far, I had not met anyone in Connemara who had a good word to say about fish farming. That weekend, there was an annual conference of the Irish Salmon Growers Association in Furbo. The use of the controversial insecticide, Nuvan, was one of the foremost issues under discussion. Nuvan is used in fish farming to kill sea lice, which feed on the flesh of young salmon. It succeeds in

66

killing off the sea lice, but the side-effects connected with the use of this chemical is still a shadowy area. It is feared that the use of Nuvan on fish farms has an adverse effect on the surrounding environment, particularly on wild sea trout and wild salmon. It has not been scientifically proven that this is so.

There is no denying that the angular cages scattered in bays around the coast of Ireland are ugly eyesores which detract from spectacular views. Neither can it be denied that fish farms in Ireland – most of which have started up in the last decade – provide employment in remote coastal areas where, outside the boom summer months of July and August, unemployment is very high. The process of feeding the smoults, maintaining the cages, harvesting the fish and packing them all provide jobs. My brother David was working for Salmara, a fish farm off Derrynane Bay in south-west Kerry, where the same controversy was going on. Visiting him the previous summer, I had been told not to discuss Salmara in public. "You could get yourself into a fierce argument."

By the time I had walked almost the entire loop of the Sky Road, the blue sky had dissolved. There were huge clouds, constantly melting into each other and changing colour. The mountains became insubstantial-looking; the faintest wash of bluish-grey on a liquid horizon. I could see banks of rain rushing over the sea.

I began hitching and as the first drops of rain began to pelt down out of a black sky, a car stopped. The lift back into Clifden was on a road that was literally more pot-hole than road. The car bucked and leaped. The woman driver had had a blown tyre that morning on this same stretch of road.

"It's said," she told me grimly, "that there's a Clifden garage which survives solely on the income from fixing cars that have to travel this road."

At Clifden, I left a note for Deirdre at the reception desk of the Alcock and Brown, returned to Leo's Hostel to pack my rucksack and waited for Pat O'Connell to collect me. Pat was the mother of one of my exiled London friends, Toni, and had invited me to stay the night at Errislannan, near Clifden.

Seal Cottage was a peaceful place, overlooking Mannin Bay, with a garden that ran down to the sea. The two dogs, Bruno and Sam, gave me a noisy welcome and then stretched out in front of the fire. We had gin and tonics and a leisurely supper, while outside, the rain and wind lashed the windows.

Next morning, when I went into the living room, Pat was looking through a pair of binoculars at seals on the rocks at the end of her garden. "I see them nearly every morning," she told me, and pointed the seals out to me. She was so used to seeing them that the slightest flicker of a fin revealed the seals to her, whereas I searched for a long time with the binoculars before I could dintinguish seals from the seal-coloured rocks.

"And there is an otter in my garden," she said, and went with me in her dressing gown into the windswept garden to point out where she saw her otter in the evenings.

I was getting the boat from Cleggan to Inishbofin at ten o'clock that morning. Pat would not hear of me hitching, so I said goodbye to Bruno and Sam, the seals and the otter's garden and we set off for Cleggan.

The *Dun Aengus* was tied up at Cleggan pier. Pat waved goodbye to me and went off in search of a friend in the village for morning coffee. I gave Paddy O'Halloran, the boatman, a hand with loading some of the island supplies. There were several boxes of groceries, shrink-wrapped crates of milk, litres of paint, mail bags and a fridge-freezer; the last of which needed the help of some bystanders.

Besides myself, there were two other travellers, a German couple, who wanted to go out to the island.

"You are coming back this afternoon?" they asked.

Paddy smiled. "Maybe. Maybe not."

"But we have got to get back this afternoon!"

"There might be a boat and there might not." He shrugged his shoulders. "It depends."

The Germans looked at each other in frustration. "It is not good enough!" They shook their heads and marched away down the pier.

A woman with a headscarf and a shopping bag got on,

went into the little cabin and began placidly reading a newspaper. An elderly man with a battered leather suitcase climbed aboard carefully and came to join me at the railings. He told me that he was from Clifden and going out to a friend for a week's holiday. Just before the boat pulled away, several island men came running down the pier, loaded on further supplies, then scattered themselves around the railings and in the cabin.

The journey out to Inishbofin was superb. From the boat, Connemara looked even more extraordinary; all blues and purples and oranges, balancing on a platform of silver-grey water. Inishbofin made a lush green curve on the horizon, looking somewhat like a sea-meadow.

The harbour was a long, meandering inlet of coves and beaches. The Clifden man told me that Inishbofin had been taken over as a penal colony for priests and bishops in the time of Cromwell. He pointed in the direction of a partially submerged rock at the harbour entrance.

"One of the bishops ended up there. Cromwell had him stripped naked and fettered to the rock at low tide. He made everyone watch as the tide came in and slowly drowned him."

We stared soberly at the rock. I thought of generations of islanders pointing out that particular rock to their children and the knowledge of its grim history being handed down orally over the centuries.

Fastened to the harbour rocks like a stone barnacle were the remains of an old fortressed castle. "That was Grace O'Malley's – the pirate queen's – castle. And Cromwell refortified it later on."

The boat slipped quietly past the straggling castle walls, which still looked formidably strong. In the shallower parts of the harbour, the water was a clear green colour, upon which small boats rocked gently. A new pier, about one-third completed, stretched a tentative arm into the sea, further up harbour than the pier towards which the *Dun Aengus* was moving. Later on that day, I was told that this new deep-water pier was being built so that in future, the ferry boats would be able to berth even in low tide.

The *Dun Aengus* stopped its engines in the harbour and

everyone, the boatmen, the woman with the headscarf and shopping bag, the man on holidays with his old suitcase, me with my rucksack, all climbed down a wooden ladder into a punt, while the groceries, the mail bags and the litres of paint were slung down by the island men, who then climbed in themselves. How they were going to unload the fridge, I didn't know. The punt riding low in the water, Paddy motored the fifty yards or so to the stony beach, where we all got out and repossessed our belongings.

"Next time you come, you'll not be doing this," the Clifden man told me. "The new pier will be finished by next summer." And he shook my hand and went off with his suitcase to greet his friend, who was waiting on the beach for him.

Everyone dispersed; the island men in the direction of the new pier, the boatmen and the woman passenger up towards the houses of Middlequarter. On the noticeboard in Leo's Hostel, I had seen a sign for a hostel on Inishbofin and I set about looking for it. I walked up past Day's Hotel and Miko's Pub and saw a sign with "Hostel" painted on it.

The hostel was a quarter of a mile or so down the narrow road; a lovely old stone building. I climbed over a home-made stile into the back yard, as the front door was locked. The back door was also locked.

I went around the front again and looked back down the road. There was a man with a walking stick slowly making his way towards the hostel. When he saw me, he raised the stick in greeting. The man turned out to be Miko Day and was looking after the hostel for his son. He took a key out of his pocket.

"So I'll be on my own in the hostel?" I said, unthinkingly.

He chortled. "There's no shortage of old men who'd keep you company!"

The hostel was bright and clean and obviously newly-decorated. There was a wonderful old radio in the kitchen and a copy of *Cooking Afloat On Sailing and Power Boats*, perhaps in anticipation of storm-bound hostellers.

In the afternoon, which was clear and blue and remained so all day, I walked around the island. This was the first day since I had set out that there had been no rain at all. I kept peering up suspiciously at the sky, but the sun continued to shine steadily and the sky remained blue.

There were two hotels on the island, Miko's Pub, a tiny shop, a church, a post office and a telephone box. There was also the regulatory island fleet of movable wrecked cars. I passed a decaying orange Volkswagen Beetle abandoned in a ditch, which looked as if it might fall apart if I touched it. The car had one headlight missing, which made it look like a battered face with an eye gouged out. Minutes later, it lurched past me on the road, in an amazing defiance of its scrap-heap appearance. All the cars I saw were like this – missing lights and bumpers, untaxed, unlicenced, with doors and windows that didn't quite shut and bodywork that was slowly crumbling away in great rusty patches.

The west side of the island was all bog and sheep and rabbits. There were thin strips of bog opened, ready for digging, and small, neat clochans of piled sods of turf. The undulating eastern side had bright beaches, lush fields and views back towards the shadowy purple outlines of the Twelve Pins. The sun turned the evening sky deep-pink and soaked the sea with colour, so that for twenty minutes or so, the island glowed and the sea radiated light.

That evening, I put my torch in my pocket and went to seek out Miko's Pub, by the harbour. Miko's Pub was surprisingly Continental-like inside. It had a slanted pine ceiling and a horseshoe bar, with an airy, light feel to the place. Gradually, the gaps in the bar filled in and John Cunnane, the man next to me, struck up conversation.

I asked him what the names of the different townlands on Inishbofin were, and he told me, but I couldn't quite make them out and asked him if he'd mind writing them down. He wrote very slowly and carefully and handed me back the notebook with the names – Westquarter, Fawnmore, Middlequarter, Cloonamore, East End – all written in exquisite copperplate.

John introduced me to his companion, Des O'Halloran, and when I told them that I was going to hitch around the Irish coast, they shook me by the hand, bid me welcome to

Bofin and would not let me put my hand in my pocket the whole night.

They wanted to know where I had been walking that afternoon. I mentioned all the rabbits I'd seen in Westquarter.

"Rabbits!" John said, slapping his cap down on the counter. "The place is alive with them!" He told me that a group of men were going to go bagging some night shortly. "We never had the myxomatosis here. Bofin rabbits are healthy buggers. They're three and four pounds weight."

"Like small dogs," another man put in.

"Sweetest of meat," said a third.

John explained to me how they were going to catch the rabbits. That afternoon, I had seen a man mending a fishing net by the shore, cutting away the torn net from its perimeter of rope. He would then have sewn in a new net. The rabbit catchers gathered up the old torn net and strung it across walls.

"And the rabbits, they'd be running for their holes and smash! They'd all be caught against the net and we're not long gathering them up. We were at it last year too. Fifty-five one night. Sixty another night."

They told me there was about two hundred people living on the island. They did a bit of fishing, a bit of farming, work on the new pier, built and maintained the score of holiday houses. Inishbofin was one of the last places in Ireland to get electricity, only going electric in 1982.

Was there a guard on the island?

"Oh Christ, we do want none of them buggers here," John said.

Was there ever any crime? I enquired inanely. Everyone roared with laughter. "Crime! This is a civilised place. We don't lock our doors ever."

A man with an American accent came up to the bar. He was introduced to me as Pat O'Brien. Pat O'Brien was Assistant General Manager at Landerbank in Hong Kong. His grandmother had left Inishbofin during the Famine and gone to America. Pat's father had always wanted to come back to Ireland, but had never been able to afford the fare. Pat himself had first come over in 1972. He had bought a plot of land on the eastern part of the island and was planning to build a house. I listened to all this, fascinated.

"You can't deny the history," he said. "The desire to see where you came from."

There was a metal plaque over the fireplace with a quotation from the American poet, Theodore Roethke, on it. I asked if he had ever visited Bofin. Roethke had visited Bofin four times in all, the last time being in 1958. John told me that Roethke and Richard Murphy had held drinking parties on boats in the harbour. Des had sung for him.

"I had Feis medals and all. He was supposed to invite me over to sing in America, but it never happened."

What had Roethke been like, what had he spoken of, what did John and Des remember of him; I tried to find out. But it was too late in the evening. They were too well-jarred to bring out such old memories. Undoubtedly, the stories were there, but they remained untold that night. To my question of what Roethke had been interested in talking about – a fairly unanswerable question by any standards – John struggled with memory and several pints of Guinness and then laughed.

"He was nearly always so drunk he didn't talk at all. Whiskey. He was a great man for the whiskey. An enormous man for the whiskey."

It was a marvellous night. I was introduced to almost everyone in the pub, my hand was shaken time and time again, I was invited back in the summer. The atmosphere of good humour and warmth filled the place. There was something innately gentle about the Bofin people and they could not have made me feel more welcome to their island.

The morning dawned pink and blue on Inishbofin. I closed up the hostel and made my way down to the pier. The tide was out and once again, just before the boat was about to go, the island men came running and we all got into the punt.

Pat was also taking the boat back to Cleggan and loaded on several pieces of luggage. He hung onto some suitcase or other and I cradled his portable computer in my arms.

Everything else was piled in the spray-soaked stern. Pat too pointed out the bishop's rock to me, now clearly visible in the low tide, but all I could think of this time was Pat's grandmother, taking the boat from Inishbofin for the last time and how I was holding her American grandson's computer in my arms, which would be sitting on his executive desk in Hong Kong within two days.

Pat drove me a couple of miles out from Cleggan and I started walking towards Moyard and Letterfrack. The first car that I hitched stopped. The driver was a travelling executive, who was based in Cavan.

"I thought you needed rescuing from the Middle of Nowhere!" he cried, when I opened the passenger door. He wanted to know if I had been waiting hours for a lift, and seemed disappointed when I said about five minutes.

Letterfrack, a tiny village built on a crossroads, seemed to be composed entirely of Veldon's. Veldon's looked to be a deceptively small place from the outside. Inside, there was a newsagents, a delicatessen and supermarket, with a large pub which you entered through an outside door.

I was wandering about with a shopping basket when I noticed a girl at the greeting cards stand. She looked strangely familiar to me. It was Mercedes, who appeared to be choosing Thank You cards, presumably for the twenty-first birthday presents she had received. I backed away quietly and peered nervously around the shop, just in case my admirer should pop up from behind some rack or other, but there were no other familiar faces in sight.

It was business as usual with the rain by the time I had finished lunch in the adjoining pub. I Gore-Texed myself fully and started walking towards Tully Cross. I walked for a long time, each new turn in the road revealing another ferny waterfall, another tea-coloured river, wandering sheep, breathtaking pot-hole or new angle of the Twelve Pins.

For a couple of hours, no vehicles at all passed me, coming or going. I was just thinking how far away from everything this part of Connemara seemed to be, when a white van appeared in the distance, coming towards me. I stopped walking and stared in disbelief as the surrealistic van came nearer. It was a Coca-Cola van, complete with three all-American looking young people, in red and white "The Real Thing" t-shirts, all of whom waved to me and laughed soundlessly behind the windscreen, revealing sets of perfect teeth.

All the time I had been in Connemara, I had been noticing donkeys at the roadsides. John Hinde postcards would have one think that donkeys were lovingly tended by the fisher-farmers and their red-haired children, but this did not seem to be the case. Most of the donkeys and foals wandering the roads had untrimmed hooves and matted coats. I had asked many people what the donkeys were used for now, but nobody really seemed to know and were unfailingly vague in their answers. "I don't know who owns them, but you hardly ever see a working donkey these days." "I think people just have them." "They're very neglected, whoever owns them."

Presumably, these donkeys were descendants of the original working donkeys. With the advent of tractors and trailers, they had been let stray and look after themselves, which they seemed to manage reasonably well, until you looked closer and saw their untrimmed hooves.

Tully Cross was another small village at a crossroads. On one side of the village, there was a row of brand-new cottages of the Rent-An-Irish-Cottage variety. In most other places where this scheme is in operation, such as Corofin and Ballyvaughan, the cottages are located on the edges of the villages and towns, looking like the peculiar touristy housing estates they are. But this peripheral location means that at least they do not intrude upon the real houses in the towns and villages. Incorporated uneasily into the main street of the village at Tully Cross, the cottages looked as if they'd been put there for a film set; empty unresonant shells.

I was hoping to make it to the hostel at Killary Harbour that evening. It was late afternoon by this time and the traffic could not be said to be heavy. I rested on a wall at the outskirts of Tully Cross, thinking it better to keep close to the village in case I couldn't get a lift and would thus only have to walk back again.

A lorry, which had been unloading goods outside a shop, turned in my direction. I had hitched it and it had stopped before I realised that all three seats in the cab were already full. But they were going to Leenane and would be passing the turnoff for Killary and there was no guarantee of another lift, so somewhat apprehensively, I slung my rucksack up and climbed into the cab after it.

The three seats were occupied by the driver, who drove the lorry like a tank, a morose young man who remained silent the entire journey – whether from embarrassment or boredom, I could not tell – and a middle-aged man (who was both drunk and randy) and upon whose bony knees I perched, all the unpleasant way. At every lurch and bump of the road, every swerve and corner, while I clung grimly to the dashboard, his arms held me in a vice-like grip and his hands inched further and further up my body.

"Are you carrying ice-cream?" I enquired of the driver wildly, desperate to avoid any more inane questions and endearments ("sweetheart" and "darling", accompanied by a squeeze every few seconds) from the middle-aged man.

He laughed. "Ice-cream, frozen chickens, frozen peas – you name it, it's in the container!"

So we lurched along in a lorryload of frozen food, while the incredible sun-washed sea and mountains slipped past and I fought a private battle with the wandering hands.

Along the way, the driver and morose young man got out to unload some of the frozen food and I slid thankfully into the middle seat.

"Ye see that house yonder?"

A small cottage a few fields away. "Yes."

"I spent the first few years of my life there and I played football with a ragball. We had no money for a real football. Imagine that, darling!"

"Imagine."

"And I'll tell you another thing, sweetheart. I have a daughter and we gave her a French name – twas the wife thought up the name. And when it came time for her to be christened, the parish priest took me aside and said, 'how would you be after spelling that?' Imagine that, and he an educated man, darling!"

"Imagine."

At the turnoff for Killary, I leapt out nimbly and thankfully. When the lorry had eventually swayed away and his arm out the window was lost from sight, absolute silence descended.

The entrance to the narrow road down to the harbour lay opposite Lough Fee; a silver tongue of water. I started walking down towards the harbour, the dark shapes of the sunless mountains barricading themselves against the horizon. It was a strange few miles. Beyond the mountains, the fjord was a steel-coloured knife, cleaving far through the mountains. There was something stark about this landscape. The other parts of Connemara had seemed softer, blazing with dying bracken and undulating with bogland, but Killary was all hard edge and cold glitter.

I knew someone who was working at the Little Killary Adventure Centre and turned down the track to a snug collection of converted stables and cottages. A dog barked furiously. Michelle Hughes came out to see who the intruder was. She stared at me incredulously.

"But you're supposed to be in Australia, aren't you?"

We had tea in the kitchen and talked. They were waiting for a big group from Dublin to arrive and people bustled purposefully in and out of the kitchen. Michelle and Neil, who was the bustling cook, arranged to bring me to Leenane that evening and I continued down the last mile to the hostel.

Killary Hostel was perched almost on the edge of the fjord, right at the end of the small Salrock peninsula; a dip of lights among the dark mountains and severe-looking water. The hostel was being done up and was both shiningly clean and warm. There was a big fire going in the common room and convector heaters in the small dormitory. This, for an An Óige hostel, was unexpected luxury. In the weeks that followed, which got steadily colder and wetter, my first question to fellow-hostellers about hostels in the direction I was heading towards, was simply, "Are they heated?"

I had supper by the fire and watched daylight fade over the fjord. The wind began to wail and howl; the rain to spit

77

furiously against the windows. In 1948, the philosopher Wittgenstein lived in the original cottage onto which the hostel was extended from, and finished writing *Philosophical Investigations*. I listened to the rain and wind and imagined him mining the spaces of the deep fjord and the stern mountains. Tim Robinson, mentioning the Killary Youth Hostel in his *Gazzetter to Connemara*, says of it:

formerly Rosroe Cottage, where the philosopher Wittgenstein stayed in 1948; he wrote that he could only think in the dark, and that in Connemara he had found "one of the last pools of darkness in Europe".

I sat listening to the storm outside and was almost reluctant to get up and go to Leenane with Michelle and Neil. It had been a day-long effort to get to Rosroe and it felt like cheating to be driven away from it so soon.

The car headlights picked out an old blue crane at the side of the road. "Left behind from the film," Michelle said. "What did they use it for?" Neither of them had seen the film yet, so I didn't tell them.

The village of Leenane, which was used in *The Field*, had been given back to 1990. The Lotto signs and telegraph poles had been reinstated. Hamilton's Pub, the facade of which had been used in the film, was quite low-key inside, with just some framed, signed photographs of the cast on the walls.

We had a couple of drinks and then I had to get back for the regulation 11.30 An Óige curfew. The curfew is not always imposed, although it is offically supposed to be. I had thought, the Killary Hostel being so far from anywhere, that it would just be a question of scrambling in a window, or locking the door after me, but I had been told quite firmly that if I wasn't in by 11.30, it was just too bad.

That night, I slept uneasily in one of the last pools of darkness, the wind waking me at intervals.

Michelle was an instructor at the Adventure Centre and I had hoped, weather permitting, to go on a long walk with her in the next day or two. But next morning, the weather had got worse. Rain slammed down out of a thick grey sky. The fjord water tossed and rippled and clawed at the shore. The wind slapped me about and sent me reeling indoors. The visibility was too poor to contemplate serious walking.

I spread my map of Connemara over the breakfast table and consulted it. Michelle had told me of a track which led over a gap in the mountains and along by the shore of the fjord, bringing one onto the main Leenane road; a walk of five miles or so. I located it on my map. Apart from climbing the mountain gap, it was a low-level walk for much of the way and I decided to go to Leenane by this route.

There were two other hostellers at the table; a German couple named Udo and Katherine. They were having a hostel breakfast, which the wardens had prepared for them. Engrossed in the map, I hadn't noticed the warden setting down part of their breakfast before them.

"Excuse me please," Katherine said, patting my arm. "But what do you do with these?"

She held up a Weetabix between forefinger and thumb. Udo was already nibbling gingerly at the side of his piece. Intrigued to discover that Weetabix was not the familiar breakfast cereal I had casually imagined it to be, I explained to them that you poured milk over it. They did so, very carefully and ate slowly.

"Very good, very funny," was the verdict. They waited eagerly for the warden to bring the next part of breakfast and looked distinctly disappointed when it turned out to be scrambled eggs and toast. No surprises there.

The mountain gap bit was at the start of the walk. The wind shoved me up one side and pushed me down the other, then pummelled me all the way along by the fjord. I could see fish farms in the fjord, which was slicing deeper and deeper inland. There were no houses in sight, nor any sign of a road. It was very beautiful and very wet. I had a soggy lunch, sheltering behind a wall, observed by several curious and friendly sheep, who nosed hopefully about my rucksack.

By the time the road came into sight, with the weather no better, I felt more than ready for the temporary shelter of a car.

Dominic and Christine, a French couple, stopped for me. They had no English and I had very little French, so we had a journey of vigorous miming. I was hoping to make it to Westport that day, which is where Dominic and Christine were also going. But my route to Westport lay via Louisburgh; the coastal two sides of a triangle. I got out of the steamy warmth of the car just beyond Glennagevlagh, having indicated my route to them on the Michelin map. They waved me off in some bewilderment.

The swollen river and Aasleagh Falls were dark-brown and roaring loudly. There was a chill edge to the wind. I set about walking onwards, in an effort to keep warm.

This was stupid. When you set off hitch-hiking, you cannot really plan anything. It is not possible to be sure of getting anywhere by a certain time, or indeed, of getting anywhere at all, since all of these things depend on getting lifts. It was a dripping wet day, all weeping trees and puddles and cold breath-filled air and there was not one car going to Louisburgh.

I had walked a sodden and dogged few miles before I realised this. There was nothing to do, except to turn back towards the main Westport road and to hell with Following The Coast that day. The Gore-Tex seams were doing their sponge trick. I could feel the rain gradually soaking through my boots. *Why* hadn't I stayed in the car and had a sensible, straightforward lift to Westport? I picked my way back among the puddles and chastised myself for straying so far from an alternative route.

Sheep huddled at the side of the road got up and bleated mournfully at my disturbing them. They were even more miserable-looking than me. They shook their fleece repeatedly like big sad dogs and wandered along, bleating and searching vainly for the least wet bit of road or grass they could find.

It took a long time to get a lift, once I'd got back to the main road. People are very good about picking up hitch-hikers when it starts to rain. It's when its been raining for some time and a potential passenger is clearly going to leave their sodden mark in your car, that a hitch-hiker can expect to wait for their lift. I began to feel like curling up amongst the sheep and sharing out the remains of my lunch with them.

Eventually, a Fiesta van pulled over. It was going all the way to Westport. I pulled off the Gore-Tex, threw them into the back and fell in myself, cold and wet and fed up. Besides the driver, whose name was John, there was one other passenger; a Norwegian man named Sven.

"I'm showing Sven around," John told me.

"Are you a hitch-hiker also?" I asked Sven, realising as I did so that Sven was certainly not a hitch-hiker. He was wearing a very beautiful, if impractical, suede jacket and had a haircut that looked as if he'd just stepped out of a particularly good barber's.

"No, no, Sven is in Ireland on business. He works with me in the fish farming industry."

I sat up straight on the back seat. "Oh," I said carefully, "that's interesting. I've just come from Connemara and I've seen lots of anti fish farming signs. Perhaps you can tell me your side of the story."

"We're tired telling our story," John said cheerfully. "And we've just spent today driving around Connemara, pulling down those signs you saw and putting up some of our own instead. There's one on the back seat beside you."

Under a jacket was a rectangular printed poster. *Fish Farms Mean Jobs/Export Fish Not People.*

We talked about fish farms all the way to Westport. Sven belonged to the parent company in Norway and was obviously attached to the managerial and financial side of things. John had been showing him some of the Connemara fish farms. In answer to my questions about some of the controversial issues surrounding fish farming, John's side of the story was this: Yes, Nuvan is used and yes, it is a "very nasty" chemical.

"But listen to me," he said, "farmers also use Nuvan in sheep dip. They are required by law to dip sheep twice a year. What do you think they do with the waste?"

"They dump it?" Sven suggested.

"Exactly! And where do they dump it?"

"In the rivers?" he said doubtfully.

81

"Exactly! And you don't hear the same racket about farmers using Nuvan, do you?"

John had been to the fish farming conference in Furbo the previous weekend. I asked him if local disquiet was being revealed in ways other than tacking posters to trees.

"It's a very nasty feeling," he said emphatically, "and it's getting nastier all the time."

He did concede that one of the reasons why fish farmers were so disliked was the fear some people had of the industry taking over the major lakes and fishing rivers to rear smoults in; a sort of knock-on effect from the rod licence controversy. There was a fear that once people had to pay the government to fish in what had previously been free waters, that there would be nothing to stop the government leasing out stretches of rivers and lake areas in which to place fish farms.

"And that, to anglers, would be sacrilegious."

He went on to say that some time previously, one of the prominent fish farmers had made a foolish statement to the effect that if the fish farming industry in Ireland was going to expand, that it would have to use lake and river sites in which to do so. Before the rod licence controversy had been settled, the government had had to give public assurances that this would not happen.

The conversation turned to alternative methods of killing the sea lice.

"Sven here tells me that they use powdered garlic in Norway and it kills the sea lice off instantly."

"*Garlic,*" I repeated, amazed. "Are you going to try it?"

"We will try anything; we would love to use anything other than Nuvan," he said, very sincerely.

Before farmed salmon are harvested, they are fed Canthaxantin by pellet form, which dyes their white flesh the same pink colour of wild salmon.

"In Norway, they are using paprika," John told me. "And we'll try that too." Garlic to kill off the sea lice and paprika to colour the salmon flesh! I wondered if the pair of them were having me on, but they assured me they were not.

It was still pouring as we drove into Westport. They would not hear of dropping me off in the town, asking me where I wanted to stay and then going out of their way to drop me to the door of the hostel, even carrying my rucksack into the hallway.

The hostel went by the exotic name of "Club Atlantic Holiday Hostel". It had only recently opened and looked somewhat like a converted warehouse but was spotlessly clean; was heated and the small dormitories had wonderfully wide pine bunks. The rain drummed down on the corrugated roof but I no longer cared.

There were not many people staying at Club Atlantic. I brought a book into the common room and struck up conversation with Marc, a Swiss boy who was on a break from an English language course in Dublin. After we had been talking for about half an hour, he got up to go and called out politely from the door: "Excuse me, but I never asked you what part of Germany you were from?"

There was one other person in the common room; a young man in a lumberjacket with a big, clean-cut face from which his features seemed to be hewn out in an exaggerated way. He was writing what looked to me like pages of poetry, on sheets of sunshine-yellow foolscap. There was a lot of sighing and pen-clicking. He looked over at me once and immediately bustled the pages into a sheaf, covered them with his arm, and sighed more deeply than ever.

I made myself some dinner in the empty kitchen and ate it in the empty dining room. The rain was still at it. The hostel was some distance from the town and I did not feel enthusiastic about putting on my wet jacket and going in search of Westport town. I peered into the common room, but it was now empty. Nobody else seemed to be arriving that night. The reception desk was closed. My footsteps echoed in the corridors.

I took a book and dashed across the road to The Railway Tavern. The only other customer, boots stretched towards a small turf fire, deerstalker pulled down over his eyes, was the sighing pen-clicker.

Thomas was originally from Virginia and had been living in Chicago for the last five years.

"I've been doing a bit of acting and a bit of carpentry. I do all that sort of stuff in between writing poetry."

Thomas' grandparents had come from Westport and Thomas had come back for a holiday to Ireland to see where they had been born. He liked Westport so much that he was going to spend the rest of his month there.

"I'm gonna stay in the hostel until it shuts."

"What do you do all day in Westport?" I asked, curious to know if Club Atlantic was livelier than it appeared to be.

"Go to the library. Write poetry." He gave me a hard stare. "Gee, Woman With the Funny Name, but your hair looks just like one of those Connemara bushes in the wind. Real wild and strange. You've got real poem hair."

The Guinness was sour and flat. Thomas continued to stare, perhaps sizing me up as possible poem-material, while I moved restlessly in my chair and tried to keep the conversation going in an effort to divert attention from the wild and strange hair.

"What sort of poems do you write?"

"Nature poems, mostly."

"You must like Ted Hughes then?"

Thomas stopped staring and looked puzzled. "Ted Hughes?"

"He writes lots of nature poems," I explained, baldly. "He was married to an American woman who was also a poet; Sylvia Plath."

"Sylvia *who*?" Thomas shook his head. "I don't know an awful lot of poets. What does she write?"

I dropped the subject of Ted Hughes and his one-time wife, Sylvia Who, and took myself and my hair to bed.

Rummaging through a pile of magazines and papers in the common room next morning, I came across a day-old *Irish Times* and looked through it. I had recently begun to take a great interest in its weather section. Along with the weather charts and forecasts and "Yesterday's Midday Temperatures", there was a fascinating daily column by Brendan McWilliams, in which the most unlikely things connected up in some way with weather. All manner of quotations turned up in this column, ranging from old newspaper reports to Shakespeare plays; from journal extracts to Omar Khayyam. The columns are entitled anything from "A Memorable Monk" to "The Smell of

Rain". In one of these columns, he admits, with a sense of glee: "Writing a daily column for the *Irish Times* leads one down strange pathways."

On the long-standing topic of rain, Brendan McWilliams is inexhaustible. The column for 16 October was headed "Troublesome Rain" and it struck a responsive chord in my sodden heart.

Heavy rain alone is troublesome, but when combined with the penetrating force of a strong wind – a phenomenon known to meteorologists as driving rain *– the problem is magnified many times. Faced with the "to-and-fro-conflicting wind and rain" – conditions all too familiar to us recently – detailed research pays dividends in finding the materials best able to "bide the pelting of the pitiless storm".*

In calm conditions, raindrops fall vertically at a speed which depends upon their size. When the wind blows, however, the drops are also carried horizontally; with very strong winds, the rain is swept along at angles close to 45 degrees - and when this happens, a vertical wall facing the wind receives a substantial wetting.

As the vertical walls, so too for people. *Troublesome rain.* I liked that delicate euphemism. It was much more lyrical, not to mention politer, than any of the adjectives I had previously been tacking onto the word "rain".

Westport disorientated me. The riverside mall reminded me of Ennis. I wandered dispiritedly in the rain and kept going around in circles, getting mixed up by the clock-tower at the end of one vista and the statue of St Patrick on an immense stone plinth at the end of another. St Patrick, clutching a crook which was entwined with a snake, looked down beningly at me, as well he might, presumably being in a place where the rain no longer bothered him.

Westport was where I did little more than dry out, go to the bank, do my laundry, stock up with groceries and have a second early night at Club Atlantic Holiday Hostel.

I shook off dispiritedness and set off for Achill the next day, glad to be on the move again.

4
ENTRANCES TO THE UNDERWORLD
Achill to Sligo

I got a lift as far as Mulrany from a man with brick-red cheeks and enormous hands, which looked as if they could easily crush the steering wheel like a crumpled can.

"I'm Rosita," I said confidently.

"Is that so," the man replied. He grunted and looked over at my map-case. "Are you hitching around the Irish coast then?"

Startled, I said yes, and he grunted again in a self-congratulatory way.

In between grunts, Is That So had some interesting things to say about Achill. "Have you ever been there before?"

"No."

"Well, all the folk you'll be likely to see in Achill will be women and young ones up to eighteen and the old ones. There's no work in Achill. All the men go away to work and all the young ones these days go for good when they've finished school."

"What about tourism?"

He laughed in an unamused way. "That's all there is and there's only a few doing that. Tourism and fishing – in the summer. It's always been the same on Achill. It's a bloody hard place to squeeze some kind of life out of, unless you work in the hotel or in a shop or you're simple."

I was still pondering what he meant by this last comment when he made what turned out to be his final remark of the journey.

"There's not a family along this bit of coast who doesn't have relations in America; or have half their own family off in England."

I sat on a wall outside Mulrany village and had lunch,

looking out over Clew Bay. A small boy on a BMX bike hovered nearby, darting from driveway to driveway, coming near me and then pedalling madly away again, squealing with laughter. Lunch eaten, I packed up and walked through the village, the small boy trailing me delightedly until I got a lift.

I asked Marita, the Achill woman who picked me up, about what Is That So had told me.

"Yes dear, it's true for a lot of people," she said. "I've been married twenty years now and for most of those years, my husband has been working in London. He comes home four times a year, for two weeks at a time. And there's a lot more like me. We have three children and they all say they want to stay in Ireland. We'll see about that," she concluded, in a voice which was somewhere between hopeful and grim.

I walked the last couple of miles to Achill Sound, the road arrowing through areas of dark-looking bog. At Achill Sound, I picked up letters from the poste restante and looked at the map to decide which way I would go towards Keel. There was a scenic road which looped round to the south; The Atlantic Drive. This looked promising.

A man with his small son in the back seat brought me as far as Cloughmore. "You're going the wrong way to Keel," he said.

I explained about wanting to follow the coast.

"You'll get no cars going further out here at this time of the year. There are no houses between here and Dooega, at the other side of The Atlantic Drive."

"I don't mind walking."

"Good." He looked across at me and chuckled. "That's what I think you'll be doing."

I saw why this stretch of road was called The Atlantic Drive. Nobody would have any need to stop, other than to pull in to admire the view or have a picnic. There were no inhabited houses to visit or rent, no shops to tarry in. You would just keep driving on if you were a tourist. I thought it was unlikely the Achill people would often walk or drive the five miles or so between the villages of Cloughmore and Dooega. The main shopping routes lay out through Achill Sound and over the bridge for the Cloughmore people, and north, either to Keel or Achill Sound, for the Dooega people.

At any rate, I had the entire Atlantic Drive to myself that afternoon. No cars passed me in either direction. There was a peculiar light in the sky. There were streaks of pink behind Clare Island and grey-blue bulging clouds beyond the bogland, which, even in that light, looked dark; the matted coat of some primitive animal. Achill seeped all around me on that walk. It was a seeping place. The huge skies were fluid with light; the bog leaked over the horizon and beyond eyesight.

Ruined cottages stood side by side with inhabited houses in the village of Dooega: a sad inversion of Tully Cross, with its brand-new thatch on the "Rent-An-Irish-Cottage" buildings standing alongside the slate roofs of the true Tully Cross people. Dooega was partly ruined, partly propped up; a bleak, windswept village hunched low beneath a hill. It did not encourage me to linger.

About a mile the far side of Dooega, I got a lift to the turnoff for River and Keel. It was still a few miles more to Keel, but although there were plenty of cars on this bit of road, none stopped. I switched on the torch and continued walking. A farmer stood at the side of the road, whistling and calling to his dog, which was moving a flock of sheep beyond the brow of a small hill.

Eventually, I was given a lift by two women; Michelle and Rita. Many of the hostels closed either in mid October or at the end of October, until the season started up again the following year. There was a hostel still open in Keel – The Wayfarer – where I hoped to stay that night. Michelle and Rita did not need to go all the way into Keel, but they insisted on driving me to Keel, finding out where the hostel was, and waiting outside to make sure it was open before waving and driving away.

All the way around, I kept meeting this sort of kindness. People would sometimes go miles out of their way to leave me at the right road or turnoff. I was invited into their homes for tea. I was often made to feel as if I had hailed a taxi instead of hitching a lift, being treated like a VIP passenger; fussed over in case I was cold from window draughts, or that the dog in the back was too smelly or that their small child was annoying me. People said things like: "I used to hitch myself, so I'd never see anyone stuck now." "I wouldn't like to see my daughter out on the road on a day like this." "My kids hitch-hike themselves, so I always pick people up now."

The Wayfarer was an independent hostel. The blurb on my *Independent Hostels Of Ireland Guide* declared: "As an association we are pleased to provide a high standard of low cost accommodation."

It was £4.00 to stay in The Wayfarer, where I had the most unpleasant hostel overnight stay of my journey. The warden and his family lived in one part of the old house and the hostellers had the rest of the house. The warden came out from behind the family door, to take my money and to tell me what room I would be sleeping in, and then vanished, not to be seen by me again.

There were damp patches on the ceilings. Water dripped methodically into the plastic containers which had been placed thoughtfully underneath the more active patches. The torn carpets had been repaired with strips of wide brown sticky-tape. The kitchen was lit by what appeared to be a ten watt bulb.

On closer investigation, I decided that it was not a place where I would wish to consider preparing food. Another hosteller leaned over the cooker, peering deep into a pot in order to see what it was that she was so furiously stirring. In that dim light, she could have been one of the witches from *Macbeth*, rustling up a little something in her cauldron.

However, worst of all was the bathroom. There was a shower fixture in the bath and there was actually hot water, but upon inspecting the bath I quickly changed my mind about having a shower; to me, the area around the plug-hole on that night resembled a small and furry animal.

I got my torch and went to seek out temporary refuge in a pub.

At The Village Inn, a dozen elderly men huddled round the turf fire with their pints of Guinness and watched *The*

Late Late Show in silence. I sat in a corner and wrote letters.

"What brings you to our part of the world at such a time of the year?" the barman asked me curiously.

"I don't know," I replied grimly, dreading closing time and the inevitable return to The Wayfarer.

Despite the walking I had done that day and the Guinness in The Village Inn, I did not sleep well or deeply. I had neglected to investigate my bed before setting off for the pub. The beds were bunk beds, as is usual for hostels. However, The Wayfarer bunk beds were collectors' items; magnificent Victorian cast-iron affairs. They had wooden bases, with mattresses on top. The mattresses were an inch thick and were stuffed with what felt like horse-hair.

I unrolled my sheetbag and knew it would be a long night. There was one other girl in the room. She tossed and sighed and yawned all through the night. I tossed and cursed. It was like lying on the back of a horse, I decided. By morning, I had come to the conclusion that it was like lying on the back of a horse with chronic mange, since the horse-hair mattress was full of lumps.

I got up very early, feeling vicious. The warden, with whom I intended to exchange several nasty words, having had plenty opportunity to think them out during my largely sleepless night, was nowhere to be seen.

It was pouring, of course. But I was so glad to get out into the fresh air that I didn't mind the daily Gore-Tex ritual.

Both Is That So and Marita had told me about a deserted village at Doogort, a couple of miles north of Keel. "I don't think it was particularly a Famine village," Is That So had said. "More that people left it gradually, through emigration."

They had been vague as to how many houses were in the village. He had said about twenty. Marita guessed there to be thirty.

There were more than seventy ruined cottages at Doogort, all spread out along a green road, gables towards the wind which swept in from the Atlantic. Most of them were more tumbledown than the houses in the deserted village near Fanore. I walked around them in the pouring rain and then took shelter in a workman's hut near the road and had some hot coffee from my flask.

When I looked down at the road again, there was a station wagon parked at the side of the road. I hadn't seen or heard it approaching. It was painted green, white and gold in sections; green boot, white body and gold bonnet. I wondered if it could have anything to do with the Presidential Election and went down to have a proper look.

Werner was German. He was rubbing his eyes and folding up a duvet in the back of the car. He offered me a lift back to Keel.

The interior of the car was a shrine to the Irish Football team. World Cup scarves, flags and badges festooned the roof. Jack Charlton's face beamed from every corner. There were stickers and tricolour teddies and stubs of match tickets. I stared around at it all in amazement.

"But you're German," I said. "Your country *won* the World Cup."

"I know," he said simply. "I'm sorry about that."

"Why do you support Ireland?"

"I *love* this country," he stated. "It's a wonderful country and Achill is the best place in the world and Ireland have the world's best – "

"– football team!" I finished.

I got a lift from Keel to Mulrany from a sharp-faced Donegal couple, who argued icily with each other all the way. I had to remind them to let me out at Mulrany, as they were so absorbed, they had forgotten they'd picked me up.

I started trying to get a lift towards Belmullet, in north Mayo. This was on the main road going north, but in an hour and a half, only two cars passed, neither of which stopped. I sheltered under an old stone railway bridge and waited. These periods of walking or waiting, caught between stasis and movement, were oddly satisfying. The landscape extended itself slowly around me and allowed me to absorb it; the minute I got into a car, it began to telescope down and move quickly past.

A Mancunian named Patrick stopped. He was driving a

battered old Hiace van which had an engine that gave a good imitation of someone screaming in non-stop hysterics. Proper conversation was impossible. I gathered, in between pauses for breath before the next bout of yells by the engine, that Patrick made his living by buying outboard engines for boats and flogging them off for a handsome profit in Ireland. For the continued prosperity of his income, I hoped the outboard engines were in a better state than the one in his van. Patrick seemed to be asking me questions but I couldn't make out what they were. I nodded and smiled and he nodded and smiled and we drove along companionably.

The area we were going through was emptier than any Irish landscape I had previously seen. Miles upon miles of bog; the same dark-looking bog I had seen on Achill. The settlements of Ballycroy, Bangor and Bunnahowen were well stretched out, with nothing in between, except the bogland. Bog oak lay in contorted piles at the side of the road. The landscape was bleak, yet compelling. Huge skies pressed down on the dark bog, which began to mesmerize me with its sameness.

Country and western music leaked out of small pubs in Bangor, where a sheep-market was taking place in the main street. People turned to stare at the van, which rattled through the town loudly and did not stop.

Patrick was going all the way to Belmullet but I changed my mind about possibly spending the night there. It was still early in the afternoon and I did not want to spend the rest of that grey day wandering sleepily around Belmullet, which the *Rough Guide* described as; "a functional little village, its streets perpetually mired with mud from the bogs."

I got out of the van just beyond Bunnahowen where the road split, and began walking down the road which goes round the top of Mayo; towards Ballycastle and Killala. I got a lift a few miles further on to a crossroads, with a man who wordlessly stopped his car for me and then, after a silent journey, wordlessly stopped again at the crossroads, indicating that this was as far as he was going to bring me.

There was a small shop on one corner of the crossroads and a garage on another corner. I stood opposite the shop and watched cars drive out of the flat landscape, stop outside the shop, the occupants go in and then emerge with boxes and bags, to drive away again; their bright-eyed children watching me from the rear windows.

A couple in a car pulled in to read the signposts and to confer with each other. The man got out of the car and came over to me.

"Can we give you a lift anywhere?"

At this stage, I had decided to try and make it to the An Óige hostel in Killala, which I fervently hoped would be clean and dry and lacking in horse-hair mattresses. He spied my map.

"Can I have a look at that? We're trying to find Carrowteige but I've forgotten where it is. We'll be going onto Ballina after that, if you want a lift. Do you mind a diversion?"

I didn't mind at all. I found Carrowteige on the map and gave directions.

Alec and Tracy were both in their twenties. Alec was from Ballina and Tracy was from Luton.

"I went over to London one summer, for a couple of months," Alec laughed. "That was years ago. I ended up staying. I'm just back on holiday, showing Trace around."

Trace sat stiffly in the passenger seat and stared out the window.

Did Alec see himself coming back? He shrugged his shoulders. "Not just yet. We'll see how it goes."

As a boy, Alec had gone to the Gaeltacht in Carrowteige, a place where he said he had had "great crack". He wanted to show it to Tracy. We turned off the main road and drove down the small peninsula, Alec pointing out the house where he had stayed. At the flat, wet stretch of sand at Carrowteige beach, Alec stopped the car for a couple of minutes. They didn't get out of the car and walk around; they just sat there together and looked out silently over the wet sand where one of them had spent summer as a child.

Music played on the car radio. Conversation died out. The car was pleasantly warm. Navigational duties over, I lay against the back seat and slept the rest of the way to Killala.

93

The Killala Hostel was warm, dry, clean; had new duvets and was furnished with comfortable bunks. It was a big old house which dated from 1892. There were pillars of polished granite outside the front door, a magnificent mahogany staircase in the hall and several lovely fireplaces. One of these fireplaces was set with hand-painted tiles of birds; another, with a mirrored overmantle, was intricately carved from oak.

Besides myself, there were four other people staying – all women. "There's no men about," the warden said. "Go and look in the men's toilet on the first floor."

The first-floor men's toilet had an extraordinary loo. It was made of nineteen-century porcelain, with enormous patterns of blue flowers painted inside and outside. It was cracked, but still in working order, and was the most marvellously exotic thing I had yet come across in a hostel.

I had a wonderfully long sleep that night and holed up beside the fire in the common room next day, writing my diary and reading.

Well-rested, I got up early next day and set off in the clear morning.

Tom, who was from the village of Kilcummin, gave me a lift into Ballina, where he worked. General Humbert had landed at Kilcummin with his troops in 1798. Tom had been an extra in the television production, *The Year of the French,*some years previously.

"I was a soldier one day, a peasant the next day. There were fifty local extras and we were all mates. Be Jaysus, we had a grand time out of it all, what with all the crack during the day and down the pub every evening."

He asked me what I thought of Mayo and I described the day spent hitching to Killala.

"Aye. It's a hard place to live in, Mayo. You can go ten miles down the road at night in Mayo and not see a single light from a car or a house. But I wouldn't want to live anywhere else than Kilcummin. And Mayo's doing all right. It might look sparsely populated, but it's Leitrim, not Mayo, that's the only county in Ireland with a declining population."

When I told him about Achill, he nodded. "Achill's

always had that tradition of people going away to work. But the best thing that's ever happened to Mayo is Knock Airport. Now people can travel from London to somewhere like Belmullet in under three hours. Before the airport, they'd have to fly into Dublin and then spend hours driving across. People come home much more often now. I tell you, it's the best thing that ever happened to Mayo."

Tom dropped me out the Sligo Road, which bypassed Ballina. I wanted to try and go to Sligo via Enniscrone and Easkey; the coastal road. A jolly, bearded man drove me to Enniscrone. The only thing which I had planned on doing on the journey was to take a hot saltwater seaweed bath in Kilcullen's Baths of Enniscrone, which I knew were open until the end of October.

"What on earth are you going to Enniscrone in the middle of winter for?" Although he was from Crossmolina, some twenty miles away, he had never heard of the Baths. "You're having me on!" he declared. "Whoever heard of a seaweed bath?"

He was so intrigued that he drove me all the way down the beach road to Kilcullen's and got out of the car to investigate the Baths with me.

Alas, the downside of spontaneous travel, where I seldom bothered phoning ahead to check if places were open, meant that I took the chance of their being closed. The Kilcullen Baths, an old whitewashed stone building, glittering pristinely under the unexpectedly blue sky, was, as I had thought, open until the end of October. But the neat little sign informed me that the opening hours for Monday to Friday in October were four in the afternoon to eight in the evening. It was still only midday.

I climbed up onto a windowsill and peered in through an open window. There was a slatted wooden dais, painted green, which covered the floor. Set into this was a huge Victorian cast-iron bath. It had wide copper taps through which the hot seawater had flowed many a time, and there were rambling sea-green stains on the tap side of the bath. A frieze of coloured Victorian tiles contrasted with the plain white tiles in the rest of the room. The ceiling was high; the room bright and sunny. The whole place smelt tantalizingly of seaweed.

I vowed to return some other time and wallow in my marine fantasies.

It was a blue day. The wide sky was deep blue; the calm sea was blue. A mother and her two children drew pictures in the sand with a stick.

I walked out the road a bit and started hitching towards Easkey. I waited. And waited. An elderly woman in a raincoat and headscarf asked me where I was going.

"It's an awful long way to Sligo," she said, plainly worried. She patted me on the shoulder. "I'll be saying a little prayer that you'll get a lift." She walked backwards down the road, waving encouragingly, until she lost sight of me.

Her little prayer didn't seem to be working. There just weren't any cars heading towards Easkey. I waited over an hour and then looked at my map. I hated the idea of having to retrace my steps to Ballina. There was a small back road a bit further on, which ran inland to join the N59; the main road to Sligo.

Once I had reached the turnoff and began hitching on the back road, the inevitable happened. Cars suddenly emerged from nowhere and whizzed past, towards Easkey, on the road which I had just left. There were nothing but bicycles on my back road.

At the entrance to this back road was a road sign, of a kind I had not seen before and which mystified me. It was a yellow, diamond-shaped sign, with the silhouettes of a car, which was in the top part of the sign, and the little figure of a running person underneath it. Whatever it meant, it gave me an idea.

I took up a dangerous position in the middle of the main road and began to dual-hitch, racing from the main road to side road as the scant traffic dictated, glancing every now and then at the mysterious, scampering and vaguely manic little figure in the sign. At last, a red Mini, which was turning sharply into the back road, came to a bewildered halt.

"Can't make up your mind where you're going?" the driver inquired, not unkindly.

There was another long wait once I'd got onto the main

road. At this stage, I was very hungry. Usually I filled a flask in the morning and made up some lunch, since I could never be sure how long I was going to be on the road, but I had forgotten to do so that morning.

Mike, a Fermanagh truck-driver, gave me a lift to Sligo town. There was something amiss with the truck, which meant that he had to drive at under 40 mph. At intervals, my stomach rumbled. I had the misfortune to say that I had only been to Sligo once before; passing through, some years back. Mike drove right through Sligo and into the outskirts, where he kindly pointed out the Tourist Office to me.

"There you go!" he beamed. "They'll tell you all about Sligo in there!"

My hunger was so overpowering that I barely waited for the truck to disappear from sight before legging it back into town without giving the Tourist Office so much as a second glance.

There was a restaurant in the O'Connell Centre on O'Connell St. I hauled myself up flights of stairs, lurched into the Tea House and began to blissfully read the menu. A motherly, white-haired waitress came over to take my order. She took one look at me and at my rucksack, dumped in the corner, and said, shrewdly and tactfully, "The roast dinner is very good value and a most substantial meal."

"Right," I said, "I'll have it."

One substantial roast dinner later, I emerged onto O'Connell St again and went to look for a bed for the night.

The White House was an independent hostel on Markievicz Road. There were some people staying at the hostel on a long-term basis; students at the Sligo Regional Technical College. Edel, who came from Ennis and was one of these students, smiled tolerantly at me in the kitchen and asked what country I was from. I had to name all the streets in Ennis before she believed that I had grown up in the same town that she had.

People were always asking me where I came from. I was not quite sure how to answer this question, which usually

97

came with another question; the second being, "Where do you live?" My accent, usually a reasonable way of pinning someone down, was of no use to anyone. It was a snowball of an accent; part west of Ireland, part Dublin, part Australian, part English.

If, when people asked me where I was from and I said "Clare," the next things they would say were "You don't *sound* like you do," or "But you don't *live* there any more, do you?"

Sometimes, I tried hard to answer these questions. "I was born in Clare, but I've been working in London," was usually a satisfactory answer. Some people kept on asking, not unreasonably, "But where do you *live*? Where is your *home*?" I admitted I was presently homeless, had no fixed abode. "Where are your *things*?" people asked in desperation. Scattered in boxes on tops of wardrobes and in attics between London and Clare was the answer. It didn't sound like much of a home.

I consulted the *Concise Oxford Dictionary* to find out what this place called "home" was. "*Dwelling-place; fixed residence of family or household; native land of oneself or one's ancestors*". Dwelling-place – nowhere permanent. Family residence – parents and grown-up siblings scattered across Ireland. Native land! That was easy, but to say "Ireland's my home", was useless as an answer to another Irish person.

Living abroad, I'd tried wrestling with this idea of home in a poem entitled "Birthright".

> *Washing her hair at the kitchen sink*
> *My mother would say that Clare water was awful hard,*
> *And I was mystified.*
>
> *Turloughs, in which the water came and went*
> *Leaving behind a rich sward,*
> *Pooled the county*
> *Like the unpredictable welling of tears.*
>
> *At schoool, we learned*
> *That the Burren was an area of limestone:*

Porous rock
Through which the rain easily sliced
And scooped grykes, swallow-holes, and caves.

As a child, it seemed stone grew
In these fissured fields
As natural a crop as oats or barley;
The flat, thin Liscannor flags and Moher slate
Were harvested for walls,
Roofs, floors, and hearths.

Away from Ireland now,
Along with its landscape of stone
The turloughs of Clare soak my memory;
Are constantly dissolving themselves,
Like my irresolute ideas of home.

The truth was that I had not yet found a home that did not dissolve with restlessness, if a "dwelling place" – the first definition of the ambiguous word "home" in the dictionary – was what was meant by home. Yet I felt *at home* in many places. I had felt at home in the strange landscape of the Nullarbor Plain, had even asked the barman if there was a job going in the roadhouse, perfectly happy at the idea of spending time in this middle of nowhere. As I travelled around Ireland, I thought it was possible to have several homes and that the word "home" was fluid; a word that I would continue to redefine for myself.

In the dormitory which I had been directed towards, was Jill, who was in the process of flinging around the room what looked like the contents of a small boutique. Jill was travelling around Europe on a Kawasaki motorbike, which pulled a trailer. She had been in Ireland for a week – a wet week – and was only now opening some of the bags in the trailer. The rain had leaked in; everything was mouldy. She scrabbled through all the bags, cursing madly and raced off to find a laundrette before everything shut for the day.

There were far more people staying at The White House than there had been in any of the other hostels: six

Australians; Jill, who was English; Andreas, a German; Drew, an American; as well as the students, who tended to be sighted only in the kitchen.

Over breakfast next morning, I talked to Drew, who had a luxuriant beard and quantities of hair, which was neatly tied back in a pony-tail. Drew had already been out sightseeing.

"I got up at five this morning and jogged out to Drumcliff to see Yeats' grave. It's very nice; you should go there too."

Drew worked in Boston with "sexually abused young girls" and studied theology part-time. He leaned towards me confidentially.

"This is the first time I've ever been out of the US! First time out of Boston! I wanted to come to Ireland for a holiday because it's a Catholic country and it'll be real useful to me in my thesis."

I asked him what his impressions of Ireland were, so far. Drew pulled thoughtfully at his pony-tail and gave me a bright smile. "It's an extremely feminine place," he said fervently. "I think it's a great womb – a womb of Catholicism and a womb of creativity." The smile vanished. "But it troubles me that the women over here seem very repressed. Ireland strikes me as being a very patriarchal society. I can understand why there's no abortion, but can you tell me why there's no divorce?"

Sligo intrigued me. I had heard it described as a small town masquerading as a city. Looking out on Sligo Bay, Sligo's maze of narrow streets seemed full of young people from the Regional Technical College. It gave the impression of being a compact, scurrying town. The big chain stores – Quinnsworth, Penneys, Dunnes Stores – were squirrelled away in peripheral locations, so that the heart of Sligo concentrated itself among those inner narrow streets.

There was a bronze statue of Yeats outside the Ulster Bank. It was signed "Rowan Gillespie" and dated 1990.An elongated, rather aloof-looking W.B., caught in mid-walk, or mid-swagger. An enormous, floppy bowtie fluttered at Yeats' throat like an exotic butterfly and all across his voluminous clothes were lines of raised writing; extracts from his work. I was told later in Hargadon's Pub that the locals had dubbed it "The Swank at the Bank". A jacket billowed out around Yeats' hips and at a quick distant glance, you could think that here was a furious cobra, ready to strike. Perhaps the sculptor had intended this visual trick to emerge – the steel and bite beneath the swank.

Over the years, I had read articles in various magazines and newspapers about Michael Quirke, the Sligo butcher who was also a woodcarver. In the last two years, he had given up butchering altogether and was now carving wood full-time.

Michael Quirke's shop was on Wine St. There were small, chunky-looking wood carvings in the window, with scraps of paper beside each one. Written in pencil on these bits of paper were legends and poems, each of which was particular to the carving beside it. I recognised some of the carved figures – Óisín, Fionn McCool – but most of them were unknown to me. Some of the carvings were straightforward depictions of mythological figures. Others looked baffling; three-dimensional story-boards in wood, with, among other symbols, nuts, fish, goats and pigs.

Presiding over all these myths were two portraits, which hung from meat hooks and were carved in relief. One was of W.B. Yeats, the other of Samuel Beckett. The sharp, stern face of Beckett stared out unblinkingly at me. Carved in the corner of this portrait, in loose, straggly letters, was the single word, "Waiting".

The shop still had the unmistakable aura of a butcher's: the functional white-tiled walls; the old-fashioned wooden counter; the Butcher Boy slicing machine; the metal rails and meat hooks.

Piled on the floor were great raw chunks of tree trunks. On the counter lay small pieces of wood; many of them partially carved. Michael Quirke, a thin, lithe man with wise eyes, stood behind the counter, whittling away.

From carving the flesh of animals to carving the flesh of wood, I thought, looking in the window.

I went inside and lingered by the counter, inhaling the smell of clean-cut wood and linseed oil. Almost at once,

Michael Quirke laid aside the piece of wood that he was carving and came over to talk to me. For the next hour, he told stories and talked, while I listened, asking the odd question, simultaneously dazzled and bewildered by the incredible depth and range of his knowledge of Irish mythology; which seemed to be populated with a vast number of characters of whom I had never before heard.

As he spoke to me, he picked up the finished carvings in the window and told their stories. He lifted pieces of uncarved wood from the counter and told me which tree they came from, the wood giving the illusion of almost leaping into his hands.

"I only use wood from windfallen trees. That terrible storm a couple of years ago felled enough trees to keep me carving for years. I use oak, ash, sycamore and elm. It's *wonderful* stuff, wood. It's still living for seven years after it's been felled."

He showed me the triangular piece of wood he had been working on when I came in. There was a dark streak on one side.

"I'll try to keep this darkness," he said. "People don't like to consider the darkness – they only want things of light – but I try to put darkness in my carvings as well. It's more honest."

There was a copy of Robert Graves' *The White Goddess* and one of Paul Durcan's – *Daddy, Daddy* – behind the counter. He saw me looking at them.

"I learned a lot from this book," he said, pointing towards the Graves. "And someone brought Paul Durcan's book in one day and showed it to me. I'm in one of his poems!" he explained, with pleasure and disbelief.

I glanced through the poem, "Antwerp 1984", while he told me that Durcan had come into his shop one day. "He came in here and talked to me for hours. I got an awful lot from him, so I'm delighted to see that he got something from me."

I asked the meaning of one of the symbols which recurred in several of the finished carvings; a pig.

"The pig is very important in Irish mythology," he assured me. "Pigs can see the wind. And artists and poets

102

can see within." He took up a squat carving of a Rodin "Le Penseur" type person, with the head almost swallowed up by the shoulders. "This is a Druidic carving."

I read the scrap of paper that accompanied it; "How Can The Knower Be Known?" And the answer?

"Look within," Michael Quirke said.

He drew diagrams of Ben Bulben and other Sligo mountains. "This area is so rich in mythology and strangeness. There are cairns on top of these mountains; the mythological entrances to the underworld. Lakes are also entrances to the underworld. There are people who say that some of these Sligo lakes are bottomless. That's all a cod! The only place that's bottomless is the rat's nest between the ears."

I had to buy something. It would have been impossible to have been so verbally bewitched and not to want a carving from this craftsman. How much was Beckett, I enquired gingerly. Beckett was forty pounds. He was the one extravagance of my journey.

Michael Quirke took down the carved portrait in Irish ash and wrote on a piece of notepaper that I should brush a mixture of 30 per cent linseed oil and 70 per cent turpentine onto Beckett's face each year "To keep the wood supple". He wrapped the carving up in layers of brown paper and string, left over from the butchering days, and handed it across the counter to me as he must have handed out thousands of parcels of meat in the past.

"I'm twenty years at it now," he said. "And two years full-time at it. And I'm still only learning!" He lifted his arms suddenly. "I'm *obscenely* happy."

The *Rough Guide* assured me that the Sligo County Museum was open daily 10.30-12.30 and 2.30-4.30, but when I turned up at the museum on Stephen St at 3.00 that afternoon, the door was firmly locked. I went into the Library, across the way, to ask if anyone local had the keys.

"Did you bang on the door?" the librarian asked me.

"No."

She sighed. "Try banging on the door and shouting. There's a heraldry section upstairs," she explained

103

patiently. "One of them should hear you eventually." She turned back to stamping books.

I duly banged on the heavy wooden door of the museum and called out.

Footsteps clattered down the stairs and the door was opened by a young woman with dark hair.

Abigail was one of the people who worked in the heraldry section. "It gets mad in the summer. Full of people all trying to relate themselves to Yeats!" she grinned.

There were just two rooms to the museum, each of which opened off the entrance hall. The left-hand room held articles of local interest, while the right-hand room was given over to things Yeatsian. The light was dim in the Sligo County Museum and I wandered about, looking curiously into the display cases, which were of a formidable size and made from dark wood.

The Yeatsian room struck me as being a rather startling waste of space. The walls were lined with prints of Jack Yeats' drawings, of a kind that are widely available for a couple of pounds; and murky photocopies of pages from W.B's notebooks. The cases were full of nondescript trivia. The only interesting Yeatsian thing was a splendid dark-blue leather case, embossed in cream, red, blue and green, which had held W.B. Yeats' Citation for the Nobel Prize for Literature. Even that was made to appear redundant, as of the Citation itself, there was no sign.

The room which contained local artifacts was far more interesting. It seemed to be a much less planned room and this made for a happy jumble of junk and history. There was a double-weight firkin of butter, weighing 112 lb., which had been found in a bog at Cloonty in 1982. The notice informed me, somewhat vaguely, that it was "thought to have been buried in a bog for over a century". The firkin resembled a tree stump, with hairy-looking "bark" at the sides, which were powdery-white in places.

There was an innocuous-looking brown-handled paper knife, "taken from the GPO Dublin, by a member of the staff, when the order was given to vacate the building during the Easter Rising 1916".

104

There were the usual pieces of china and glass and some extraordinary objects, which seemed to be there for no other reason than to fill up space, such as a "section of a rail for drying clothes over a hearth". Mr McElhanney of Castle St had donated a pair of leather doll's shoes, about two inches long, handmade by himself. They were perfectly stitched, with stout little heels and strong laces and sat on a shelf near an Inquisitional-type black cast-iron rat trap.

But the things which I found most fascinating were two "Unclassified Objects" which bore the polite query, "Can you identify any of the objects?" The two objects in question were something that resembled a crude knife and a wooden-handled skewer-like prong, which had a mysterious loop in the middle.

Abigail came over to see what it was that was making me laugh. "Oh, they have storerooms full of things that no one knows what they are," she said. "Every now and then, they bring out a couple of them."

Whole rooms full of "Unclassified Objects"! There is probably the makings of an entire Folk Archive languishing in Sligo storerooms. Why not make an exhibition of "Unclassified Objects" and invite the public to try and puzzle out their identities?

That evening, the entire hostel went to Hargadon's Pub on O'Connell St. Hargadon's was a dim cave of smoke and shining glasses, honeycombed with snugs, which were hung with old Guinness advertisements. There was an uneven stone floor and two counters. One was the bar counter and made of marble; the other was on what had been the grocery side and was wooden. On the wall behind this wooden counter were layers of shelves and drawers. They were all so old that they now slanted and sagged, at such peculiar angles that they must have been greatly disorientating to any patrons of Hargadon's who, over the course of an evening, had drunk too much.

The Australians asked Jill to tell them the story of the Moor's Murderers. Jill, in turn, asked for Man-eating Crocodiles and Deadly Snake stories. Andreas remained silent. I had not yet heard him utter a single word and wondered if perhaps he had no English. The only

105

alternative to the exchange of grisly stories was Drew, who questioned me earnestly about Irish Catholicism.

At closing time, Andreas came out with his one remark. "I know a place we can go and buy beer."

Myself, Jill, and Vanessa, one of the Australians, were all so amazed to hear Andreas speak that we found ourselves obediently following him down the street. Everyone else had gone back to the hostel. Andreas led us down Castle St and stopped outside a ramshackle old building which was covered in scaffolding and banged on the door. This door-banging ritual was obviously the Sligo *Open Sesame*. I had a vague idea of someone peering out and handing him a bottle of whiskey, wrapped up in brown paper.

He banged and banged. There was no sign of life; not a glimmer of a light to be seen anywhere. Eventually, we could hear tentative footsteps. Suddenly, as soon as the door was opened a cautious few inches, Sligo people appeared silently from the shadowy street. We all melted swiftly through the entrance and climbed flights of rickety old stairs. The man who let us in locked and bolted the door behind us.

Somehow, in the course of the previous night, Andreas had managed to bloodhound out the Sligo United Trades Club.

The Sligo United Trades Club was apparently a very old institution. It had originally been established as a meeting place for tradespeople. It was now the local Ceolthas Ceoltoirí Éireann headquarters. The interior of the Club was all dark paint and formica, with carefully shuttered windows. It was a small place and somewhat run-down, but despite its unpromising appearance, there was a remarkable assortment of people squirrelled away in the Sligo United Trades Club that evening.

Well-dressed women perched on bar stools. Old men cradled pints of Guinness. Men in suits lounged by the doorway. Student types, wearing the regulatory Doc Martens, tapped time to the people who played music in one corner; fiddle, bodhrán, tin whistle.

The music played until about 1.30 am, when the wooden shutters behind the bar were brought down. This did not interrupt the flow of drinking that night, however. The barman now merely nipped in and out the door at the side of the counter, with pints of Guinness and glasses of whiskey. People continued to arrive and bang on the door below.

When the music finished, cards were brought out, the chessboards were unfolded, games of draughts were set up. The chess games were quiet and serious; the draughts riotous and noisy.

Ronan, one of the younger patrons, gravitated over towards us. Ronan had lived in America, Australia and England. "Sligo's the place to be," he declared. "There's the best crack to be had here."

A group of young men were playing Twenty-Five with rigorous concentration. They called for another player and Jill volunteered. They looked staggered.

"A bird! A card-playing bird!"

Jill had to have the game explained to her. The man opposite me snorted into his whiskey.

"She doesn't know how to play," he said. "She's got no business playing."

"They asked her," I retorted, somewhat defensive for the Bird.

"Aye. And now she's holding them all up!"

I looked across at the card table. Jill looked slightly harassed. Two of the men were explaining the rules to her. Two others were making forays to the bar door and returning with glasses of whiskey, which they stowed on a shelf under the table, presumably for consumption at a later hour. Two more were loudly declaring they wouldn't play if a bird joined their table.

The man beside me had a pasty face, apart from his long hooked nose, which was crimson. He wore a smart-looking shirt and tie.

"I play Twenty-Five myself," he told me, "but I wouldn't bother my arse playing with those fellas. They're all pissed." He belched.

He eyed me sourly. "You're a stranger here, aren't you? Well for some, to be off on holidays. I don't work myself."

"So you're unemployed then?" I said, rather curiously, eyeing the shirt and tie and the double whiskey.

Pasty looked outraged. "I didn't say I was unemployed! I said I didn't work! I have money. I don't need to work. I have *income*." He looked shiftily at me.

I considered this revelation and wondered of what nature this *income* could possibly be.

He dug me in the ribs and addressed me in a deep and sullen voice. "Very important money. *Serious* money."

That was all he was prepared to give away. I knew it was useless to ask any more questions. He went back to snorting into his whiskey.

We prepared to leave at 3.00 am. The place was still buzzing with talk; drink was still materialising from somewhere.

The barman crept down the stairs in front of us, peered through a spyhole, opened the door a crack and put his head out. Then he beckoned us from the stairs, where we had been told to wait, and shooed us out quickly. The door melted shut behind us and we were alone on the deserted street.

5

THE TWO PARTS OF THE COUNTRY

Drumcliff to Letterkenny

I could have quite happily stayed on in Sligo for another few days, exploring its narrow streets more fully. I would have liked to have looked at the Art Gallery and stayed to see a performance of Seamus Heaney's *The Cure at Troy* at the Hawk's Well Theatre, the following day. Sligo was the sort of place that quickly absorbed its visitors. After such a short time, it began to look familiar to me; as if I had dashed in and out of its post office and taken the riverside walk by the Garavogue for years.

But I decided to move on. The weather was clear and dry; too good to spend browsing through the streets of the biggest town in the north west. It was perfect hitching weather.

Walking out the Drumcliff road, I could see the mountain-top cairns which Michael Quirke had pointed out to me. Ben Bulben raised its odd outline to the sky.

Drumcliff Church was a simple, stone church. W.B. Yeats is buried in its graveyard. His grave is protected by the clean, ecclesiastical lines of the church and shadowed by bare Ben Bulben's head; nestled between religion and the primitive nature. I wondered if he had ever secretly wanted a pagan burial in a mountain-top cairn and then decided not; nowhere for his desired epitaph to be carved out.

The grave itself is unprepossessing and the impression is of coldness and hardness. The epitaph, *Cast a cold eye/ On life, on death./ Horseman, pass by!*, was chiselled out in white letters on the headstone. The concrete grave was covered in white quartz chips; no earth in which to plant flowers or rose bushes; a tight, sealed grave. "All that is personal soon rots. It must be packed in ice or salt," Yeats had himself written.

To me, the most poignant thing about the grave was a little slab of stone, in memory of Yeats' wife George: a telescoped memorial, which rested at his feet like a small and loyal dog. The letters on this piece of stone were not fresh and white; they were faded and grey.

I looked about the windswept churchyard, watching people trail in and out to take photographs of Yeats' grave. There were several charming headstones, with epitaphs of unrestrained expressions of affection. In the Kerr plot, a husband, wife and son were remembered as "three who were lovely and pleasant in their lives".

The epitaph which I liked most was on a simple obelisk of stone to the east of the church, in the Henry plot.

> *Rough and unpolished*
> *   this stone stands erected*
> *Bearing no pretensions*
> *   to foolish pride*
> *Ah no, tis simply to mark*
> *   the humble bed*
> *Where kindred clay rests*
> *   side by side*
> *This is enough for me*
> *   for you however great*
> *Knowing man's length*
> *   and breadth is his sole estate*

Danny, an Englishman, gave me a lift to Bundoran. He was a terrifyingly bad driver. Danny kept telling me to gaze upon Ben Bulben and did the same himself. Oncoming drivers flashed lights, tooted horns, shook fists. Danny took not a scrap of notice. He kept gesturing towards Ben Bulben as if trying to cradle it within his hands. I thought he would simply abandon the car and run towards Ben Bulben with outstretched arms.

"I *love* that mountain!" he cried passionately. "That mountain made me buy a holiday house in Sligo, just so I could look at it all day long."

He craned and stared and kept imploring me to regard the bare head from all angles; to observe the changing light upon it; to see how the shape recreated itself, as we, sadly for him, drove away from it. Danny continued to peer in his side-mirror and breathe, "Oh, that mountain, that *mountain,*" while I clung to the dashboard and thought that Ben Bulben had bewitched him. Perhaps he had been investigating the cairn entrances to the underworld.

Danny settled back into his seat reluctantly as Bundoran came into view. He told me that I'd have to come back the following summer, because the Bundoran Waterworld would have opened by then.

"There's going to be a Wave Pool and a Spider Slide," he said.

"What's a Spider Slide?"

Danny hesitated momentarily, then flowed on. "Whatever it is, they're saying it's going to bring the tourists in by the coachload!"

I leapt out thankfully at Bundoran, grateful to be still in one piece.

The first thing that struck me about Bundoran was the obvious garda presence in the town. Bundoran is only a few miles from the Fermanagh border. The gardaí in Bundoran that day sat tensely in a car on the main street. As I scribbled in the notebook I carried permanently in my jacket pocket, I realised that they were watching me. When I put the notebook away and started walking briskly up the hill, the squad car followed, at a discreet distance.

There was a strange atmosphere in the town. There wasn't a soul on the streets apart from myself. Everyone else was presumably inside, having lunch. Every second house had a Bed and Breakfast sign; there were posters announcing the forthcoming opening of Waterworld in the window of every shop. The Spider Slide was to be a novelty water-slide for children. It seemed a tenuous attraction for luring coachloads of tourists. On a piece of waste ground, there were several more gardaí, nosing around a parked Hiace van.

Painted on the front wall of a house at the top of the hill was a mural in memory of Kieran Doherty, with the words, "Kieran Doherty T.D./ was the eighth hunger striker to die/ to achieve five, just basic demands. August 2nd 1981".

The man who brought me to Ballyshannon also told me about Waterworld. At Ballyshannon, I was shouldering my rucksack and zipping up my jacket when I turned to glance down the main street. Two pairs of eyes were firmly fixed on me. The squad car had followed me to Ballyshannon. Annoyed at being trailed in such a manner, I went to have lunch. The car had eventually disappeared, for good this time, when I emerged onto the street again.

I had a lift in a sleek BMW with a sleek businessman to Donegal town. There were several gift shops and craft shops clustered around the Diamond, always a good yardstick by which to measure the volume of tourists passing through.

One of the Australians in The White House had told me that the independent hostel in Donegal town was "ace" and so I went to find it.

"It's behind that red shed," a woman obligingly said.

The Bridge End Hostel was a small house in a terrace. There was one very small room which served as kitchen, dining room and common room. There were four small dormitories. The hostel slept twenty-six. The rooms for sleeping in were dim and crammed with bunks. It was a bright sunny afternoon outside. In the Bridge End Hostel, it was like having tumbled into the Black Hole of Calcutta. There were half a dozen people staying in the hostel that night; less than a quarter of the advertised capacity. Even so, we fell about each other in the kitchen, waited impatiently for our turn with saucepans and squashed up to eat at the one table.

I had come down to the kitchen and was beginning to chop vegetables when two Australians, Grant and Mike, burst in. They looked distraught.

"Have you heard?" Mike cried out.

In the early hours of that morning, 24 October, five soldiers and a civilian had been blown up by an IRA bomb at Derry's Coshquin checkpoint. In Newry, at the Cloughoge checkpoint, one soldier had been killed by a similar bomb. Both devices had been carried to the

112

checkpoints by civilians under force, who acted as human bombs. The 67-year-old grandfather who had carried the Newry bomb had managed to shout a warning and dive for cover, 30 seconds before the bomb exploded. Patsy Gillespie, the civilian at Coshquin, had not had time to escape.

The Australians had heard the news on the car radio of the person who had given them a lift. They told it to me by turn, shocked and white.

"We *were* heading on towards Derry tomorrow," Grant told me, "but we've changed our minds now."

"Jeez, there are some real madmen in your country, ain't there," Mike said, flatly.

The Australians discussed the killings all night. They could not get over the brutality of the human bomb bit. Unclear on the politics of it all, the Australians fastened onto the human dimension in a way that Irish people do not always have the emotional energy to do, after so many years of similar outrages. Some threshold – of the ability to be shocked; to feel pain – was constantly widening. The use of civilians as human bombs widened some intangible threshold of pain to a new extent.

Writing on the "Opinion/Home News" page in the *Irish Times* of 31 October in an article entitled "IRA brings anarchy one step nearer", Mary Holland opened with these lines.

The publican had just come across a human arm in the glass and debris on the floor of his bar and was, understandably, a bit upset. "You think you've absorbed it, that you're lucky to be alive. Then something like this happens and it really gets to you." He had been allowed back into the pub at Coshquin, on the main Derry to Buncrana road, to pick up a few momentoes.

We switched on the RTE Six-One news. The checkpoint bombings got scant coverage, RTE's main story was the escalating furore about the Lenihan affair. The *Irish Times* claimed it had evidence that Brian Lenihan had telephoned Patrick Hillery at Áras an Uachtaráin in January of 1982. The previously rather dull Presidential Election campaign had become a saga which was gripping the nation as, day by day, more bizarre facts, denials and counter-denials were revealed.

Since I had set out, on 1 October, 24 days previously, seventeen people had been killed in the North; one of the most intensive periods of violence for many years. In this one day, six soldiers and a civilian had been killed, yet the subsequent media coverage in the South was far outweighed by "The Lenihan Affair" Bombs in the North were usual. Political scandal was not. The checkpoint bombings were dealt with more as if they were an accessory to the news, rather than news itself.

This did not go unnoticed across the border. Later on in her article, Mary Holland writes:

Over and over again on Thursday and Friday, people said to me: "Did you see the RTE news? At least the BBC seemed to think that what happened here was important." There was incredulity and considerable bitterness that RTE could devote almost all of its news bulletins to the Lenihan affair and that the human proxy bombs in the North, a terrifying escalation in the IRA's methods, warranted so little attention.

I cannot recall a time when the two parts of the country have seemed so separate, each indifferent to what is happening to the other.

The two parts of the country. The image which that phrase presented rang some distant and far-off bell in my head. After a couple of days, I remembered what it was that Mary Holland's words had reminded me of.

I had been a small child when what is termed "The Troubles" – as prudish a euphemism as "The Emergency"in 1939-45 – began to escalate to the degree that seven people could be murdered in one day and it did not seem particularly newsworthy. Aged about eight, I had been flicking through an *Armada Quiz and Puzzle Book.* There was one page in which the outlines of various countries were shown – some sideways, some upside-down. You had to guess which country they were; the idea being that you were initially flummoxed by their odd position.

I stared for a long time in amazement at Ireland. This was not an outline with which I was familiar. *Was* it Ireland? I peered intently at the page and then scrabbled through the pages to find the Answers section. I forget now the exact answer; presumably, it was either "The Republic of Ireland" or "Éire".

What I had been looking at was an Ireland minus the Six Counties.

It was a tremendous visual shock. I have a vivid recollection of feeling very confused. I knew that I was Irish and that I lived in Ireland, but the *Armada Quiz and Puzzle Book* had me living in an island which I had never seen before. It was like looking at a jigsaw with a vital piece missing and it was the first time that I began to be aware of terms like "the Republic", "the Six Counties", "the South", "the North"; the two parts of the same country.

That evening, I prodded my conscience. Would I have been as shocked by the day's events; would I have been as keenly aware of the balance in RTE's television news if I had not been journeying in this manner and trying to observe and listen to what I saw and heard along the way?

Perhaps these were empty and useless questions. I knew that wherever I had been, I would have been equally appalled by the checkpoint bombings. As for the media coverage – I had to admit that I might not have taken much notice of its small portion of that evening's news, having grown up watching countless news programmes in which bombs and murder were dutifully reported. The names of the dead and the locations of the bombs varied, but each "incident" was reported in a similar way: the long-shot of the scene, cordoned off, with a few grim-faced RUC officers looking on; the bewildered, kindly testimony neighbours gave of their fellow-neighbour who had been shot down; the grief-stricken faces of the bereaved at funerals.

People had said to Mary Holland: "At least the BBC seemed to think that what happened here was important." It seemed forcefully clear to me why the BBC had given priority to the bombings. Of the seven killed, six were British officers. To the BBC, it was nothing more or less than news.

115

The Bridge End Hostel was not a cheerful place to be that evening. I had almost finished eating when another hosteller, a Frenchman, arrived into the kitchen. He was very drunk. He staggered around, demanding of everyone in turn that they cook dinner for him, singing and belching in between each request. Ordinarily, I would have laughed and ignored him, but in this cramped area, with the Australians at the other side of the table, still discussing the bombings, I felt that I had to get out.

I went upstairs to grab a book and then went straight out into the nearest pub. Between leaving the kitchen and entering Campbell's Pub, there was hardly five minutes. I vaguely noticed two other people sitting at the bar and had ordered a drink before I realised that one of them was the Singing, Belching Frenchman; he too had obviously made a beeline to the nearest pub.

I opened my book.

"Irish people are unfriendly!"

The other man at the bar got up, raised his eyes at me, and left.

"Irish people are *very* unfriendly!" he said, glaring at me.

He eventually cleared off in search of food, with a parting comment, "Irish food is shit!"

"What a drunkard!" I couldn't help exclaiming to the barlady.

She looked genuinely surprised. "Oh, I don't think he's drunk. He's been around for a couple of days and he's always like that."

I felt bad. Had I misjudged him?

I made some reference to the bombings. The barlady told me she had heard no news that day and knew nothing of what had happened. It was a Wednesday; the Lotto draw was to take place as usual after the 8 o'clock RTE news. She switched on the television and we watched the news in silence. After the news, she turned to me and simply said brightly, "It's the Lotto now! Maybe this will be my lucky night!"

Any guilty feelings I might have had about possibly misjudging the Belcher swiftly evaporated when he kept me awake all night by staggering down the corridor at intervals to throw up noisily in the bathroom – which was, unfortunately, next to the room I was sleeping in – and then returning to his bed to snore like a prehistoric monster, clearly audible through the thin walls.

I was up and out of the Bridge End Hostel next morning at a very early hour.

A series of short lifts brought me to Killybegs, Ireland's major fishing port. It was not difficult to be aware of this fact, since long before Killybegs came into view, I could smell it. On the left-hand side of the road from Donegal we passed IAWS, a fish-meal factory, known locally as "The Perfumery". The fish-meal factory was not a pleasant sight, looking something like a fish-abattoir. Blood poured from lorries full of mackerel. I could understand why the local people I talked to were indignant that the factory eyesore had been located so near the main road.

The man who brought me the last few miles to Killybegs told me that there was probably more money in Killybegs than in any other town in Ireland.

"And you'll see some grand houses roundabouts – fishermen's houses – but not near Killybegs itself. Too smelly for them."

Killybegs itself was a functional-looking little town, with basic services and ordinary shops. But the cars parked along the quayside street hinted at an affluent population: Mercedes, BMWs, Volvos.

Apart from the overpowering smell of fish, the most striking thing about Killybegs were all the seagulls. Even at dumps, I had never before seen so many gulls gathered scavengingly together in one place. The gulls were thick, flying clouds, endlessly reforming as fresh catches were landed and unloaded. The Killybegs roofs were white with bird-droppings. The gulls were everywhere: weighing down telegraph wires; wing to wing on rooftops; flapping manically over trawlers and lorries. These birds were the best-fed looking gulls I had ever seen. They were positively *fat*.

I looked around until I could bear the smell no longer and then hitched out. On my lift to Kilcar, the driver

117

roared with laughter when I said something about the strong fishy smell at Killybegs.

"Think it was bad today?" he hooted. "This is a good day!"

Kilcar was a small village in a valley, set in lush green fields, backed by mountains. I walked the few miles from Kilcar to Derrylahan; green and undulating generous miles after days spent in towns. Although I wasn't hitching, several people stopped and offered me lifts, but the country was too wild and peaceful to hurry through.

The townland of Derrylahan nestles between Muckros Head and Carrigan Head, perched up from an inlet of the sea, with Slieve League in the distance. Everyone I had met thus far who had travelled through Donegal had told me that the independent hostel of Derrylahan was simply not to be missed. But I had also been told that the Bridge End was "ace" and so approached Derrylahan like a Doubting Thomas.

Derrylahan Hostel was an old cottage, set back in a field, with views down to the sea. Patrick Raughtery, the owner, saw me coming and came to the door to greet me. He was a white-haired oldish man, with a tum and a ridiculously cartoonish sort of smile – either full up or full down, so that he looked either ecstatic or dismal. Mostly, the smile was full up. He bustled about, making me tea, opening the biscuit box, sitting me down by the range and generally making me feel as if I was a favourite niece come to visit. It was exactly like being in somebody's home. The small dormitories looked like bedrooms, not dormitories; furnished with homely wooden bedside lockers and immense, grandmotherly-type dressing tables with swing-top mirrors.

As I was having tea, the telephone rang. It was a girl who had arrived in Kilcar and was wondering where the hostel was. Patrick got out his car and went to collect her.

To get to the kitchen, you had to go through a room set up as a shop. There were all sorts of things that hungry hostellers would appreciate – fresh fruit, vegetables, soda bread, chocolate bars. They were all just left there. Patrick Raughtery trusted the hostellers who passed through Derrylahan not to pinch anything.

The rain had finally got to me. I began to sneeze and cough to the accompaniment of a banging headache. I holed up in front of the range at Derrylahan for two days. It was a waste of a fleadh at Carrick, a couple of miles further down the road and a waste of some wonderful hill-walking, but I couldn't have been in a more pleasant place in which to feel lethargic.

I had forgotten that it was the weekend of the October Bank Holiday. Derrylahan, almost empty when I'd arrived, filled up with Dubliners, up for the Carrick Fleadh. The track in front of the hostel was crammed with cars, the kitchen was a-rattle with Superquinn bags and the new arrivals swopped stories of lengthy tailbacks in the bank holiday exodus from the capital.

I fled further west, to Glencolumbkille, and caught up with my diary. Ireland was displaced that weekend. Few people were staying at home. All across the country, people were on the move. Towns and villages were inhabited by a fluid population. Nobody was where they usually were, yet everywhere seemed to be crowded with people.

The Dooey Hostel at Glencolumbkille was also full of people who had abandoned cities for the weekend. On Sunday morning, I stood at the edge of Glencolumbkille and attempted to hitch along the road which runs through the Glengesh Pass. The road I was trying to hitch on was one of the thin white strips marked on the Michelin map as "other roads", which cobweb between areas of low population. These roads tend to be the most remote, least travelled and usually worst-kept of Irish roads.

Hitching out of the "other road" from Glencolumbkille that morning was doomed to fail. The members of the floating population were not on the road, having already driven far enough to get to where they were. The local people were relaxing in their homes, eating Sunday lunch or watching bank holiday television.

I tried hitching on the road that led back to Killybegs. This was more successful. Matt and Dave, up from Roscommon for the weekend and staying in a caravan at Glencolumbkille, were on their way to Killybegs in search of a cash point. They were both suffering from bad hangovers. Matt drove like a lunatic, the car hopping along the road and bouncing over the hump-backed bridges like a demented flea. Five minutes earlier, I had been cursing the lack of traffic. Now, I was merely thankful that there were no other vehicles in the flea's path.

There were no cash points in Killybegs.

"Jaysus, we'll have to go all the way to Donegal now," Matt groaned, while Dave, who was sitting in the back and feeling the worst of the car's gymnastics, looked as if he was going to throw up at the prospect of this lengthened journey.

I got out beyond Killybegs and hitched on towards Ardara, where I had lunch at Nisbett's Hotel and read the Sunday papers. It was typical bank holiday weather; dull and cold, with intermittent showers of hail and sleet.

Walking up the steep hill out of Ardara and getting a lift from a Kiltimagh couple who were trying to find a friend's house at Annagary, and unsure of where I would spend the night, I decided to just keep travelling as long as there was daylight. On bad-weather days, I sometimes did this, reluctant to leave the warmth of cars, or to cut conversations short, or to face into the rain again.

The Kiltimagh couple took one of the "other roads" through The Rosses to get to Annagary, thus bypassing Burtonport. I regretted missing Burtonport. Flicking through the *Rough Guide* while waiting outside Glencolumbkille earlier that day I had been intrigued to read, in the section headed "Upper Rosses"!

... their departure (a colony of post-hippies known as The Screamers) coincided with the arrival of three eccentric ladies from England, who live in immaculate, formal Victorian style in the white mansion at the entrance to Burtonport. Known as the Silver Sisters, Miss Tyrell, Miss Lucinda and their young maid are an engaging sight, doing their village shopping dressed in bonnets and sober black garments edged with white lace. They welcome only visitors with a serious interest in their anachronistic way of life, and not the merely curious.

Being bank holiday Sunday, I guessed that the Silver Sisters would not be "At Home" to visitors of any sort. They would be more than usually protective of their anachronistic way of life from any strangers who were temporarily dipping into Burtonport life. I guessed their front door was firmly shut and that Miss Tyrell and Miss Lucinda had hung up their bonnets for the weekend and had retreated to a back parlour, where they were, at this moment (it now being 3.30 in the afternoon) partaking of tea and sandwiches and little cakes, served up to them by their young maid.

I got out of the car of the Mayo couple at Annagary and into the car of a Scottish couple. The clocks had gone back the night before and I was unsure of the hour when darkness would begin to fall. We had driven into the Gweedore area when light began to drain from the sky.

Drowsy, I hauled myself out of the car and set about looking for a B & B. I knocked on the door of one house which had a sign hanging outside its gate, but was told by the woman who answered that she was not doing B & B at this time of the year. The migratory bank holiday population didn't seem to have made it to Gweedore. She directed me to Bunbeg House, a B & B down a side road which led to Bunbeg Harbour, where the mailboat leaves for Tory Island.

Twilight fell as I followed the empty, winding road down to the harbour. Bunbeg House was the last house on the road. It overlooked the narrow slit of the harbour. Standing at the front door, I could hear the water lapping quietly.

The doorbell resounded twice through the house. Nobody came to answer it, although there were lights on inside. After the third ring, I opened the door and walked inside. Hearing a television on in a room off the hall, I knocked and pushed the door open.

As strange and unexpected a sight in the lounge room of Bunbeg House as the three eccentric ladies in the pristine mansion at Burtonport. Ten African men were huddled around an enormous turf fire, watching *Rambo III*.

I was pulled into the room, sat down in the chair nearest

the fire and plied with questions. One of them went to find the owner of the B & B. Another threw yet more turf onto a fire that was already almost at the chimney fire stage. My jacket was hung neatly over a chair. *Rambo* was put on pause.

"What your name?"

"Where you come from?"

"How long you staying?"

Jean, the owner of the B & B, came into the room. She, apparently, was not doing B & B either at this time of year. But she looked out of the darkened window when I went to put on my jacket again, and hesitated.

"Come with me," she said. "I'll fix you up, somehow."

Jean showed me into a room overlooking the harbour and then wheeled in an electric Dimplex heater to warm up the room. I went down a warren of stairways to a room off the kitchen and had coffee and sandwiches.

When I returned to the television room, *Rambo* was again put on pause, the fire was stoked up and despite my protests, the best armchair vacated. Five of the ten were living in digs at Bunbeg House. The other five, who had left by the time I came back, were living a mile or so away in other digs.

The Bunbeg House five told me their "easy names" which sounded like; Gerard, William, Peter, Buzz, and John. They were all Kenyans and all studying telecommunications at a Bunbeg factory, with the aim of going back to set up a similar factory in Kenya. Some of them had only been in Ireland a few weeks, while others, like Peter, had been in Bunbeg for months.

"Ireland is so *cold*," they all chorused and gave a collective shiver. I noticed the layers of clothing and the way they sat close to the roaring fire, sitting two to an armchair: one in the seat and one on the arm.

I asked them how they spent their time, apart from working and studying. Anything that involved staying indoors, where there was relative warmth, it emerged. Mostly watching television and videos. There was a tall stack of video cassettes by the television. I looked through them: *Rambo II, Crocodile Dundee II, Halloween II, Dirty*

Dancing, assorted soft porn movies. It looked like they were working their way through the contents of the local video outlet.

The Kenyans had young faces. Huddled close together to the fire, they bombarded me with questions in ragged English, anxious to keep me talking and in the room. It was not difficult to sense their loneliness and boredom.

"You stay here long time?"

"No," I admitted, feeling guilty. "I'll probably leave tomorrow."

They stared at me reproachfully.

"How much longer are you here?" I asked Peter.

"Forty-seven days," he shot back, without a second's hesitation.

That instant answer reminded me of the home-made calendars pinned up in school alcoves, which had each day heavily scored through the moment you got up in the morning. We always knew exactly how many more months, weeks, days and hours were to be got through until it was the holidays. I had not enjoyed those periods of measuring out a life with pen-strokes.

Forty-seven days. I shivered.

I breakfasted alone next morning. The Kenyans, on their bank holiday, had asked not to be called until midday. Passing closed doors on the way down to breakfast, I had heard the sound of snoring and wondered if they were dreaming themselves back in warmer climes.

Before walking back to the main road, I looked about the harbour. There were a dozen boats jogging quietly on the dark water: most of them were flying the black flags associated with the IRA.

It was a wet, blustery morning in Gweedore. I got a couple of lifts which took me as far as Bloody Foreland.

"It's the windiest place in Ireland," the driver said cheerfully, handing out my rucksack as I clambered from the car and immediately staggered with the impact of the wind, slamming in from the Atlantic with the force of a stone wall in flight.

The shelving arm of the Foreland sank grimly into the bare sea. Rainclouds hid Tory Island from sight. Apart

123

from the eerie *wheeing* of the wind, Bloody Foreland was silent. I had coffee, sitting on a bank at the brink of a field, gathering that grey place around me.

The Gaeltacht area of Gweedore, stretching from the townland of Bunbeg to the village of Gortahork, is a large area of land in which settlements are scattered out instead of grouped together at village intervals. There was a chemist shop here, then twenty far-flung houses and a pub there, another score of houses, another mile and then a post office. The townland of Bunbeg seeps onto the townland of Derrybeg; Derrybeg seeps onto Bun na Leaca and so it goes. You are never very far from a building of some sort, yet the place somehow seemed desolate to me.

I walked for an hour or so. There were stacks of turf banked up like walls against the gable of every house and every house had a watchful dog, who barked shockingly loudly and ran out at me from front doorsteps. All along the coast road, the dogs waited for me to pass by their particular house, warned of my approach by dogs I had already passed and their barking surged along the road like a wave of the sea.

The only proof of life in those scattered houses, apart from the dogs, were the thin lines of smoke which rose from every chimney and from which I got a single, acrid smell of domesticity each time I passed under the dissolving lines of smoke.

The rainclouds lifted from Tory Island and it revealed itself on the sullen horizon. Over a summer, I had once spent three strange weeks on Tory. Looking out at the long, low lines of the island, the east side of which was serrated, as if some amphibious giant had taken bites out of it, the memory of those weeks flooded back.

The day of my first visit had coincided with the departure of a controversial priest, reputedly asked to leave by the local bishop as a result of a letter written by one of the friends I was visiting, on behalf of the islanders and at their request. The priest, it was said, had offended the islanders by the methods of his regime. Allegedly because of him there was no pub, although you could buy bottles of Guinness in one of the shops. If there was a session of music going on with too much volume, or dancing in the Hall going on too late, the priest sent the merry-makers home to bed. I was told it was not uncommon for people to be read off from the altar.

Once gone, the islanders instantly wanted their priest back.

My first night, we were pursued from West Town to East Town, by islanders baying for blood, but content to fling sods of turf at our retreating backs.

The next morning, there was a knock at the door and a sheepish-looking islandman offered both an apology to the two girls about the Turf Throwing Incident, together with a request that the two girls sleep in the "hostel" and not in the same house as the two young men. The "hostel" was a crude prefabricated hut, painted a deceptively cheerful red, which had been set up that summer to accommodate a workcamp, the members of which all fled the island before their period of employment expired.

We girls had no choice but to decamp from the House of Sin, relations already being more than strained between our friends and the islanders.

During the week, the Calor Kosangas cylinder ran out in the House of Sin and a new one could not be obtained by any means. I found this Cold War no more or less extraordinary than the island in general. East Town and West Town were misnomers. In that summer of the mid 1980s when I visited the island, the population was around the one hundred mark. There were two ill-stocked shops in West Town and one in East Town. The mailboat, which brought supplies, only came twice a week and then only in fair weather, making it almost impossible to stock fresh fruit and vegetables. West Town also had the tiny island school, the church, the priest's house, the Community Hall, the "hostel", a round tower, a Tau Cross and the post office. Into this last, the entire population gathered, spilling onto the road outside, whenever the mailboat from Bunbeg arrived. The names on the envelopes were called out loudly and distributed to eager, waiting hands.

There were two island vehicles. One was a tractor. The other was an electric milk van, which had been converted

125

into a minibus, with the words "Coras Iompair Toraí" painted on the outside. It's sole purpose was to transport elderly people from East Town to West Town for Sunday Mass, at which there was a strict division of the sexes: men on one side and women on the other.

The fantastically high and intricate rambling cliff walls at the east end of the island made the 660 feet Cliffs of Moher seem laughably tame in comparison. The cliff walls, busy with all manner of seabirds, were stunning. We were told by our friends, both of whom had been there for several months, that small children growing up on the island had been scared off exploring the dangerous cliff by stories of Bogey Men living there. Some of these children had made it to adulthood without ever having been to the cliffs, although they were perhaps a mile and a half from West Town and a quarter of a mile from East Town.

My second visit to the island had been for two weeks, the last week of which I had been desperate to flee, the relationship with my boyfriend having soured. But storms had suddenly whipped up and the mailboat from Bunbeg had not been able to make the eight miles out to the island. Marooned on the island, I had scanned the horizon each day with the same feeling of having been irrevocably abandoned by the world that I imagined Crusoe to have experienced.

I had finally flown out in the helicopter which brought the doctor in from the mainland for one afternoon a fortnight, hearing later that the mailboat had not put to sea for a further two weeks. I had not returned since, nor did I have any desire to do so now, but these memories made for strange company on the bleak and windswept coast road of Bloody Foreland.

When a car eventually came along and stopped, the driver, who told me he was from Magheraroarty, pointed Tory out to me and said he'd never been there himself, "but I hear they're right queer folk". I kept my peace. It cannot be easy to live on islands, particularly one eight miles from an uncertain mainland, which, if you were travelling to as a Tory Islander, you called "going over to Ireland".

Apart from this one comment about Tory and telling me he lived in Magheraroarty the driver was silent for the rest of the journey. As I was getting out of the car at Magheraroarty, he stared out over the steering wheel.

"This is a staunch Republican area," he said suddenly. "And it always has been," he finished and directed a fierce stare at me before driving away.

I was taken aback by this parting comment. Usually people said something like "All the best", or "Hope you're not waiting too long". But I was not as taken aback as I would have been ten days before. I remembered the black flags which I'd seen flying from the boats in Bunbeg Harbour that morning.

Even after such a short time, I could feel the curious in-betweenness of Donegal. Donegal is something of an island: a good two-thirds of its county boundary touches the Atlantic and of the other third, all of it shares borders with Derry and Fermanagh, save the narrow neck of land that connects with Leitrim. In Donegal, more than any other "southern" county that I hitched through, there was a much less pronounced sense of distance between it and the counties beyond the border. There was a keenness and an awareness in Donegal; a sense of eyes and ears being turned, ever watchful, ever attentive, eastwards toward the border counties; that the political goings-ons in Dublin were little to do with them, although they jangled the same coins in their pockets.

To some of the people who gave me lifts in the "South" the six counties across the border could well have been as foreign to them as another country – for example, many people admitted to not having crossed the border for years. But in Donegal, it was the "South" that seemed shadowy and distant and the "North" which was the reality.

Although I continued to get lifts easily, people were much less forthcoming in telling me their names, which was understandable since I was a stranger in a sensitive area.

The thin, pinched-looking man who brought me to Creeslough and did not volunteer his name, told me that

127

he had moved from Donegal to Kerry because he could no longer bear being so close to the border. He spoke about the checkpoint bombings with great bitterness. "No wonder the English despise us," he said softly. "It was the work of animals."

I got out at the turn-off for Trá na Rossan peninsula. It was freezing. The road struck up chill as iron and the rainclouds bellied over Muckish and the hard, conical shape of Errigal. The mountains appeared and disappeared through the clouds. It would be possible to drive through Donegal on a bad day and not to know there were mountains there at all.

I hopped from one foot to the other and beat my hands together, all of which felt more like lumps of pack ice than hands and feet. Hot coffee from the flask helped. The £4.99 investment from Quinnsworth was proving to be the single most useful item in my equipment.

There was not much traffic heading my way, but there was still tantalizingly enough cars to keep on trying. Back on the road which I had just left, the main road towards Letterkenny, the returning bank-holiday makers drove by in their scores. I decided to wait another half an hour and then head for Letterkenny.

The half hour was almost up when a car stopped. The driver was a young lad who lived in Downings. He asked if I'd been waiting long for a lift. I told him about an hour and that there'd been plenty of cars but none had stopped.

He laughed. "Most people around here won't pick you up unless they know you."

Trá na Rossan was a small peninsula, lying between Ball Head and Malin. I got out where the road forked and walked the rest of the way to the An Óige hostel. There were masses of wide beaches, vast skies, distant headlands and capricious mountains. It was beginning to get dim when I arrived at the isolated hostel: a century-old granite house with pointed eaves; an Irish pastiche in stone of a Swiss wooden chalet.

The hostel was due to close in two days, not to reopen until 1 April the following year. I was the only person staying there and it had the deserted, waiting atmosphere of a holiday house. There were bird-charts and jars of shells in the common room and magnificent views of Trá na Rossan beach from the dining room.

It must be wonderful in the summer, I caught myself saying.

People who gave me lifts were always amazed that I should want to travel the coast in winter.

"But you should be here in the summer! This place is *heaving* in the summer. It's dead in winter."

I had deliberately chosen winter time to travel. On my coastal route, I felt it would have been impossible to try and see the places through which I was travelling if I'd had to peer through the crowds of a temporary summer population. But there were times such as now, when I could not avoid contemplating how a bit of sunshine and the long summer evenings would make a place like Trá na Rossan somewhere you would have to be forcibly dragged from.

The only blur on the landscape and on many other beautiful landscapes I hitched through, was the appalling rubbish which was unfailingly dumped in the most scenic locations.

The dining room was a corner room, with windows on two sides. From one side, you could look out and see the wide beach; from the other, you could see a graveyard of abandoned cars, strewn halfway up a hill. Cars in the first stages of rot looked as if they'd sicked up their innards before they died. Car seats, steering wheels, mirrors and rubber mats surrounded the wrecks.

There were at least a dozen cars in various stages of decay, which had somehow been transported halfway up this hill and then left to fall apart. It wasn't even a case of out of sight, out of mind. I imagined the local people directing strangers to the hostel: "Oh, you can't miss it. It's the house at the foot of a hill where there's a load of crocked cars."

A storm blew up that night and I slept uneasily as the rain and wind launched themselves furiously against the windows. I woke up several times during the night, always just in time to catch the dying rattle of a demented screech of wind which, half awake and half asleep, startled me horribly each time.

Next morning I got a lift straight away from an old man who drove very slowly and with a certain erratic grace. He was on his way to the garda station at Carrigart to collect a form for his driving test, "Because I'm over seventy now and they think I'm suddenly going to start crashing into everything."

I spent some time in the village of Carrigart, vainly searching for the post office, until someone directed me to Sweeney and Son, General Drapers. Tucked away at the back of the shop, almost hidden behind rails of shirts and jerseys, was a little counter that served as post office. I counted ten mission boxes on the counter, all ranged neatly together, their open slits like so many gaping eager mouths.

The storm winds had dropped, but the rain, with its usual tenacity and staying powers, was continuing to belt down. My next lift brought me to the formal, rather grand-looking village of Rathmelton, where I was forced to take shelter in a telephone box by the Leanna River.

I had a peaceful lift to Letterkenny in a Mini that never went faster than 30 mph, driven by an old man who told me that Letterkenny for him was no longer the place it had always been. "It's full of strangers now. They brought a whole crowd down from Dublin to work in the Welfare Buildings and the town never got over it, in my opinion."

The independent hostel at Rosemount Terrace was a good place to come upon that wet day in Letterkenny. The house was a second house of the warden's, who came down each day to light an enormous fire and distribute front-door keys. The showers were hot, the house was warm and I had a room to myself. All this for £3.50. The day I arrived, I let myself in by pulling a key on a chain through the letter box.

6
THE FLOATING DRIFTWOOD OF THE ROADSIDE
Derry to Portaferry

Standing on the Derry Road on the outskirts of Letterkenny next morning, I was unable to rid myself of the feeling that envelopes one at airports and ferryports – the imminent feeling of crossing a distance. Apart from two short visits to Belfast to see a friend, I had not spent time across the border.

This had not been a conscious decision on my part; it had somehow evolved over the years. It was a combination of having no family ties there and the insidious feeling that beyond the place called "border" was latent violence. I was, in short, a passive victim of television newscasts, even though I knew something of the reality of the situation in Northern Ireland and of the remoteness of any possibility of coming face to face with acts of terrorism.

Yet, while I waited for a lift to Derry, I reflected soberly on the fact that I had somehow never before considered exploring a great chunk of land only a couple of hours drive from where I'd lived most of my life. Looked at like that, it seemed laughably stupid. I stood beyond the Letterkenny roundabout, hitching towards Derry for the first time, and felt an absolute fool.

I felt like kicking something. I kicked the grass in the roadside verge. What was that? My eye drew back, found the place in the flattened grass. I'd uncovered a four-leaved clover. As I leaned down to pick it, a car pulled in.

Barbara wore bright lipstick and huge bright glasses. She'd been brought up in Antrim, had lived for a time in Derry and was now living in Downings. Her first question to me was an inquiry as to what part of England I was from.

131

Barbara spoke of Donegal as "the forgotten county" with a degree of bitterness. "There's never been any money put into it. There are no nice little villages, geared towards tourists, like you see in Connemara. Lots of Donegal people, particularly the older generation, regard themselves as Ulster people – which they are of course, but *this* Ulster" – Barbara indicated the road to Derry – "not *that* Ulster," and she jerked her head backwards, towards Letterkenny.

Of Derry, she said that when she'd lived there first, she'd not liked it, but that it had grown on her. "Derry people are very warm, very friendly."

I asked what she'd thought of the checkpoint bombings.

"Oh, you get used to it," she said distantly. Then she amended this remark. "No, you never really get used to it. You just think you've seen it all and then something like that happens. I think they've cleared the Coshquin checkpoint by now, but we won't go that way. I couldn't face it," she said frankly.

We drove past an unmanned checkpoint and then approached the main checkpoint. There were zig-zags of square concrete blocks set into the road to prevent cars speeding through. The road had a protective neck of ugly galvanised iron sheeting; there were coils of rusted barbed wire everywhere; the apprehensive face of the soldier who waved us through was shockingly young.

"I *hate* this," Barbara said suddenly, with great feeling. She'd been open and talkative up to this point. But the border crossing rattled her. Her hands were gripped whitely on the steering wheel, she pulled her lips tightly together and stared out grimly and silently until she had put the checkpoint well behind her.

Derry, or, as the Northern Ireland Tourist Board brochure says tactfully, "Londonderry (also known as Derry)", was sheeted in rain. It looked extraordinarily large to me.

As a rule, on my journey, I was not interested in spending time in cities. Cities are whole, complex worlds onto themselves and I felt that there was little I could glean at random from such dense places.

Barbara was going into the Pilot's Row Centre, on the edge of the Bogside, and she offered to keep my rucksack with her so that I could walk about freely.

We'd passed the famous white gable with the words painted on it in black, many feet high, *YOU ARE NOW ENTERING FREE DERRY*. On another gable wall, this one opposite the Pilot's Row Centre, was a mural of Dessie Ellis. Around his throat was loosely knotted a tie, patterned with the Union Jack; the tie gave the illusion of a noose. "Don't let British justice kill Dessie Ellis," the graffiti read. At the side of the mural were the words "21 days on hunger strike". "Every morning, they come and paint in the next number," Barbara had told me.

The Dessie Ellis graffiti was everywhere I went. It was painted several feet high on the city walls; on the sides of shops; on the gables of houses; on the pavements. It was a kind of liquid news, flowing through the streets; the same headlines on every corner. "Free Dessie Ellis now." "Don't let Dessie Ellis die." "No Extradition."

Dessie Ellis had gone on hunger strike at Portlaoise Prison twenty-one days previously, in protest against imminent extradition to Britain to face charges of conspiracy and possession of explosives with intent to danger life between 1981 and 1983. He faced being the first person to be extradited to Britain under the 1987 Extradition Act. With the release of the Guildford Four the previous year and the release of the Birmingham Six drawing ever closer, there was strong feeling about the proposed British trial for Dessie Ellis.

Dessie Ellis was duly extradited to England. His case went for trial, he was later released and subsequently returned to Dublin.

The city walls, many feet thick, made a rough encirclement of what appeared to be Posh Derry: large department stores, coffee shops, bookshops, craft shops; banks; professional practices. In the plaza between the Guild Hall and the city walls, people were working through the pouring rain, erecting platforms and installing seating.

The Foyle Arts Festival was due to open that night,

133

which was also Halloween night. Two men climbed ladders and fixed an enormous witch's head to the city walls. Other workers were busy stringing a cobweb made from thick rope between trees and lamp-posts. A man in a dinner suit and a woman in a black silk cloak and immaculately pointed witch's hat, stepped into a waiting car and were driven away.

Derry did not look like any other Irish city with which I was familiar. I floundered on the wet streets and tried to see what it was that made it different, beyond the surface trappings of British stores, red pillar boxes, tanks rolling through the streets, barbed wire coiled on the rims of walls and the Bogside murals, which were largely faded.

In cities such as Paris or London, it is certain landmarks or buildings which reveal themselves, both visually and aurally, in advance to the traveller – the Eiffel Tower, Sacre Coeur, Big Ben, Trafalgar Square – but in Derry, it was the *names* of areas of which I had prior knowledge: the Bogside, the Creggan. Derry had been filtered through to me aurally, rather than visually.

I walked around the Bogside, pacing the fluid boundaries of a place within a place. It was not something definable and solid like a building which one could blithely photograph and say "I saw that": Derry was the least "been there, seen that" place I had ever been to. It swelled. I floated on the grey tide of rain and was washed out again, feeling none the wiser, except now having some immediate visual sense of place to affix the name "Bogside" to.

It rained and rained and rained. I collected my rucksack from the Pilot's Row Centre and took a taxi out to Brook Hall, where I had been invited to spend the night by Jennifer Johnston.

Next morning, back in Derry centre, I read the *Irish Times* over coffee. "October rainfall double average" an article by Dick Ahlstrom declared. *Only double*? I thought, frankly disbelieving Dick Ahlstrom.

The witch's head on the city walls opposite the Guild Hall was still intact, although now looking much the worse for its prolonged exposure to double the normal rainfall.

Looking around the Guild Hall, I was struck by the old

stained glass windows for which it is justly famous. There were a series of windows commemorating the 1688-89 Siege of Derry and windows in honour of those who had fallen in the World Wars and a modern window by Peter Rooney, in memory of those who died on Bloody Sunday in 1972. In the Guild Hall, it was possible to trace major events in the history of Derry by looking at these stained glass windows. There was something uplifting about examining events from the history of a city in these windows which, although it periodically resounded to the sounds of violence, bravely continued to record itself through the fragile and tenuous medium of stained glass.

I crossed the Foyle by the Craigavon Bridge and walked a couple of miles to get out beyond the suburbs. A new car, possibly stolen, lay abandoned in a ditch. As I drew level with it, another car pulled in, the driver jumped out, photographed the abandoned car, resolutely ignored me, and then drove away swiftly.

I got a lift to Limavady with a Speed Merchant. As a hitch-hiker, one of the drawbacks of good roads is that it's possible to achieve great speed on them. You can only hope you'll arrive safely. The superior roads of Northern Ireland are no myth. It was pleasant not to have every bone jolted every five minutes as the car temporarily disappeared into a pot-hole: however, it was frankly terrifying to be on a well-maintained road with a Speed Merchant, who considered anything under 100 mph to be a sluggish pace.

The Speed Merchant worked at the Foyle Meats Abattoir, where he made a stop to deliver a message and where I had the doubtful experience of inhaling the smell of fresh blood for five minutes.

At Limavady, I had a very late lunch and consulted the map. It was late afternoon by now and would soon be dark. But I felt like continuing on a bit further and trying to get within sight of the coast again.

I went into the Limavady Development Centre and asked if there were any B & Bs out the road a few miles. The four men in the Centre were amazed to see me and expressed doubt at the possibility of there being any B &

Bs open at this time of year: doubtful indeed if there were any B & Bs within a ten-mile radius of Limavady. They looked at me with some concern and began to rifle through Yellow Pages and local directories, assuring they wouldn't see me stuck.

Several minutes and several phonecalls later, they tracked down a B & B for me. "Ballycarton Farm," one man said. "It's Mrs Craig's place. She's a widow – her husband died on her a while back. It's out the Bellarena Road a few miles."

I set out walking on the quiet road, noting that although this was a country road with a scattered population, each house I passed had a number. I discovered that this was common practice in the North: a curious illusion of living cosily in a street, cheek-by-jowl with your next door neighbours, whereas in fact the people occupying the houses on either side of your number were often miles away.

The driver of a Texaco lorry stopped to give me a lift and brought me all the way to Ballycarton Farm, 239 Seacoast Road: no neighbours within sight. Ballycarton Farm was located at the foot of Benevenagh Mountain, which had been visible long before we reached the farmhouse.

Benevenagh was the most extraordinary mountain I had ever seen. From its base to about two-thirds of the way up its slopes, Benevenagh had been planted with a patchwork of trees. The plantations were in blocks of varying size and the trees were many different colours: deepest green, golden brown, orange, palest green. Where the mosaic of the tree-line stopped, the tonsured bald head of the mountain rose up, crumpled and furrowed grey rock against the rain-washed sky.

Ballycarton was a long, low house, with a geranium-bright porch and a small grey-haired woman waiting to greet me at the door.

Mrs Craig gave me a room which overlooked Benevenagh and then went bustling off downstairs. There was a roaring fire on in the living room and after a wash, I went downstairs and wallowed in an enormous armchair by the fire, suddenly exhausted. A young boy put his head around the door. "Would you like to come into the kitchen for some dinner?" he asked.

The kitchen was warm as a nest: an ancient Aga stove radiated heat and the smells of good cooking. I sat down and ate with the family. Mrs Craig's two grandsons lived with her and she also had a permanent lodger: the local clergyman. I was gathered into the warmth of that kitchen and fed great quantities of delicious food.

The grandsons dashed off into the night, the clergyman made a brief appearance and then melted away again. Mrs Craig was a solidly frail woman; about seventy, stooped with rheumatism, bright-eyed and wise. She moved about the kitchen with slow, considered movements, saying little, but somehow making me feel at ease in her home, so that I found myself helping to clear away and wash up as if I had long been familiar with where the cutlery and crockery were stored.

We went in and sat by the fire, where Mrs Craig fell asleep over household accounts. The room was warm, the house was silent, apart from the gentle snoring of Mrs Craig. I dozed off too for some time, and we both ascended the stairs with loud yawns.

I woke up to a watery sun pouring itself over Benevenagh. "My grandsons love that mountain," Mrs Craig told me, over a veritable feast of porridge and grapefruit, home-made bread and home-made jam, not to mention the usual fry-up. "They're forever climbing it." Kylie the cat also came into the kitchen for her breakfast – "the children named her after that pop-star. Have you heard of her?" – along with her nameless grey kitten, whom I was invited to christen.

Mrs Craig and the clergyman asked me if I had any Free State coins, as they had not yet seen either the 20p nor the £1.00 coins. I fished some out of my pocket and they examined them with great interest. Free State coppers, I was to discover to my embarrassment, were so unacceptable an offering in the North that storekeepers handed them back to me with something close to outrage. Fumbling for that extra penny or twopence, and forgetting to check its origin before presenting it with the rest of the

137

change, I was told icily "That's *foreign* money", or "That's *Irish* money". I let the harp coins sink to the bottom of my rucksack.

Ready to journey on again, I asked if I could settle up. The price of all this unobtrusive welcome, dinner the evening before and a gargantuan breakfast?

"We'll say seven pounds," she said and absolutely refused to accept any more. Before leaving, I presented her with the four-leaved clover and a Free State coin: each as exotic and useless an object as the other.

Mrs Craig waved me off into the thin morning and I walked for a couple of miles. Something felt wrong. After a while, I realised that it was one of the few mornings in which I had not woken up within sight of the sea.

The first car I hitched brought me to Downhill; a tiny village dominated by Mussenden Temple, which perched dramatically at the edge of the cliff overlooking the village. Mussenden Temple and a dovecote are the only surviving buildings of Frederick Hervey's eighteenth-century estate, which is now maintained by the National Trust. The entrance gates to the estate went by the name of "The Lion Gates" but I would swear to it that the animal atop those gates was either a bulldog or a most peculiar and very bald lioness.

The house was built to extend backwards; each section neatly leading one into the next. The house led into a courtyard, the courtyard to outhouses, outhouses to stables, stables to storerooms, and storerooms to an arch in the outer boundary wall, through which, if you walked in a perfectly straight line for a hundred yards or so, you would reach the Temple door.

The passing of time had clearly revealed the layout of the estate to be perfectly symmetrical. I stood at the doorless entrance to the old house and looked right down through its exposed interior and outbuildings, also precisely planned, and had an uninterrupted view of the Temple door. It was a vista which would have rarely revealed itself in the days when the house was occupied: too many closed doors and gates and the constant movement of people blocking the sightline.

The Temple itself was beautifully preserved and brazenly steadfast in its survival at the cliff edge. Sitting in there and looking out, people must have felt as if they were adrift on the Antrim coast.

Built in underneath the Temple was some sort of storeroom, protected by an iron grille. I peered into the dimness and read a little sign which proclaimed the contents of the storeroom to be "fragments from the Castle; architectural and decorative pieces, antique statuary" etc. In the gloom, I could just make out the headless torso of the mate of the peculiar animal masquerading as a lion, and the weathered heads of several statues, regarding me solemnly from strange angles. There were also fragments of cornices and stucco; white and gold pieces of plaster, lying crumbled on the floor like bits of icing from some ghostly wedding cake.

Inga and Iona, a mother and her small daughter, originally from Newcastle in England, picked me up beyond Downhill.

"Rosita?" Inga said, when I told her my name. "I once had a friend called Rosita. She was an acrobat and a bareback rider in a South American circus. You wouldn't be in that line yourself, I suppose?"

Reluctantly, I admitted to not sharing the same occupation as my circus sister.

Mother and daughter were out on a day's drive around the Antrim coast. "We're having a lovely time, aren't we Iona? Still, we've got to be back in time to see *The Generation Game* on telly, don't we?"

Iona looked up from her teen magazine and agreed. She looked up politely each time her mother pointed out something scenic and then returned to the magazine.

They planned to stop in Coleraine for lunch and then continue onto the Waterworld at Portrush. Would I like to look around Coleraine and then travel on with them? It was raining hard by this time and I didn't feel like a long walk beyond the Coleraine suburbs before reaching a suitable hitching point, and so gratefully agreed.

The hub of most Northern towns was centred on a place called "The Diamond"; a place called "The Square" in the state of foreign money. Neither Diamonds nor Squares adhered strictly to their allotted shapes, but for sheer impact, the Diamond had it over the Square. "Meet you at the Diamond" had a far more exotic ring to it than "Meet you at the Square".

Coleraine was a somewhat grim town and certainly looked none the better for being wrapped in rain. There was a great visual display of charity and Christianity in Coleraine. I counted ten charity clothes shops and every other shop was a Christian bookshop. Hardly any of the towns I had travelled through since starting out had had even one decent general bookshop, but when it came to Christian tomes, Coleraine bulged.

I bought groceries in Stewart's supermarket, which was doing a special weekend offer of an "Ulster Fry Pack" for 99p. This was a bargain. Stewart's Ulster Fry Pack contained two soda farls, four potato cakes and four pancakes. I'd never known that you were supposed to fry soda farls and the result was delicious.

Portstewart and Portrush were both Victorian seaside towns. Inga told me that Portstewart was like an Irish Blackpool in the summer. "And at Easter, all the Northern Ireland bikies come and tear up and down the streets. They see the lads over the water doing it at seaside towns over there and Portstewart seems to be where they do it here. But Portrush is much smarter. Lots of elderly people go there to retire."

Portstewart seemed forlorn. Even in winter, some seaside towns never lose their sense of vitality, while others – particularly those with the trappings of amusements, promenades and kiosks – look almost unnaturally deserted without the influx of holidaymakers for whom the structure of the town has been recreated.

The Portrush Waterworld was closed, to the visible relief of Iona, who stared at the water shute with horror and declared, "There's no way you'd catch me going on *that* thing!"

Inga dropped me off in the town with the parting information that in summer, Portrush had the largest cockroach population in Ireland.

"How do you know that?"

"Oh, *everyone* knows that," she assured me.

On the surface, Portrush did not seem all that different from Portstewart, other than the fact that it was larger. But while Portstewart was an empty place which was clearly missing its summer population, Portrush though similarly quiet, had a hidden population behind many of its faded Victorian facades. These old seaside boarding houses were no longer places you came to holiday in: they were places where you came to live out the rest of your days.

Portrush was full of discreet signs for Retirement Homes and Nursing Homes. I gradually became aware of curtains twitching as I walked past and looked up in time to see yet another white-haired man or woman peeping down at me. There were wheelchairs and walking sticks in every front porch, where in former years there would have been prams and buckets and spades.

It looked as if the people who frequented the Christian bookshops of Coleraine came to Portrush for their holidays. Many of the hotels and guesthouses displayed signs saying that they were unlicenced. The first time I saw one of these signs, outside the West Bay View Hotel on the Coast Road, I thought it was a mistake. But I had not been mistaken. To advertise as a dry house was obviously to advertise an attraction.

A few doors down from the West Bay was a guest house whose sign proclaimed it to be a "Christian Guest House". I wondered if the people who chose to retire to Portrush considered themselves to be thus taking their first steps towards some final spiritual journey, since at every corner, you came across evidence of a God-fearing population.

I considered the idea of staying overnight at the Christian Guest House. Regretfully, I decided they would discover me to be agnostic sooner rather than later, and eject me post-haste from the premises.

I spent a fruitless half-hour wandering round the Portrush newsagents in search of postcards. Postcards, a rack of which stood in every newsagents in the South, were rare commodities in the North. Apart from the cities, it was impossible to buy a postcard in Northern Ireland. When I asked for them, I was told things like, "Oh, we ran out a long time ago," or, "We only sell a few in the summer," or, most often, *"Postcards?* No, we never sell those. No demand for them."

This scarcity of picture postcards was a direct result of the lack of tourists. The Introduction to the 1991 Northern Ireland Tourist Brochure bravely sells this fact back to potential tourists: "Even minor roads are smooth, well signposted and remarkably free of traffic."

The 1989 Northern Ireland Visitor Report gives a figure of 1.1 million tourists for the year. A similar Visitor Report issued from Bord Fáilte gives the figure for tourists to the Republic for 1989 as 2.8 million. These figures are deceptive. On paper, the Republic has an average of three visitors to every one to Northern Ireland. However, over 90 per cent of those visitors to Northern Ireland came from no further afield than the Irish Republic and Great Britain. The *expenditure* by visitors – a far more telling statistic – in 1989 in the Republic was 1300 million as compared to 136 million in Northern Ireland. The number of North American visitors alone to the Republic in 1989 was 427,000 as compared to 55,800 to the North.

Bord Fáilte states that 75,000 people, or 7 per cent of the total workforce, were employed in the tourist industry in 1989. Although I studied the Northern Ireland Report closely, nowhere was there any mention of the number of people employed in tourism.

It is possible to gauge the differences in tourist earnings between the two tourist boards without ever reading either of these Reports.

The Bord Fáilte Report is a glossy brochure, printed on high-quality paper, with a coloured photographic cover. It is well laid out, has several photographs inside and professionally designed graphs and charts. The Northern Ireland Report is a badly-bound photocopied typescript, with acetate over the plain lettering of the cover. There are no photographs anywhere and the pie-charts and line-graphs give the impression of having been drawn by hand.

Yet the Introduction to both the 1991 Bord Fáilte and Northern Ireland Tourist Brochures offers the potential tourist exactly the same thing – natural beauty.

Bord Fáilte tells one of "this beautiful island under pearly skies with hills as green and lakes as blue as you ever dreamed... There is a magic in the Irish air to be found nowhere else." The Northern Ireland Board declares: "This is a land of blue mountains and forest parks, mazy lakes and windswept moors, white Atlantic sands, an inland sea... the rain keeps the land a magical emerald green."

The Northern Ireland Visitor Report for 1989 admits in section 4.3 of its analysis of "Tourism trips and nights to Northern Ireland" that its lack of visitors is due to "increased political tension". The missing visitor population is surely one of the most frustrating and cruellest results of media coverage, of which I discovered I was by no means the only passive victim.

The afternoon had cleared up chill and blue. I reluctantly left Portrush behind and started hitching towards White Park Bay.

The road to White Park Bay was empty and glorious. From a distance, the dramatic ruins of Dunluce Castle, built right on the edge of a headland, looked like the rambling, exotic sandcastles that children make, but Dunluce had been built to last longer than sea-washed sandcastles. I looked it up in the *Rough Guide* that night and discovered it dated back to the sixteenth century and had been built by Sorley Boy MacDonnell, whose clan had ruled northeast Ulster. It's history was as exotic as its appearance and I laughed at one of the matter-of-fact *Rough Guide* coments: "In 1639 Dunluce Castle paid the penalty for its precarious, if impregnable, position when the kitchen, complete with cooks and dinner, fell off during a storm."

White Park Bay Hostel, where I was going, was one of the six official hostels in the Youth Hostel Association of Northern Ireland. There were only two independent hostels in Northern Ireland listed in my Independent Hostels Guide. This made for a far smaller ratio of hostels per area in Northern Ireland than in the Republic, and this, again, was a direct result of the lack of tourists to use them. Consequently, the price of an overnight in official hostels was a good deal more expensive than their An

Óige counterparts in the Republic: £5.50 (sterling) per night for someone over 18 and £4.50 for someone under 18.

The White Park Bay Hostel had a superb location. It was halfway between the villages of Bushmills and Ballintoy, well off the main road and built snugly into a curve of a small hill. It looked right out over White Park Bay – a wide, sweeping bay lapped by miles of sand; the surf and foam surging like liquid grass in a windy meadow. Rathlin Island lay sleek on the sea, already winking with lighthouse beams and Scotland was clear and sharply outlined on the far horizon.

There was a notice on the hostel door: "Hostel shut until 5 pm". It was still only 4 pm and the air was chill and sea-washed. I skulked about the hostel, trying doors and windows. The table in the dining room was set for a child's birthday party. I camped out on the doorstep and watched the white-edged waves breathing tirelessly.

By the time the warden spotted me, I was almost reluctant to stop watching the mesmeric rhythms of the sea. The warden's eleven-year-old son, whose birthday party it was, was on his way up from the beach where he'd been playing football with his friends. I hid out in the dormitory until the children had eaten.

White Park Bay was a calm place, islanded between the villages. Within sight of Scotland, it made me feel curiously distant from Ireland, perched on the edge of its north coast as I was.

That evening, I phoned Paul and then Nick, friends in London, whose voices crackled down the line as they each asked me to describe where I was.

"I'm at White Park Bay, near the Giant's Causeway. I can see *Scotland!*" I said, almost disbelievingly, knowing that the smoke-coloured shape of Islay on the horizon unfurled itself in an unbroken piece of land all the way down to London, where in Forest Hill at that moment, Nick was looking at a map of Ireland and locating White Park Bay.

This feeling of liquid distances and indefinable boundaries was heightened next morning when I was having breakfast and looking out to sea again. A young man appeared, seemingly from nowhere, and gestured towards the door, asking me to open it. I had gone to bed the night before at about eleven and it was now sometime after eight. In the time I had been sleeping, Rob had travelled to Stranraer, got the ferry to Larne, slept there on a bench for a few hours and then hitched up to White Park Bay at daybreak.

I was about to set off on a seven-mile walk along the North Antrim Cliff Path to the Giant's Causeway. Rob, still full of energy despite a largely sleepless night, asked if he could join me and so we set off companionably.

It was a glorious day. The huge sky was deepest blue, the sea glittered with small, silver-coloured waves, the white sand crunched underfoot like fresh snow. The tiny settlement of Portbradden lay across the far sweep of the bay. The tide was out and so we walked across the beach to Portbradden, making diversions to do some cave-exploring with a torch, but we found nothing more exotic than shells and dead birds.

Portbradden was charming: a string of brightly-painted houses which gave the illusion of floating on the sea, situated as they were at the foot of a steep cliff. Portbradden boasts what is reputedly the smallest church in Ireland. There was little to see in the twelve feet by six and a half feet space when we looked in the window, apart from a small altar, a wooden pew and a highly erotic statue.

The path hugged the edge of the cliff-tops and you are advised not to walk along it on a windy day. But there wasn't a puff of wind on that clear, calm day, as we followed the path along the Antrim headlands, the long grass seeping down over the cliff face and the gulls swooping close to our faces.

As we came closer to the Causeway, the strange volcanic landscape began to gradually reveal itself. Sixty million years ago, the earth erupted on this stretch of coastline, bringing to the surface a great body of molten basalt. When this cooled, it took the form of thousands of perfectly hexagonal columns, of differing heights.

The result makes for a peculiar and spectacular landscape. Columns of rock pressed their stone flanks deep into the sides of the cliffs. Out at sea, clusters of rock reared up like stalagmites. The crystals of stone were everywhere and took many illusory guises – pan-pipes; church organs; Gothic cathedral facades.

The part of the Causeway which is most visited is the part closest to the road and Visitor Centre. We rounded a headland and saw a mass of shorn Causeway columns, projecting out into the sea in an irregular honeycomb of stone, the people swarming over them like bees. Although it was November, the car-park was quite full and there were a lot of people about.

We decided to hitch back to the hostel and began walking in the direction of White Park Bay on a quiet back road. We shared out the remains of our lunch and the talk turned to tales of food.

In Switzerland, Rob (who was from Melbourne) had met up with an Englishman, with whom he hitched for a couple of days. "For lunch, he took a tin of catfood out of one pocket and a tin-opener out of the other and ate the whole lot in front of me!"

I squawked in disbelief. "You're *joking*!"

"I'm not. The chap said he'd worked in a petfood factory in England and that the standards of hygiene and quality of food were much better than any of the stuff they can for human consumption – because he'd worked in a meat canning factory before he'd worked in the petfood place," Rob said cheerfully.

We got a lift from three Englishmen over from Birmingham, all of whom, including the driver, were happily smoking joints.

"The Giant's Causeway was a good place to trip!" one of them laughed, and we had the not unpleasant sensation of driving the remaining miles to White Park Bay in a warm fug of marijuana.

There had been several new arrivals by the time we returned to the hostel. There were people having tea at the table in front of the picture window and they were all staring out to sea with much the same glazed and mesmerised expression as I had felt to be on my face the day before, while waiting on the doorstep. They broke off staring to

146

introduce themselves and then their gaze drifted inexorably out to sea again.

"It's just like watching television," Julie, a woman from Sydney explained, as I made some more tea and joined them in watching this hypnotic television programme.

That evening, myself, Rob, Julie and Jerome – a New Zealander – all went to Fullerton's Pub in Ballintoy. Fullerton's was very small and had the look of a pub which had been "done up" in the seventies or perhaps the sixties. Everything was brown: the nicotine-stained ceiling, the formica tops, the beauty board. There were a few stools at the bar. Other than that, the only seating was fixed padded benches and formica-topped tables, of the sort one sees in greasy-spoon cafes.

We were the only people under sixty in the pub, but were welcomed loudly by everyone present. All the young people, it emerged, had gone to a disco in Portrush. Beside the door, there was an electronic keyboard, a microphone on a stand and a couple of speakers. Would there be music, I asked the barman. "And the best around!" he assured me. We sampled the Guinness and waited.

The musician arrived. Behind him, Pied-Piper like, in swung through the door what looked like the entire population of the village of Ballintoy, bar the teenagers who mistakenly thought that there was better crack to be had at a disco in Portrush.

What ensued was one of the most extraordinary evening's entertainment I'd ever had in a pub. The musician struck up old-time waltzes and as many people as could squeeze onto the tiny floor space, did so, waltzing with tremendous style and formality. The audience gave a rowdy appreciation to every waltz and cheered roundly for each new couple that took to the floor.

And then the whole tempo changed. A singer joined the musician and together, they began belting out a series of country and western songs. The music hopped and jerked its way through the pub, which was now crammed with people. "Now *that's* what I call music!" the barman hollered and the bewildered Southern Hemisphere visitors asked me if most Irish pubs were like this, or if they played this sort of music all the time.

It was impossible not to laugh at the whole wild scenario or to fail to want to dance in such an atmosphere, to the crescendo of crazy music; evocative of tossed lassoes, cracking whips and galloping hooves. Jerome and I tumbled onto the floor and we launched into a completely mad dance, half Irish reels, half thigh-slapping American, trying our best to keep pace with the music which got faster and faster, everything blurring into one tremendous swirl of people clapping and stamping feet and yelling encouragement until we realised that there was no end to the music: that they would play as long as we could dance. We collapsed exhausted into each other's arms and were rewarded for our efforts on the floor by a standing ovation.

After such a performance, I was fit for nothing else.

The music gradually subsided in volume and tempo. Julie told one of the locals that her grandmother had come from Downpatrick and the musician played *The Mountains of Mourne* for her, greatly to her delight. She was less delighted, however, when the man who had got the song played for her then asked her up to waltz for its duration. He looked like someone from a lost generation: all Brylcream and black hair, with ruddy cheeks, who stood a head shorter than Julie, clutched her firmly to his chest and steered her around the floor with barely disguised lust.

Julie's expression of amazement and horror, veiled by an enormous effort at politeness, made us laugh until we felt sick, and her waltz with the man from the lost generation received the loudest applause of the night.

I stayed for a further day at White Park Bay and could easily have stayed for several more. I spent most of that next day down on the expansive beach, exploring the profusion of sea-arches at the Ballintoy end of the beach. The rock there seemed to be moulded by the wind: all intricate arches of dribbling stone. It was another superb blue day, with a clean edge to the wind.

Next morning, I discovered to my dismay that the nearest branch of my bank was back in Coleraine and so was faced with the prospect of having to partially retrace my route. There was a back road which ran inland from Bushmills to Coleraine and I decided to travel by this way.

I hurried on through Bushmills, home of the oldest legal distillery in the world, where whiskey has been made since 1608 and took the inland road to Coleraine. At Coleraine, I went to the bank, had lunch and was then anxious to get back on the road again. The B67 ran inland from Coleraine to Ballycastle, on the far side of White Park Bay, and so I walked through the town, struck out along this road, and began hitching.

I had been hitching for perhaps fifteen minutes when a car flashed its lights at me and the driver gestured in front of him. When I turned to see what it was that he was pointing out to me, I saw that a red car had pulled into the kerb some yards down the road and was waiting for me. Usually, when drivers wish to give you a lift, they signal to you that they will pull in by putting their indicators on. I thought it somewhat odd that this driver had not done so, nor, as a second sign had he sounded his horn after pulling in.

I went up to the car, opened the door and looked across at the driver. Some purely animal instinct of warning jolted through me, sensing something peculiar. It was nothing that would hold any credibility or that I could explain logically, but all I knew was that I instantly felt frightened and unnerved.

"Where are you going?" he asked.

Almost always, I managed to be the one to ask this question first. It allowed me an opportunity to size up the driver and to decide whether or not I wanted this lift, without giving away any information about my destination. But I had been so rattled in this instance that I hadn't been able to say a word and now found myself automatically answering "Ballycastle," although it was the last thing I actually wanted to say.

"Get in and I'll bring you part of the way."

The driver's eyes were unfocused and he looked somewhat drunk, although I could get no smell of drink. Other than that, he looked perfectly ordinary, but something made me absolutely determined not to get into the car. "Where *exactly* are you going?" I asked, playing for time.

He sighed. "Look, I'll bring you all the way to Ballycastle if that's what you want. I'm on a day off and I'm just driving around, so I've plenty of time. Just get in and I'll bring you all the way."

I stared at him. "No," I said. "No thanks," and I shut the door and walked back up the road again towards Coleraine.

When I glanced around a few minutes later, he was still there, watching me. As soon as he saw me looking back, he reversed the car until it was level with me, and beckoned. I shook my head, noted the number plate and make of the car, and kept walking. I found that I was shaking. When I looked around again, the car had disappeared and its driver now knew where I was trying to hitch to. Ballycastle suddenly seemed a very long seventeen miles away.

Nothing had actually happened to me. I had not been threatened or physically forced in any way. But despite this, I felt the vital confidence and nerve which a hitch-hiker has got to possess in order to hitch in safety and enjoyment, just draining away.

Hitching, you set out to arrogantly cross uncertain distances by placing your faith in your ability to swim: to choose the right lifts. But I had floundered and taken in water and was now aware that there was the possibility of not always making it safely to the other side. But with a good half of the Irish coastline still to see, the only thing to do was to keep hitching. So I hauled myself onto the floating driftwood of the roadside and struck out again, but this time with less confidence and more fear. I hitched nervously, but not the red cars, and am quite certain my face was set in such a grim expression that people gave me one look and kept going, since it took a very long time to get a lift. By this time, I was beginning to consider the unhappy possibility of having to get a bus.

The car that stopped had a woman driver and I was so relieved that I found myself telling her about the other car.

"Oh, but you must report him!" she exclaimed. "Haven't you heard about that German girl who was raped and murdered in 1988? She came off the ferry at Larne and was hitching up north. They found her body in the back of Ballypatrick Wood, just south of Ballycastle. They never found who did it. I wouldn't hitch round here for *anything!*"

In 1988, I had been in Australia and so had never before heard this grim tale. Every driver who picked me up for the next few days told me this story and implied that I was a sitting duck for a similar fate.

Nobody who spoke to me about "the German girl" knew her name, something which perhaps depersonalized her to them and made it easier for them to recount her fate with such horrified fascination. The German Girl and Ballypatrick Wood seemed to have entered the same black mythology as the anonymous bishop who had perished so cruelly on Bishop's Rock at the entrance to Inishbofin harbour.

The woman from whom I first heard this story, dropped me off in Ballybogy, urging me to go to the police. These two experiences combined in making me thoroughly scared, although commonsense told me that the possibility of a murderer still being in the same area of his crime after two years was remote. But I did feel scared and for the first time, wished heartily that I had a travelling companion.

I didn't have much time to feel edgy as the driver of a Texaco lorry stopped very soon after and brought me the rest of the way to Ballycastle. He commented, as most people did, on the fact that I was travelling alone. He added, however, as most people did not, that it was dangerous to travel alone.

"You're the first hitch-hiker I've seen this year and I'm always on the road," he said reprovingly. "Haven't you heard about the girl –"

"*Yes,*" I said desperately.

It was no good. He related the whole grisly story to me again and let me off at Ballycastle with the information that the next part of my journey would bring me through Ballypatrick Wood, "where she was done in".

If I was ever going to be made feel paranoid about hitching alone, it was happening here. I felt absolutely no desire to report my thin story to the police. But I had been unnerved by the whole experience and so horribly shaken by the fate of my fellow hitch-hiker that I found myself asking where the police station was.

The Ballycastle Royal Ulster Constabulary Station was on the outskirts of the town and had the sort of protection usually accorded only to money: the commodity being protected within these particular walls was lives. I had to speak into a video monitor outside the metal gates, and state my name, address and purpose before I was allowed to enter. I said my piece to an officer in the bare reception area. He made me relate it again over the telephone to a woman detective who was still working on the murder case. Telling of my experience for the third time that day, I began to feel worried as well as foolish. Was I going to put somebody under suspicion, simply because I'd had an inexplicable instinct? The officer started tracing the car. I reiterated the fact that no physical threat or force of any kind had been imposed upon me and prepared to leave the RUC station as quickly as possible.

It was not my day. I was told that they would like me to make a statement and would I mind waiting until somebody was ready to take it? It was getting dark by this time.

"Don't worry about any more hitching today," the officer said. "Our boys will run you over to Cushendall."

Given a choice, I would have preferred to take my chances on the murky stretch of road rather than be driven along it in an RUC car, but I had walked myself into this.

I waited: gloomy, embarrassed and miserable.

For the fourth time, I told my story, to an officer in a small room where an old-fashioned ceramic sink gurgled at intervals behind his chair and the row of uniform jackets hanging on pegs were casting disturbing shadows in the half-light.

The officer wrote down what I said. "Apprehensive," he said, grinning across at me. "That's a big word."

Everyone who talked to me at Ballycastle RUC Station was courteous and friendly, but the very obvious presence of so many revolvers and rifles made me uneasy. By the time I gave my statement, I was nervous. By the time I left the station in an unmarked car with two of "our boys", I felt irrationally guilty.

The boy in the passenger seat had a rifle across his knees. I found myself wondering why neither of them wore seatbelts and thought the reason might be to allow a swift reaction to any threat. The windows were the standard practice bulletproof type.

I was an uneasy passenger in that car. The men I was travelling with were marked men, by virtue of their job. They might leave the RUC tomorrow, but they would continue to be potential IRA targets for as long as "The Troubles" went on. In that car, I knew what fear was: knew just a little of that underlying fear which those men, no matter how much they push it away from them, must always carry with them.

I asked them the clichéd question about being policemen in Northern Ireland.

"If you thought about it, there's no way in the whole world you'd ever do it," the driver said, flatly.

"If you thought about it, you'd go mad. Absolutely crazy," the other said.

I got the hint and said no more.

There was silence for some time and then they began pointing out places of interest to me.

"That's Loughareema, a famous vanishing lake. It can be there for weeks and then it suddenly disappears overnight. People windsurf on it, but sometimes, you could turn up with your windsurfer and there'd be no lake to surf on!"

"That's Cushendun, a lovely little village."

I was being driven to the hostel at Cushendall, which lay deep within the verdant Antrim glens. Cushendall Hostel, described in the Youth Hostel Association leaflet as, "A large old, once family house, set in its own grounds on the hillside of the Antrim coast overlooking Cushendall Bay", appeared to be all these things, inasmuch as we could see in the complete darkness.

The hostel was some good distance from Cushendall itself and lay in darkness within large and rambling grounds. The house was certainly large and old. It was also empty. There was no sign of anybody within the silent, unlit house. The officers got out of the car with me and shone their torches around. The front door was open. They found the light switches and called out, but there was no reply.

"Are you sure it's open?" they asked me.

I was as sure as you can be from consulting the official information, but looking at the empty hostel, I was not so sure. Apart from the silence and the smell of disuse seeping through the house, it was shockingly cold.

The officers had homes and dinners to go to. I bade them goodbye and when the sound of the car had melted away down the driveway, the silence spread out again through the hostel. A sloppy, laughing sound made me jump. It was the urinals, which periodically laughed up water all night: an unpleasant sound in that empty place.

Under the section headed "Staying in a youth hostel" in the 1990 Accommodation Guide for the Youth Hostel Association of Northern Ireland, I read: "All the Hostels are well cared for, with warm comfortable lounges for relaxing and recounting your tales." Alas, the Cushendall Hostel was sepulchral. I clattered upstairs, opening doors as I went, finding nothing but rows upon rows of empty bunks.

My breath made white clouds. Outside, it was below freezing. Inside, the temperature was not much higher. There was a fireplace in the empty, icy lounge. I ferreted about for signs of fuel, but found only coal-dust at the bottom of a plastic bucket. I had not yet removed my jacket or gloves. The camaraderie around the fire at White Park Bay the previous night seemed like a memory from the distant past.

I was looking through the *Rough Guide* for a B & B listing in Cushendall when a car pulled up outside and a young woman arrived in.

I have remembered her as Marylee, although I'm not sure if this was her real name or not. Marylee was American and was more or less a self-appointed temporary warden. The official warden had apparently hated his job so much that he had begged her to look after Cushendall for a couple of weeks and had then promptly absconded to Scotland. Marylee had been visited by someone from YHANI, who discovered she did not have a working visa. She told me that she would now have to leave and the hostel would subsequently close for the remainder of the winter.

So far, the day had been one I would rather forget. I seemed to have temporarily lost control over my plans. As the day had evolved, so it finished. I fully intended to abandon the ice-box in favour of a B & B, but, distracted by Marylee's tale of the vanished warden, I found I had signed myself in for the night.

"I feel sick with the cold, so I'm going to bed," Marylee announced. "Make yourself at home."

"The fire?" I inquired, grimly and pessimistically.

"The coal ran out last week and the YHA haven't brought any more. They were *supposed* to put central heating in this month, but... " She shrugged her shoulders dismissively. She presented her back to me and went upstairs. "By the way," she called down to me, "there's no hot water in the showers."

I tried the hot-coffee central-heating method. It didn't work. I wrapped my numb fingers around my pen and tried to write, but it was too cold.

After some time, Marylee resurfaced. "Let's go to the pub," she said. "They've got a heater there."

The pub Marylee brought me to had a Super Ser gas heater, a juke-box and four men sitting up at the bar. She drank Seven-Up, played the juke-box and ignored my attempts at conversation. I fell silent, as *Nights in White Satin* finished playing and caught the last of a conversation from the four men at the bar, who were discussing kneecapping.

Marylee said she was going to stay by the heater until she was thrown out. She put another coin in the juke-box and closed her eyes. I put on my jacket and wound a scarf around my neck.

"Oh, you're going," she said, with obvious relief, opening one cautious eye and then settling back against the seat again. "Bye bye."

I hurried back to the ice-box, piled several blankets on

the bed and burrowed down. I didn't bother taking off my clothes. It would have been a punctilious act and I'd had more than enough of being punctilious for one day.

To be fair to Cushendall, when I later wrote and complained to Reg Magowan, the Chairman of the YHANI, he promptly wrote me an apologetic letter, enclosing two complimentary overnight vouchers, saying somewhat mysteriously that there had been "extenuating circumstances, but these would have been of little comfort to you during the visit." He assured me that "the Hostel has now been refurbished with full central heating."

In the frosty blue morning, Cushendall looked spectacular. The wide bay was blue and the Antrim glens and mountains were green and orange, islanding the village at their feet. Looking out from a window at the top of the hostel, Cushendall seemed like an Italian village at the edge of the Mediterranean.

Already dressed, I lost no time in departing the ice-box.

I had a lift in a leather-lined Volvo to Carnlough with a couple from Castlerock who were out on a birthday celebration. It was Winifred's birthday. Her husband had taken the day off to bring her on a drive. Winifred sat in the passenger seat and knitted.

"Oh good for you, dear," she said, when I'd explained I was doing a bit of travelling and yes, I was doing the travelling without anybody else. "You'll meet a nice man soon and that'll be the end of your wandering."

Her husband agreed. "Yes, everyone needs a mate and a home and children. You'll settle down one of these days, so enjoy your freedom while you can."

The village of Carnlough was spread out along a high sea-wall. I had actually walked right out of it, looking for the centre, before I realised my mistake and turned back. Carnlough's speciality seemed to be home-made ice-cream. Every second shop was offering it: McKillop's; McMullan's; McAuley's.

I splashed out and had lunch in the gracious Londonderry Arms, where even the women's loos were sumptuous. Mounted on the wall in the lounge was the horseshoe worn by Arkle when he won the 1965 Cheltenham Gold Cup.

It was a short day's hitch-hike. Ballygalley was only six miles away and I arrived there mid-afternoon. The hostel overlooked the sea-front, there was a fire blazing in the hearth and the whole place was toasty warm.

I made a phonecall to Pat Thompson in Saintfield, mother of Elaine; another exiled friend working in London. I had a standing invitation to come and stay any time. The hospitality I'd received previously at Cotswold Drive was far too tempting to pass up on, and it didn't take much persuasion on Pat's behalf to make me agree that I would phone when I reached Belfast next day and she would drive in to pick me up.

After that, I did nothing more strenuous than fall asleep by the fire for the rest of the afternoon. The water in the showers was hot. The dormitory was warm. I undressed before getting into bed that night.

It was only a four-mile distance from Ballygalley to Larne, which I hitched swiftly the next morning. Larne looked grey and featureless under the dull sky; sprawling with ugly factories. While waiting for my clothes to be washed and dried at the laundry, I walked out towards the port.

Although there were ships in port, the terminal building at Larne was quiet. I looked at sailing times. Cairnryan was two and a half hours away. Stranraer was two hours and twenty minutes. Ships to both destinations were due to sail within the hour, at 11.30am. For £14.50, travelling as a foot passenger, I could have been in Scotland by the afternoon, leaving my clothes to spin themselves to bewildered dryness and go unclaimed at the end of the day. It was gloriously tempting: the idea of sinking into the horizon of Cairnryan and making my way up through the Highlands.

I turned my back on the port and walked slowly into Larne, collected my clothes and kept walking resolutely out of town.

Judging by the banners, Carrickfergus was still empathically saying "NO!" to the United Ireland, popery and all the rest of the package.

I had lunch in McCullough's Home Bakery, where "battered fish" was on offer for £1.05 a portion.

Back on the Belfast Road again, a car stopped. The driver was the only occupant of the car. There was a briefcase in the passenger seat. Yes, he was going into Belfast.

"The front seat's occupied, as you can see," he said matter-of-factly, when I hesitated, waiting for him to move the briefcase.

And so, I was chauffeured into Belfast.

This man, it emerged, was going out to east Belfast. "It'd be much handier for your friends to pick you up over there for Saintfield, rather than go all the way into town."

Two short trips to Belfast had given me some sense of the city centre, but I was a blank with suburbs.

"I'll be going out Newtownards way," he offered. He looked at me in the mirror. "Don't worry, I'll look after you!" he laughed.

I wasn't particularly easy about being driven into a tangle of unfamiliar suburbs, but for some reason, sitting in the back seat of the car gave me the happy illusion of being in control.

He drove down the M2, along by the dockyards and the towering gantries of Harland and Wolff, down the Newtownards Road and up Holywood Road until he reached Park Avenue. His destination was 45 Park Avenue: the Mount Mason Social Club.

The Mount Mason Social Club looked like a cross between a small factory and a third-class hotel and was set back from the road. The hallway had an institutional smell: food and disinfectant mixed up together. There was a telephone in the hall.

"You can call your friends," he said. "If you need directions, just come and ask."

He disappeared behind a door to the left. There was frosted glass in the door beside the telephone and a sign on the door said "Masonic Brethern Only". I tried it. It was locked. I telephoned Pat and gave her the address, but not the name of the place. I didn't think she would have believed me anyway.

There was a long piece of doggerel pinned to a noticeboard in the hall. I copied down a few lines from it, keeping one prudent eye on the door through which the man had disappeared.

> Be always faithful to your trust
> And do the best you can
> Then you can proudly tell the world
> You're a Mason and a Man.

> Do you measure up?
> What really counts lies buried deep

But here I had to put the notebook back in my pocket, since the Mason and the Man emerged and asked me to come through.

The room he brought me into was part dining room, part bar, part reception area, with a couple of slot machines. The furniture and decor was unremarkable. There was a handful of men around the bar.

"I didn't think the Masons allowed women into these places."

He found this very amusing. "Oh, anyone can come here and have a meal and use these facilities, if they want. These are social facilities for all. It's our *meetings* we don't allow the ladies into." He wagged a finger at me and laughed again.

It was an uncomfortable wait. He played the slot machines and the men stared. It was made clear to me that I was to wait here, with them and that they were watching me and for some reason, were perpetually on the brink of laughter.

It took Pat a long time to find No. 45 Park Avenue.

"Ah, here's your friend now!" he exclaimed jovially, as Pat drove up and parked outside. I watched her get out of the car and cautiously approach the entrance. As I went out to greet her, the Mason and the Man handed me over formally, winking widely to his mates, and Pat and I drove away like a pair of conspirators.

I stayed in Belfast for a couple of days. As in Derry, the graffiti about Dessie Ellis was everywhere. "Another Hunger Strike for Justice". "Remember 1981, Don't Let

Him Die." "Irish = Guilty". Painted several feet high up on the hills; "Support Dessie Ellis".

Daubed on walls and pavements, the paint had been splashed and slapped on so quickly that the words dripped clumsily into each other. When I looked at the neat formality of the Republican and Loyalist murals, painted carefully onto gable walls with controlled brush-strokes and compared them to the wildness of the hastily-painted extradition graffiti, there seemed something terrifying in the urgency with which the graffiti had been carried out. I did not doubt that should Ellis die on hunger strike, trouble would erupt on the streets of Derry and Belfast.

While I was in Belfast, Mary Robinson was elected President. She was the first woman President of Ireland, the youngest person ever elected, and the first non-Fianna Fáil candidate. I was elated. We could not get RTE television in Saintfield, but I followed the progress of the count through the *Belfast Telegraph*, which made the election front-page news on 8 and 9 November. "Robinson edges nearer victory", "Jubilant Robinson waits for a sensational victory", the headlines ran.

Les Thompson was frankly amazed. "Ireland isn't ready for Mary Robinson," he'd said, before the results of the poll became known. When he heard the news, he greeted it with a mixture of delight and a kind of wry sadness. "You're lucky. There's a real chance now in the Republic for change in outlook and of freshness and progress. We don't have any of that up here, for as long as this killing goes on. Politics up here are stagnant and that's one of the great tragedies of the last twenty years."

Having long been fascinated by the *Titanic*, which had been built at Harland and Wolff, and by the extravagance of her tragedy, I decided to go and look at the memorabilia connected with the ship in the Ulster Folk and Transport Museum. Bidding goodbye to Les, Pat, and "wee" Kaiser, their German Schnauzer, I hitched up through Comber, Scrabo and Newtownards.

The open-air Ulster Folk Museum, a collection of replica and reconstructed cottages, farmhouses, churches and schools, necessarily involves a lot of walking. Unthinkingly,

I asked in the Museum shop if I could leave my rucksack there while walking around. Bulky items left by a stranger for safe-keeping are not welcome in Northern Ireland. The woman behind the counter eyed me sharply.

"It's not really fair to ask people here if you can leave your luggage with them," she said coldly, looking me up and down in a professional manner.

The buildings in the Folk Museum were a hotchpotch of styles and periods. There was a row of six terraced houses from Belfast city, known as "Tea Lane", which had been built in the 1820s, occupied until the 1970s and then knocked down and rebuilt in the Museum grounds. There was a byre dwelling from Derrybeg in Donegal, a forge from Newtownbutler, a national school from Ballycastle: all transplanted to form part of the Folk Museum. The idea behind the construction of the Museum is to illustrate the social history of the people of the North of Ireland.

Wandering from the Cushendall Court House to the Donaghadee Weighbridge House, I found myself thinking, *so what?* There was something unsettling about the planned village, with its careful cross-section of buildings gathered from several counties. I peered dutifully in schoolroom windows and clattered up the wooden stairs of farmhouses and eyed yet another pair of china Staffordshire dogs, but I came away from the "village" unmoved and with the feeling that it was all somewhat two-dimensional. The abandoned, tumbled, deserted villages in the Burren and on Achill had been far more powerful experiences by way of a history lesson.

Across the road, at the Transport part of the Museum, all the *Titanic* memorabilia was away on a travelling exhibition. I had to settle for a tiny metal brooch of the doomed ship, and pinned it to a strap on my rucksack, the purpose of which strap the assistant at the Outdoor and Adventure Shop in London had explained to me was "To hold an ice-axe".

I got a lift back down to Newtownards with a man who, when I asked if he travelled down South much, replied, "To be honest, I never go down. It's too expensive."

The drive down the inside arm of the Ards peninsula to

Portaferry, was through a strange and haunting landscape. In the late afternoon light of November, with a mist beginning to rise, the hundreds of little islands in Strangford Lough bobbed in and out of sight, each one with a distinctive landscape of its own: a hump-backed island here; a single tree growing there; and over there, an island riding so low in the water that it barely broke the surface of the lough. Everything was tinted grey and palest blue. The mist wavered before the car, the water trembled, the islands slipped past and eventually sank beneath the evening's darkness.

By the time Steven and John, two Portaferry men, had dropped me off in the village, I felt slightly bewitched and wandered around the quay blankly for some time, watching the brightly-lit car-ferry cross over and back from Strangford, at the other side of the lough, before remembering that I was supposed to be looking for a B & B to put up in for the night.

Early next morning, I climbed up to the old windmill on the small hill beyond the village and looked back over Strangford Lough, where the islands were beginning to gradually emerge from the mist. It had been a frosty night and the people of Portaferry had been lighting their fires. Dozens of thin lines of smoke rose straight up into the air, like the stiff pencil-rods of smoke coming out of the chimney of the symmetrical houses that children sometimes draw. I could see across to the North Channel and over to the huddle of brightly-painted houses that was Strangford. The water was perfectly still and purest blue.

Apart from the lines of smoke, the whole insubstantial landscape of the morning appeared to be without movement. There was something elusive and mysterious about Strangford Lough. I longed for a boat, to explore the islands with, but the only boat I stepped into that day was the ferry, which whisked me over to Strangford in ten short minutes.

7

A SEVERED HEAD

Newcastle to Rosslare Harbour

At Newcastle, where the mountains of Mourne sweep down to the sea, the mountains were invisible; hidden under a grey sky and sheets of rain. The promenade was deserted; I was the only person staying at the Newcastle youth hostel. *It must be wonderful in the summer,* I thought grimly, looking at the mass of grey cloud where the Mournes were supposed to be, completely fed-up with the appalling weather.

Before leaving the mountainless town, I called in to see Martin and Rosaleen Waddell, who lived on the Central Promenade. Martin, whom I knew from working in publishing in London, was holed up in his den at the back of the house, quietly celebrating the publication of his hundredth book. Master of the picture-book text, Martin can put more into five hundred words than most people can in fifty thousand.

In the book-lined study, Martin tugged at his beard, smoked pipe after pipe, and showed me books at every stage of development. There were copies of newly-published books, fresh from the printers; there were stacks of proofs waiting to be checked; there were rows of folders containing old stories, half-written stories, abandoned stories, ideas for stories. There were teenage novels, short novels, stories to be read aloud, stories for a child starting to read alone, and picture-books to be shared with a toddler. The place was alive with stories.

I told Martin a few of my own stories from the journey. He asked if I'd come down the outside of the Ards peninsula, through Donaghadee and when I said no, tapped his pipe reflectively. "We lived at Donaghadee for a while," he said, "and the air came in like dollops of cream."

When I told him about searching for the carved hand of Tim Robinson's Burren map, Martin looked as if I'd given him a present.

"Carved hand?" he said excitedly. "There's a story in that!"

He sat down at once to his typewriter and tapped out the words, and then stared at the page in fascination.

It was the perfect moment to make an exit.

A foggy mist had risen from the ground while I had been inside. All the way to Warrenpoint, telegraph poles poked up through the fog like the masts of ships that were drifting aimlessly through the fields.

Across the border, I knew that many people were beginning to work themselves into a collective frenzy, as they found various ways in which to ensure they would be near a television that afternoon. It was the day that Ireland was to play England in a European Football Championship qualifier. In the World Cup summer of 1990, Ireland had followed the progress of the Republic's football team with something close to euphoria. I knew that across the border, the tricolours were out, the pubs were packed, the excitement was palpable. In Warrenpoint, I did not expect and did not find, anything of this anticipation at all. I had purposely lingered on an extra day so that I could have the opportunity of observing the impact of the match, if any, at this side of the border.

I looked into several pubs in Warrenpoint, but they were all empty, apart from a handful of people eating lunch. Since kick-off was only a few minutes away, I settled down to watch the first half of the match in Mac's Bar, on the quay.

Mac's Bar was masquerading as an American bar; painted a brash cherry-red inside and filled with various bits and pieces of Americanism – registration plates, baseball caps, brass eagles and a *Spitting Image* puppet of Ronald Reagan. There were four men sitting up at the bar, working their way through lunch. They all completely ignored the television and glanced over at me once or twice, clearly surprised by my interest.

I watched flatly the first flat half, coffee-cups clinking on one side of me and cigar smoke billowing at me from the other. At half-time, I left and walked across the square to a small, unprepossessing pub called "The First and Last", its interior dim and the walls and ceiling stained with smoke. The football match in The First and Last had an attentive audience of perhaps thirty men.

I ordered a glass of Guinness and sat back cautiously to watch the second half. Apart from calling for more Guinness, the men didn't say much; muttered abuse and encouragement to the players and stole glances at me.

England scored. There was a thin, dull silence. Pints were lowered. Nobody said a word. It was a peculiar, unnerving silence. I was unsure how to read that silence, or the neutral expressions on the faces around me.

The concentrated silence continued for the rest of the match. And then Ireland scored an equaliser. There was one collective bellow of joy. The barman pulled a score of fresh pints and then there was total silence again until the match finished, the score one-all.

By this time, everyone in the pub had drunk a lot. Wanting to keep my wits about me and having long since discovered it was pointless trying to remember conversations with any clarity the next day with a sore head, I had drunk little. Sitting next to me were a sandy-haired man and a dark-eyed man.

Sandy asked me where I was from.

"Dublin," I said this time.

He stared unblinkingly at me. "Don't get me wrong now, just because I'm here in Warrenpoint. *I'm Irish myself*, make no mistake about that. We just have the misfortune of having the wrong government up here."

Dark-Eyes was keeping a close ear on this conversation. The barman hovered, wiping and rewiping a glass. I felt guarded and apprehensive, not wishing to become involved in a conversation that could turn nasty in an instant, but sensing that I could learn something if I stayed. So I stayed, trying to guide the conversation a bit, and constantly aware of being observed and overheard by the entire bar.

"I'm a peaceful man myself," Sandy assured me. "I

wouldn't know how to use a gun if you put one down in front of me on the counter."

Privately, I doubted this.

"Let me ask you a question," he said. "If everyone laid down arms peacefully and if there was a vote tomorrow with a peaceful solution, would you vote yes or no to a united Ireland?"

Dark-Eyes stared at his pint and groaned. The place fell silent. I felt that I was beginning to tread on thin ice.

"There's no point trying to give an intelligent answer to an impossible question," I said carefully.

Everyone laughed. "That's the right answer!" Dark-Eyes said, relieved.

"Yes or no?" Sandy insisted angrily, but I didn't answer. "You're a *Southerner*," he said, pronouncing the word "Southerner" with something like disgust, as if this explained everything and that as such, I could not possibly be interested in anything that was happening in the North.

A few days previously, a party of four men on a wildfowling expedition to Lough Neagh, two of them RUC officers, had all been shot dead by the IRA. Sandy went back to talking about guns. "Anyone who goes out with a gun with the intention of killing deserves what they get," he said sourly, mentioning the wildfowlers.

Dark-Eyes laughed at him. "There's a difference between killing ducks and killing people!"

Sandy glowered and blustered, but Dark-Eyes had taken over control of the conversation and was beginning to steer it towards safe topics. But I was still reeling from Sandy's casual remark about the wildfowlers. Somewhat unwisely, I said, "Look at those people shot at Lough Neagh. Two of them were RUC officers but the other two were civilians. I can understand that the RUC officers were IRA targets, but why did they *all* have to be killed?"

Sandy stared at me. "The other two were from the UVF," he said softly. "None of those four were really *people*."

The barman stood in front of Sandy and said, very quietly, "That's no talk for a pub. That's dangerous talk and I don't want to hear it in my pub."

I settled my glass down carefully on the counter and

166

took up my rucksack. The barman looked at me.

"Enjoy your holiday now and I promise the next time you come in here, *he* won't be here."

Sandy caught my arm. "What did you say your name was?"

I hadn't said what my name was. "Anne," I replied, and left.

It was raining outside. I wanted to put as much distance between myself and The First and Last as possible. I had never been so chilled by anything in my life as by that cold-blooded remark of Sandy's. If Sandy was a typical representative of an IRA supporter, then I suddenly understood with horrifying clarity why the years of violence had gone on so long and seemed as if they would continue indefinitely.

Later in the journey, in a pub late one night in the south-west of Ireland, I struck up conversation with an Englishwoman and a Belfast man, both of whom were passing through the area independently. They had been drinking together all day. Several pints behind, I listened to, and contributed to, their conversation with a mixture of horror, amazement, and cold professional interest.

In the way that drunk people often do, the man suddenly came out with a statement completely unrelated to what we had been talking about.

"My brother joined the British Army," he said. "He was never allowed back into the house again, except for my mother's funeral. There was no excuse for him to join up. He should never have done it."

Jolted, I looked at him. "Were you involved yourself?"

He leaned back against the wall and closed his eyes. "I was."

"D'you ever kill anyone?" the Englishwoman asked casually, rolling a cigarette.

"I wouldn't like to answer that question," he said slowly.

"Well, did you?" she pressed, lighting a match.

There was a small silence. "I did."

She let the cigarette go out. My hand closed tightly on my glass.

The man told us the story in a slow, low voice. He and a friend had been moving arms from one location to another when an RUC officer came around the corner and saw them. "He knew bloody well what we were up to. He fired a shot over the car. I had to shoot him. It was a case of shoot or be shot. I found out later that he was only nineteen and I thought, Christ, what the fuck was he doing there at that age?"

"You shouldn't have told us that!" she burst out. "I don't want to know that you *killed* someone! Why did you tell us?"

"You shouldn't have asked me that question."

"I didn't expect you to answer it!"

He shrugged his shoulders.

I found myself echoing the barman at Warrenpoint. "That's dangerous talk..." I had no doubt but that this man was telling the truth and was both shocked and amazed at the ease with which he told this story. Even if he had been spinning a drunken yarn, it was indeed dangerous talk. The woman was, after all, English. And he hadn't the smallest idea who I was; did not even know my name.

"Are you out of it now?" I asked, suddenly aware as I did so that this was an even more tactless question than the Englishwoman's.

"I got out of it after that," he said. "But it wasn't easy. The IRA came looking for me for a long time afterwards, to take a parcel here, a cache there. I had to get out altogether in the end. I was advised to go away and lie low."

"You killed an innocent man!" the Englishwoman said.

"T'is easy condemn me but it's us who had to live up there. And there are intelligent people in the IRA, you know. Mairéad Farrell who was murdered by the SAS in Gibraltar, she was a lawyer, that's how intelligent she was."

"But what did you think of those people who used civilians as human bombs?" I asked.

He put a finger to his head and twisted it. "Mad. Crazy mad. They're not sane men. Nobody could understand it. T'is the people who agreed to the Anglo-Irish Agreement they should be using, not innocent civilians.

"We have long memories. We don't forget things likes

Bloody Sunday, Loughgall, the Hunger Strikers, Gibraltar. The British just let those people on hunger strike die. They just let them die. The only one who would never have come off was Bobby Sands. He wouldn't come off even for his own mother. But the others – they would have come off if the British had gone even a bit of the way to meet them. And we'll never forget that.

"I didn't like doing what I did, but it's hard, you know. There are no jobs for us Catholics. What do you do, when people come looking for you to do a job for a bit of money? It's impossible not to get drawn in after a while. There's an awful lot up there only in it for the money. Everyone knows it's not a war of Protestant versus Catholic. There's a whole lot more to it than that. And money is a big part of it. There's big money in the IRA and the people who have it don't want anything to end, as long as the money keeps rolling in from America."

This man was echoing every cliché I had ever heard about Northern Ireland. It was like bad dialogue from a bad political play. But he was saying it.

"You know, don't you," the Englishwoman said, "that by British justice, you could still be tried for murder? It doesn't matter how many years afterwards."

She looked dazed. I don't think she had taken in a single thing after the shock of that first confession.

"I know that," he said. "But it's me who has to live with it, not you." He laughed bitterly. "British justice! It's British justice that has the Birmingham Six in jail all these years."

This encounter was to occur later on in my journey. Leaving The First and Last that night in Warrenpoint, I legged it down the sea-front and went into the first B & B I saw. The Diplomat was a large semi-detached Victorian seaside house, and at £15.00 an overnight, was the most expensive place I stayed.

The room I was shown to at the back of the house overlooked the fire-escape, was full of ugly furniture and there was barely room in it to swing the proverbial cat. In the bathroom down the corridor, the shower ran alternately freezing and scalding and since they were in the process of redecorating the resident's lounge, there was nowhere to sit except in the public bar, where I was made to feel uncomfortable since I did not order a drink.

Next morning, in search of a better shower, I picked my way past the decorator's ladders and outspread sheets and went down to the first-floor bathroom. This had just been papered in a pink-striped wallpaper. It was the same story with this shower and I skitted under the capricious whims of its freezing-scalding nozzle until, infuriated, I gave up and had a bath instead.

When I'd finished and had put in my contact lenses, I realised I had just undone the decorating work of yesterday. The pretty pink-striped wallpaper above the bath was peeling away in great rolls. I stared, fascinated. *Stupid place to put wallpaper*, I thought, and went off to eat breakfast among the stale smoke of the public bar.

I left The Diplomat, having glanced into the bathroom just before leaving. The wallpaper was continuing to lift itself off and flap sadly like the wings of a foundering flamingo.

Warrenpoint overlooks Carlingford Lough; a long, thin neck of water which stretches up to Newry. I walked out along the Lough as far as Narrow Water Castle and then got a lift from a woman who had a very sexy black négligé on a hanger in the back window, the source of many blasts of the horn from other cars, none of which she took the smallest bit of notice.

I tried hitching on the Carlingford Road, but nobody would give me a lift and so I turned back into Newry again. Newry, an ugly, sprawling town, to which the incessant rain gave a raw, dull aura, seemed to go on for ever. I walked for a long time along a horrible stretch of road on which trucks and lorries thundered past, spraying me with dirty water. All the bushes and berries in the hedgerows were black. I had almost reached the border when a Dundalk man stopped to give me a lift.

The *Rough Guide*, in its Dundalk entry, states flatly: "Dundalk you should avoid...dead when not deadly." The most surprising thing to me about Dundalk was its size; reputedly the largest town after the cities. If Sligo had been described to me as a small town masquerading as a city, then Dundalk struck me as a very large place masquerading as a small town.

The narrow streets huddled into each other, giving the impression that they contained a small place, but I kept walking and turning corners and discovering yet another warren of streets. Trying to puzzle out why it was that Dundalk gave this curious illusion of being a small town when it so clearly was not, I thought that part of the answer lay in the shops that lined the streets.

There seemed to be very few of the chain stores that usually punctuate, with monotonous regularity, the streets of a similarly-sized town. Nor did I notice many of those shops which are almost chameleon-like in their appearance; tacky boutiques and gift-shops that are here today and gone tomorrow, always poised on the brink of being turned into something else. Compared to the ephemeral retailing trade of the 1990s, the Dundalk shops and pubs looked as if they'd been there for centuries; solid, old, family-run businesses, with resolutely unchanged shop-fronts and a distinct feeling of endurance.

Walking out the Dublin Road, I passed the turn-off for the Dundalk Regional Technical College. I'd heard on the grapevine some months previously that Bennery Rickard, an old friend whom I hadn't seen for years, was working in the college library and wondered if she was still there.

Bennery, still sporting Doc Martens and a perplexed expression, was amazed to see me poking my head around the corner of her office in the library. Almost the first thing she said to me was, "Are you going to stay in Dundalk? There's a book out called the *Rough Guide* which tells people to avoid the town and the council want to ban it."

I did stay in Dundalk: I invited myself to stay at Bennery's house overnight and we yacked on for all hours, exchanging news of mutual old friends and starting every other sentence with "Do you remember?"

In my haste to depart the scene of the crime at the pretty pink bathroom that morning, I had forgotten to take away my contact-lens case, an annoying fact which I only discovered late that night. I sank my lenses into a glass,

171

which I covered with a tissue and peered dubiously in at, feeling like the owner of exotic and potentially neurotic fish.

Continuing on the next day, on the Dublin Road, just beyond the turn-off for the RTC, I quickly got a lift to Dunleer, with a local farmer who was thin and nervous, with dark eyes and dark hair and who smelt so overpoweringly of unwashed flesh that I had to discreetly open the window.

"Are you going to be long in Drogheda?" he inquired.

In the course of my journey, I'd wised up to the real meaning behind this question. "I'm only passing through Drogheda, visiting friends," I lied firmly.

There was a silence.

"Would you go out with me some night?" he blurted out suddenly. "Or have you got a steady? You *have* got a steady?"

I sighed. "I'm sorry, I've got a boyfriend." At the time, this was untrue and a lie which I resented having to make, but it was a lie that usually saved me further hassle.

"Oh." He became more nervous than ever. "You don't mind me asking you?" he said anxiously, peering down the Dublin Road as if he expected my mythical "steady" to materialize at any moment and take a dim view of all this.

"No, not at all," I said lightly, adding, "aren't there any women in Dunleer?"

He seemed to shrink away to nothing at this question. "My wife died in an accident," he said flatly. "I was left with children."

I felt sure he was telling the truth and was sad that he seemed to be so desperate for a partner that he was asking a complete stranger to go out with him. But I also found myself being annoyed, as a single female hitch-hiker, at being thought of as fair game for the asking.

Beyond Dunleer, the road towards Drogheda was even more unpleasant a stretch of road to hitch on than that outside Newry, the previous day. It was an awful black and oily road; the air full of flying dust and grit from the lorries which splashed past, soaking me within minutes.

An owl-eyed man pulled over. "I'm exhausted," he said. "I've been up for nights on end with my mother, who's

172

dangerously ill and I've got to fly back to Sydney tomorrow morning. And I've only been here a week!"

He told me he'd emigrated to Australia and was now married to an Australian woman.

"Will you ever come back?"

"No," he said decisively, and changed the subject. "Are you going to Drogheda to see the head?"

"The Head?" I was puzzled. "Is it a pub?"

At least I made him laugh. The head he meant was a real head. A holy head. The miraculously preserved head of St Oliver Plunkett, on display in St Peter's Church in Drogheda.

When Oliver Plunkett was canonised by Pope Paul VI in 1975, the nuns of my convent school in Ennis presented each child with a calendar by way of celebration. I have a distinct memory of a classroomful of ten-year-olds all staring in collective horror at the image on the calendar, which was a colour picture of Oliver Plunkett's severed head. As told, I obediently displayed it on my bedroom wall and subsequently had nightmares off and on for weeks, until, in a furtive act of rebellion, I guiltily tore it up and buried it deep within our kitchen bin.

In size, Drogheda seemed to be on a par with Dundalk, but the wide Boyne River bisected the town and gave the impression of making the place seem even bigger. The docks opened up Drogheda; the ships at anchor suggested trade and movement; the Boyne was a great liquid thoroughfare, spanned by the magnificent viaduct. Many of the shops looked new and smart and somehow temporary, but the piecemeal layout of the town was interesting and there was plenty of character to be found among the sloping back-streets.

There was supposed to be a hostel on William St, called Harpur House Tourist Hostel and so I set off in search of it. Harpur House was in a quiet row of Georgian houses and displayed a B & B sign. This did not look promising. I banged on the door, which was eventually answered by a flustered-looking man.

"Is this the hostel?" I asked, knowing at once that it no longer was. I'd been looking forward to having company in Drogheda.

"Not any more," he said. "We only do bed and breakfast now."

My heart sank. I didn't feel like another dose of Diplomat-type experiences so soon.

"Come in anyway," he said. "We only do bed and breakfast," he repeated firmly, when I was standing in the hallway.

"I'm a hosteller," I said, just as firmly. Too many overnights in B & Bs and I wouldn't be able to afford to finish the journey.

He looked me up and down. Finally, he said, "I can offer you a room for a fiver."

"Done!"

I followed him upstairs and he pushed open a door at the top of the stairs. The room he showed me into was a cavernous high-ceilinged room, with two huge windows, complete with wooden shutters, four beds, three tables, two sofas, two armchairs and a splendid marble fireplace. And it still looked empty. The entire ground floor of The Diplomat would have been swallowed up in this enormous room.

"Will this do?" he asked.

I set my rucksack down and assured him that yes, it would do, do very nicely indeed.

It was raining again when I went outside; a cunning fine mist of a rain that gradually got heavier so that Drogheda slowly began to disappear from sight. The immense viaduct bridge just melted away to nothing. Church-spires and the roofs of buildings vanished into thin air and I ghosted along the empty streets in an insubstantial afternoon.

I climbed the stone steps of St Peter's Church, curious to investigate the source of my childhood horror. Halfway down the church, there was a small side-chapel; a shrine dedicated to Oliver Plunkett. Tucked into the side of the chapel was a high marble altar rail, with a padded kneeler at its foot. There were two elderly men and a woman kneeling down together, staring intently at the glass box set into a tabernacle beyond the rail, all of them beating their breasts and muttering aloud a prayer to the saint, which had been set into the altar rail. The head in the glass box; eyes closed, shadowy, shrunken-looking and altogether ghastly, filled me with horror all over again. There was something both faintly ridiculous and disturbingly primeval about the sight of those three old people, beating their breasts and praying to a severed head.

In a glass cabinet at the side of the chapel, displayed on red silk, like precious jewels, was an assortment of shrivelled brown bones: less well-preserved parts of Oliver Plunkett's anatomy. On display was his left clavicle, right scapula and a selection of his ribs; holy relics that looked to me like something the dog had left behind.

Printed on a card among the bones were these words:

Only by kneeling in front of these relics can one express the whole truth about historical and contemporary Ireland and also touch its wounds, confident that they will heal and not prevent the whole organism from pulsating with the fullness of life.

Making dinner at Harpur House, I was kept company by the owner's small son, who arrived in at intervals on his scooter, sporting a pair of sunglasses with glorious oblivion to the weather outside.

That evening, I pushed my way through the rain and went to spend an hour in Bean Uí Carberry's pub, around the corner. The walls and ceilings of Carberry's were papered with posters and pamphlets; layered with these like a palimpsest. Over the years, the paper had been glazed with sunlight and turf-smoke and had now faded to a rich golden colour, glowing like old oil-paintings. The bulbs in the Japanese paper shades were red and orange; the turf-fire blazed; there were thick woollen rugs draped over wooden benches. The floorboards were warped and worn. I could see no sign of a cash register, but behind the high counter, there were a number of small wooden bowls, containing coins of different denominations.

Mrs Carberry's hair stuck out in grey wisps and she had a huge smile. She told me that the pub had been in the family for generations. Carberry's is renowned for its

175

traditional music sessions. She gestured to the worn floorboards.

"I'm afraid of my life that someday it'll collapse with all the dancing."

Carberry's was popular. Within half an hour of my arrival, it was packed with young people, all greeting Mrs Carberry affectionately.

"Students from the Art College," she told me.

I felt lonely. Everyone seemed to be either in large friendly groups or coupled together intimately; all self-contained. It wasn't a pub for a single traveller on a Friday night. I left and went into a telephone box on my way back to William St.

Dublin was just down the road from Drogheda and in Dublin city were friends whom I knew I could depend on to welcome me for the weekend, rucksackful of dirty washing and all. I was tired of finding myself the only person in hostels and sick of the weather. My oldest friend, Fiona Carrigg, also a recipient of one of those Oliver Plunkett calendars, was currently living in Malahide. I hadn't intended stopping in Dublin city but Malahide was not Dublin city, I reasoned.

I grabbed the phone.

I spent that weekend in Malahide being pampered by Fiona. I slept in in the mornings. I ate my way through the contents of her fridge. I put away my diary and devoured a stack of *Hello!* magazines in front of the television. It was *bliss*.

On Monday, I took the train from Malahide to Connolly Station, then changed onto the DART, which took me to Bray.

The next few days that followed were so wretched that I felt like giving it all up. It was very cold and wet; the hostels were all of the ice-box variety and were empty; the lifts were unremarkable and the landscape was dull and flat.

I slid down the east coast, never staying in one place for longer than a night. How did travel writers cope with writing about times when nothing happened and the few lines you ended up writing in your diary were dull and bad-tempered? I wasn't sure but felt that just because I was making a journey with the purpose of writing about it, it didn't follow neatly that everything I did or saw subsequently became charged with interest.

So in those blank days from Malahide to Rosslare Harbour, the eastern coastline resisted my attempts to trawl through it and I found myself recording nothing more than a series of impressions.

Passing through Wicklow town at midday, I went to have lunch at The Coffee Inn on Fitzwilliam Square. There were four small tables, all prominently displaying non-smoking signs. One of the tables was already occupied. The waitress came to take my order, just as a woman at the other table lit up.

"I thought this was a non-smoking place," I said, pointedly.

The woman who was smoking ignored me. The waitress looked distantly at me. "That lady is allowed to smoke because she's a regular," she said icily.

The logic in this eluded me. When my lunch arrived, a woman at the third of the four tables, who had just come in, also lit up.

"I suppose she's a regular too?" I said wryly.

"*That* table is a *smoker's* table," the waitress hissed. And so it was, for she stepped over to that third table and pocketed the non-smoking sign.

Hitching out of Courtown on 22 November, I switched on my pocket radio and discovered that Margaret Thatcher had just resigned as Prime Minister.

"Ten years too late," was the gloomy consensus, all the way to Wexford.

The man who drove me from Wexford to Rosslare Harbour told me that there were more people killed on this stretch of road than anywhere else in Ireland. He pointed out accident-sites to me as one would point out places of historical or cultural interest to a sightseer.

"Young lad on a motor-bike was killed over there...Three people in a head-on there... Foreigner off the boat who didn't last long... "

"I'm late for work," the man who drove me from Rosslare Harbour back into Wexford told me.

He roared into Wexford town, doing ninety on the notorious road. Pulling to a halt, he said that this was as far as he went. I got out, glad to be still in one piece and watched him stride briskly into his place of work – Wexford Garda Station.

When I was writing this book, people asked me if there were going to be photographs in it. "It's not a guide book," I kept explaining. "If anyone wants to see pictures of the places I went through, there are dozens of coffee-table books to look at." But if I had wanted to include photographs, they would have been of that part of the coastline that eluded me – Wicklow, Arklow, Courtown, Wexford, Rosslare Harbour – a visual attempt to put in what has been left out.

8
MY WIFE'S OVER THERE IN THE DRAWER
Wexford to Baltimore

Halfway up the deep and narrowing indentation of Waterford Harbour, a small car-ferry runs between Ballyhack in Wexford and Passage East in Waterford; a shortcut up to Waterford town. I decided to back-track to Wexford and then take the R733 through Wellington Bridge across to Ballyhack.

The man in a white Mazda with immaculately combed hair and a powerful, curved nose, who drove me to the roundabout for the Ballyhack Road, was on his way to Knocktopher Abbey for the day. He handed me a computer-printed letter.

If you were "lucky" enough to receive one of these letters and also be: married; gainfully employed; between the ages of 18 and 65, then by attending a two and a half hour tour of Abbey Estate, "Holiday Estate of Distinction", you were assured of an "award". These awards were not to be sniffed at: a seven-day holiday to Jamaica, the Bahamas or Gran Canaria; a Sony Camcorder; a television; £100.

"I don't know what the catch is," he admitted. "But you never know, I might come home with a holiday to Jamaica!"

The road to Ballyhack was a mean one to hitch on. I had to walk some considerable distance down the twisty road before finding a good safe place to hitch from. Cars there were in plenty, but they all whipped smartly by and did not stop.

It was bitterly cold. After an hour, I abandoned the R733 and tramped up to the next roundabout where the N25 branched out towards New Ross. I stuck out one stiff hand and wondered if I'd slowly freeze into that policeman-directing-traffic pose.

Eventually, one car sorted itself from the whizzing multitudes and stopped. The farmer's small son scrambled into the back to allow me the front seat and I got in awkwardly, thawing out slowly as we drove through miles of flat green countryside.

I told them I was going to New Ross and asked if there was anything special I should see while I was there.

The farmer laughed. "There's nothing to see there. Nothing ever happens there."

New Ross, perched high up the estuary, was very quiet. It was a Saturday afternoon, but the streets were empty. Shambles junk shop had an invitation to "Come in and Browse". I was a solitary browser in the shop, where, for £18.00, I could have been the proud owner of a pair of "rideing boots".

There was something missing in New Ross, something that had been present in other towns now for some weeks. I puzzled over this sense of something missing until I realised that nowhere in the narrow, sloping streets of New Ross was there any sign of Christmas. Not a flitter of tinsel, a scrap of holly, a whisker of a Santa Claus, or a whiff of a pine-needle.

I found this both refreshing and curious. The farmer *had* told me that nothing ever happened in New Ross, but did this also include Christmas?

I walked out over the wide bridge and past the docks, from where great thudding noises were emerging. Something was certainly happening in there.

Frank and Margaret, a couple from New Ross, gave me a lift to Waterford. Frank had a passion for old roads. All the way down the N25 to Waterford, a newly-built road, he kept pointing out to me where the old road had wandered through this new road; showing me boreens and grass-spined scraps of road that branched off from the N25 like sombre and mysterious tributaries of a lost river.

"It was a road with character," he told me, and then said sadly, "but I suppose this one is better. It's straighter. You don't spend as long a journey on it, but there's not as much to see as there was on the old road."

They told me of places in Ireland they had been to.

"But do you know something, for all our years living in County Wexford, we've never managed to find Boolavogue," Frank said.

"That's right," Margaret agreed happily. "Although we've set off in the car time after time, we've never been able to find it."

The turn-off for Boolavogue, where the rebel priest Father Murphy set the heather blazing at the start of the 1798 Rebellion, had been pointed out to me on the N11 into Wexford. It would have been a simple matter of driving up the N11 from Wexford town and looking for the signpost. But I didn't say a word. I don't think Frank or Margaret ever really wanted to find Boolavogue. I imagined that it had attained a mystical, unobtainable quality for them over the years; a landscape of the mind that the reality would never measure up to. I could imagine them sitting into the car for a day out and setting off to look half-heartedly for Boolavogue, always glad to abandon the search.

The estuary made a long, grey slit through Waterford city. On the New Ross side of the estuary, there were wharves and angular dockside buildings, with Jury's Hotel squatting on the hill behind. On the opposite side, there was a bright display of well-kept quayside houses and shops.

I liked Waterford at once. There was a liveliness in the streets and a remarkable number of young people. Although Waterford had lost many jobs, the city seemed to me to be prosperous, in brave defiance of the nationwide recession and continued trend of emigration.

Christmas had very definitely arrived in Waterford. The shop windows were all beautifully dressed. The windows of Shaw's Almost Nationwide Store were filled with trees trimmed with silver bows and strings of silver bells. The town was packed; the cash-registers sang; everyone on the streets appeared to be carrying bulging bags. Perhaps the people of New Ross shopped in Waterford on Saturdays.

Waterford wandered. Streets darted off in all directions. I spent a couple of hours walking around and felt that I hadn't seen half the city. It was a local's city; a place that you would have to discover slowly.

On Barron Strand St there was an immense grey building, which looked like a courthouse from the outside. The building turned out to be the United Trinity Catholic Church; the interior of which consolidated my impression of Waterford as a prosperous place.

Outside, dusk was falling and the only light inside the church came from one brightly-lit crystal chandelier: one of ten magnificent chandeliers which had been donated by Waterford Crystal, the internationally-famous glass-blowers.

Stations of the Cross had been painted onto pillars which marched down the centre of the church. The colours were rich and glowing and the fresco-like effect was worthy of an Italian church of the High Renaissance. The music organ was a delicate arrangement of icicle-like white pipes, the lower parts of which looked as if they had been dipped in gold; cold and pure. The stairs to the balconies were made of old wood and smelt of beeswax. The Gothic pulpit was also carved from wood and could easily have doubled as a throne for an Eastern King.

Everything in the United Trinity Catholic Church was opulent. In the dying light, the one illuminated chandelier blazed with the glory of a solitaire diamond; the mystery and tragedy seeped out of the paintings; the stained glass windows glowed with the last fragments of daylight. It was all dim and glittering and breathtakingly sumptuous. Take away the rows of seats and padded kneelers and you would have had a ballroom of Gothic proportions; waltzes being played on the icicle organ; crystal chandeliers glittering on the dancing couples.

Later on, I looked into the church again. Evening Mass had just started and the place was packed to capacity. All ten chandeliers were lit, the organ was playing and the congregation were on their feet, singing *Glory to God in the Highest*. As an extraordinary display of the Catholic Church at its most extravagant and worldly, the United Trinity Church in Waterford takes some beating.

In the Book Centre, I bought a copy of Paul Theroux's *Riding the Iron Rooster: by train through China*, in the hope that reading about train journeys in China would make me feel warm.

Further down from the Book Centre was a stonemason's yard. Gravestone slabs leaned against the walls, awaiting names and dates. A small boy broke away from his father and stuck his hands through the railings.

"I want to go in there, Daddy," he piped. His father picked him up, hugged him and carried him away down the street.

There were posters up everywhere, advertising a production of Farquhar's *The Constant Couple*. The Red Kettle Theatre Company were playing in the Garter Lane Theatre. I would have liked to have seen it. Alas, that night was a rest-night for the company.

I looked into the Olde Stand, Geoff's, and The Pulpit. All three pubs were packed and resounded with loud music. I went in search of somewhere quieter to start my book.

The bar in the Granville Hotel on the quays was filling up with people toting shopping bags and having post-shopping drinks. I ordered a glass of Guinness and opened the Theroux. I was mistaken in thinking I'd feel warm. The opening chapter was about a train journey through Germany and Poland in winter. I shivered.

Every second settlement in Ireland seemed to have an O'Connell St – Ennis, Limerick, Sligo, Athlone, Dublin. There was one in Waterford too, and I eventually found a B & B there.

The O'Connell Bed and Breakfast was a Georgian house, a few doors down from the Garter Lane Arts Centre. The man of the house opened the door, informing me that "herself is out".

He took me up two flights of stairs. The room he showed me into had wallpaper embossed with velvety green and brown flowers. The carpet had a pattern of muddy-brown and yellow swirls. There was little room for movement, the space being almost entirely filled by a double bed and enormous wardrobe.

"Now!" he said.

I stared at the carpet and the wallpaper. There was no way I could spend a night suffocating in that brown room.

"Haven't you got anything brighter?" I asked.

"*Brighter?*" He stared at me. "What do you mean, *brighter?*"

Grudgingly, he closed the door and opened the one next to it. Everything in this room clashed, as if it had been done up gradually over the years, with a new colour scheme each year. The curtains were pink and purple. The wallpaper was brown and yellow. The bedspreads were blue and purple. Everything was patterned with flowers and all the patterns were different. Looking at it all made me slightly dizzy. But it was brighter than the other room.

I'd already spent some time tramping around other B & Bs, which were either full or closed for the winter. It was dark outside and it was either the O'Connell House Bed and Breakfast or a hotel.

"It'll do," I said, noting with foreboding that there was no radiator.

"Will it now!" the man replied, clearly offended.

It was a miserable night. Nobody had bothered to empty the waste-paper basket after the last occupant of the room, who had been a heavy smoker. I put the basket outside the door, but the smell of stale cigarette smoke still permeated the room. There was no heating of any kind. I searched hopefully for an electric blanket on the bed, but I searched in vain. I ended up taking all the blankets from the other bed and piling them on top of my own bed. I wrapped one of the blankets around myself and wrote up my diary.

There were two places set for breakfast next morning. I was halfway through my breakfast when the door opened and a young Japanese man came in and sat down opposite me.

Yuno was on a two-month holiday of Europe and was taking the boat from Rosslare Harbour to Le Havre that afternoon. His English was rudimentary. I wondered how he had got on in his week in Ireland, where he was unlikely to have encountered any Japanese speakers.

Speaking slowly and very simply, I asked if he had liked Ireland.

Yuno considered. He said, "It is very noisy. Very busy. And there are many, many pub!"

He sounded shocked at this last. Yuno pronounced the word "pub" in the way some people enunciate the word "sex-shop". With our language barrier, it would have been

184

too complicated to explain the peculiar role that the pub holds in Irish society: not just a place where you go to drink, but a place to talk, to listen to music, to dance, where meetings are carried out; a place where you sometimes hear poetry readings, see plays, participate in a writing workshop, where you can find yourself buying anything from roses to poetry pamphlets and where a great deal of canvassing for support in elections is done.

I concentrated on the rest of his impressions. "Noisy and busy? Where did you go?"

Yuno had travelled from city to city: from Dublin to Belfast; from Belfast to Derry; from Derry to Galway; from Galway to Waterford.

"Connemara?" I tried. "Kerry? County Cork? Donegal?"

He shook his head. "I had a book," he said carefully. "It said life was slow in Ireland. It said go to the cities. I went to the cities, but they were not slow. I know nobody here. I did not ask anybody. My book tell me."

I was desperately sorry for Yuno, saddled with a crazy guide book and a reluctance to ask for help.

"Dublin is a big-noisy-dirty-city," he repeated and looked pleased at the prospect of leaving it all behind.

Dear-Old-Dirty-Dublin certainly deserves its wryly affectionate nickname, but I couldn't help feeling that Yuno was being just a shade hard on Ireland's capital city. After all, Yuno came from Tokyo, the largest city in the world, a city which *was* probably cleaner than Dublin but definitely bigger and noisier.

Yuno gave me his card, which was in Japanese and English. The English words said: "Japanese Massage for Healthcare by Yuno". The drawing on the card was of two portly men, one rubbing the other's stomach in a decidedly libidinous manner.

"In Japan, as many massage parlour as Irish pub!"

Yuno asked me if I would go to Tokyo with him. "I would look after you!"

It wasn't an unattractive offer, considering I'd only known the man for twenty minutes, and had never been to Japan. As breakfast conversation, it beat "pass-the-milk" any day.

185

"I'll think about it," I said, trying to be tactful.

Yuno took the card back and carefully wrote his address on it. He beamed at me. "I will be waiting for your letter!"

I packed up, left the O'Connell House and started walking through Waterford to get onto the Tramore Road. I'd gone past an automatic bank-machine before deciding that I would use the machine after all and so turned around sharply. Ducking into a doorway a few paces back, was Yuno, who had obviously been trailing me.

I went over to him. Sheepishly, he emerged from the doorway, smiled at me and pointed to a camera. "I take many pictures of you!"

"*Of my back?!*"

He touched my arm and pointed to his camera again. "Please? More pictures?"

"Only one more," I said firmly and gave a hideous grin to the camera.

"I am waiting for your letter!" he called after me.

My walkabout of Waterford the previous afternoon paid off. I took some back-streets and managed to give Yuno the slip.

For once, the rain kept missing me. The clouds were travelling before me, at a ferocious rate and everywhere I went through, the roads were dark with newly-fallen rain.

The Waterford man who brought me to Tramore was going to give his two dogs, Brandy and Max, a run on the beach. He drove me around the town, which seemed somewhat honky-tonk to me; all fast-food restaurants, amusement halls and shoddy-looking holiday houses.

"You wouldn't be able to move here in the summer," he assured me.

This echoed what the locals of almost every seaside town and village said to me. The summer, when everyone put up their B & B signs, opened craft shops and tea-shops, held country markets and festivals of all sorts, was when money was made that often had to last until the following summer.

He pointed out tall white markers to me, which were high up on headlands overlooking the bay and told me that they were known locally as "the brownstones" and used as navigational points for ships.

From Tramore, I took the T63, a narrow road which squeezed its way along Waterford's south coast. I got a lift for a few miles with a Frenchwoman, in a car whose passenger door would not shut properly and which I ended up clinging onto with a mixture of determination and alarm.

From Fennor through to Dungarvan, I got a series of short lifts and walked a lot in between. At Bunmahon, I left the T63 and walked one of the "other roads" that ran right along the coast to Stradbally, a distance of about six miles.

This stretch of coastline amazed me. I had never heard anyone talking about it. I had never seen any pictures of it. It was indescribably lovely. There were hardly any houses, just green fields undulating gently to the north of the road and the spectacular coastline on the other side of the road. The tiny beaches were of buttery-coloured sand, formed in perfect arcs between wild and rugged headlands of rock. Every so often, I came across a miniature sheltered harbour in which a handful of fishing boats were moored. Every turn of the road revealed a beach or cliff or headland or harbour even more beautiful than the last.

Stradbally was a pretty village of neat Georgian houses and pristine thatched cottages, worthy of a John Hinde photographer. At the foot of the hill that led out of the village, I came across a surreal sight.

Islanded on one side by a steep hill, on another side by the road, on a third by a stream and the fourth by a sandy cove, was a small green field. Between the road and the sea, the hill-face and the river, several sheep with black faces and black legs grazed peacefully among the hulls of a dozen brightly-painted upturned boats.

A couple of miles beyond Stradbally, I picked up the T63 again and hitched the remaining six miles to Dungarvan.

I had a very late lunch in Lawlor's Hotel and then kept going. After the bit of coastline which I had just come through, the town of Dungarvan seemed big and clumsy with a beach that was posted with signs which warned me of "Shellfish Unfit for Human Consumption".

I had no clear idea where I wanted to spend the night,

but thought that I would try hitching on the road that led to Ring. Ring is one of the few surviving Gaeltacht communities, almost all of which have now been pushed out to the furthest reaches of Ireland – the Aran Islands, the Gweedore area of Donegal, the tip of the Dingle peninsula. These enduring Irish-speaking areas cling like barnacles to the most remote and rugged regions of the Irish coastline.

I stood at the side of the road for Ring, quite prepared to wait a long time, but I had only been waiting a few minutes when a car pulled in.

Doirín Uí Mhurchadha had just come from watching an under 21 hurling match; Mount Sion versus Lismore.

"Who won?"

"Lismore, of course!"

Doirín wanted to know where I was going to stay that night. When I said that I didn't know yet, she told me that I could on no account miss the opportunity of staying in Maher's B & B.

"It has a wonderful view and you couldn't find friendlier people. They have visitors who come back to them year after year."

"Yes?" I said warily. So far, my experiences of bed and breakfast had been more miss than hit.

Tom and Bríd Maher's B & B was on the road from Dungarvan. Ring, being a Gaeltacht settlement, has no centre as such, but is scattered over an acre of several miles. Maher's had a magnificent view over Dungarvan Harbour. Alas, there was no answer at the door.

"She might be in the garden," Doirín said, correctly assuming the front door to be unlocked, and calling into the rooms and garden beyond with the confidence of one long-used to neighbourly ways.

"They'll not be gone far," she said. "Why don't you come back to my house and have some tea and we can ring them from there later on?"

Doirín brought me back to her home, lit a big fire, sliced up the Sunday roast and fed me tea and sandwiches and brack, talking away easily all the time. She did all this so gracefully and with such friendliness that I accepted several cups of tea without hesitation, not feeling at all uncomfortable about sitting in someone's house and eating the remains of their Sunday lunch.

When her daughter Áine and three grandchildren, Tadgh, Liadhin and Diarmuid, arrived into the house, Doirín said, matter-of-factly, "This is Rosita. I picked her up on the road." They all accepted this, as if used to seeing strange people in front of their fireside, wolfing down great quantities of food – they probably were.

All the Mhurchadha's spoke Irish as their first language. I was able to follow more than I would have believed, considering I had always received very poor marks for the subject during my school-days.

There was still no reply from Maher's. I knew that Doirín had to prepare a report on the Mount Sion-Lismore match. I'd bought Sunday papers in Dungarvan. Doirín had told me that it was likely there'd be traditional music in Mooney's Pub that evening and so I said that I would wait there, read the papers and try phoning Maher's myself.

Áine drove me over to Mooney's and introduced me to the barman. I waved herself and the children off from the lounge door and then went into the bar. There were about six men standing at the bar, discussing me in Irish. Appearing at such a peculiar time of the year, they naturally assumed that I was a foreigner.

The conversation back in Mhurchadha's had awakened long-dormant sounds within my memory. While unable to speak Irish fluently, I was able to follow the conversation of the Ring men with a fair degree of comprehension. I listened, amused, as they speculated on the country of my origin and my purpose in Ring at such a time of the year. They argued among themselves who would be the first to come over and talk to me. They were certain I was German. Eventually, one man came up to me.

"Do-you-speak-English?" he said, slowly and carefully.

I replied that I did, in Irish.

There was no music in Mooney's that night, but there was plenty of talk. The conversation that followed over the course of the evening flowed easily in and out of Irish and English; a few sentences of each language at a time. In this way, I was amazed at how much I could understand. Woven so closely together, the two languages cast light on each other and if an issue started out by being discussed in English, then I could usually follow it through in Irish.

For someone with as small a grasp on the Irish language as myself, that unexpectedly fluent night of talk in Ring was an almost miraculous succession of bright connections between the two languages.

For a time, the meaning of the name of Thomas Meagher's men-only pub in Waterford was discussed in a heated and lively manner.

"The straight turf," one man said.

"The red turf," another argued.

The pub was called Moondharrig, a name that initially resounded in my ear as a partially English word. "The red moon," I offered.

This conversation about the correct meaning of words continued; this time, about the way the same word could mean something different in England than it did in Ireland.

"Look at ditch, now," one said. "A ditch over here is something you'd climb onto. You'd be climbing into it if you were in England."

"What's a dike, so?" another said, puzzled.

"The dike's the ditch in England!"

"So it'd be The Hurler In The Ditch instead of The Hurler On The Ditch if you lived in England?" one laughed.

"What's a dike, so?" the same man puzzled, who'd already asked the question.

"Sure, we've no dikes over here at all. We call the ditch a ditch and the dike is a ditch too. It's all ditches we have here."

Commanding a corner stool at the bar was a man who looked every bit as certain a foreigner to me as I had looked to the Ring men. This man had long dark hair and a rakish moustache. He wore a trilby and a long coat that some people would call scruffy and others would call eccentric. To me it looked less like a coat than a cloak. There were feathers in his hat and a red rose in his buttonhole. On his wrists were wide silver braclets, with

190

spiral patterns on them that I recognized from those on the kerbstones at Newgrange. He had merry eyes and he was taking snuff. *English?* I thought to myself, puzzled. *Or maybe French?* No one in the bar seemed to be in the least fazed by his presence, as if they all knew him. To take snuff in an Irish bar and for this to go uncommented made me wild with curiosity.

Liam de Staic was a Dungarvan-born man who now lived in London and worked as an actor. He had come back to his home county that month to play in the Red Kettle production of *The Constant Couple*. He had just finished filming the role of Michael Davitt in the BBC television adaptation of Hugh Leonard's book, *Parnell and the Englishwoman*.

Liam had a beguiling voice. It was not a loud voice, but there was a certain tone in it that made you want to listen to it. It was the trained voice of an actor and it was impossible to ignore. Liam had the entire bar by the ear as he sat at the counter, telling stories, rolling cigarettes and extinguishing matches in an unselfconscious pattern of spirals.

He'd asked me where I'd come from that day and I had told everyone, for this was communal conversation, of the lovely walk I had had from Bunmahon to beyond Stradbally.

"Stradbally?" Liam said. "And did anyone there mention the story of the Missing Postman to you?"

"The missing postman?" I repeated, bewildered.

"The Missing Postman!" Martin Hession exclaimed. "I'd forgotten about that story!"

Martin had already told me that himself and Michael Quirke, the Sligo woodcarver, had been schoolfriends. A college acquaintance of mine, Judy Friel, turned out to be the director of the Red Kettle production. If, instead of stopping when I reached Clare again, I continued to circuit Ireland and meet more people, I'm sure I would have discovered that the entire population connected up with each other in some way. Talk to a complete stranger for five minutes and if you're both Irish, the chances are that you'll discover common friends or acquaintances.

The Missing Postman had been a Stradbally man named Larry Griffin. Liam told us that after "the war", the Irish government had placed those who had been shell-shocked or psychologically damaged in some way, in gentle positions of state employment.

Larry Griffin had apparently been shell-shocked. He was given the job of local postman. One Christmas Eve night, many of the Stradbally people were gathered together in the local pub; among them was Larry Griffin. Apparently, the drinking went over time into the early hours of Christmas morning. In a drunken state, one man tried to pick a fight with the postman.

At this point, some of the other men in Mooney's began contributing to the story. They argued as to what exactly had happened next. Some said that the postman had been knocked over by a blow and hit his head so badly on impact that he had died instantly. Others said that the postman had been at the top of a stairway, been hit and fallen over the bannisters. All agreed that Larry Griffin had died that night in the pub in some sort of terrible accident.

"The people in the pub got together," Liam continued, "and decided to keep it quiet. They carried his body away and buried it somewhere nearby. Then they went home and kept silent.

"Nothing was ever heard of Larry Griffin again. They sent people down from Dublin and the guards searched the place, they questioned everyone, but they got nowhere. Nobody said a word. It was known as "The Missing Postman" case. Eventually, they stopped searching. His body was never found. To this day, the Stradbally people refuse to discuss it, although everyone who was in the pub that night is probably long dead now.

"And I've noticed," Liam finished, "that whenever I've been hitching on that bit of road you came through today, and I've got a lift through Stradbally from a local person, they always bless themselves when the car passes a certain field outside the village. And if I ask them why, they won't answer me."

I later searched through newspapers in the National Library for coverage of this story. But although I spent several hours looking through the January issues of newspapers, I couldn't find the right year. I might perhaps have thought that Liam de Staic had been spinning a yarn, but for the fact that when I was looking, many people a generation older than me said that they had distant memories of The Missing Postman case. "Christmas Eve it was," they all said, but none could remember the year.

I had been so absorbed by this conversation that I had completely forgotten about phoning Maher's and it was now after ten.

Bríd Maher answered the phone, waving aside my apologies for ringing at such an hour. They'd love me to stay, she assured me.

"Is it Mooney's you're in?" she asked. "Well, stay on there to finish your conversation and would you like me to collect you in about an hour, or is that too early?"

I hadn't said anything about being engrossed in talk, nor did I expect anyone to collect me. "I'm sure someone here would drop me out."

"Not at all!" she said. "Sure, it's just down the road."

Prior to making this journey, as an Irish person myself, I had accepted the whole Ireland-of-the-Welcomes and Céad-Míle-Fáiltes with a fair degree of cynicism. But in the course of those three months, I encountered hospitality and friendliness time after time. I wasn't a foreigner, so there was nothing exotic or special about me, and neither was I well-heeled. In money terms as a tourist, I was poor value: no credit cards, no hotels, no meals out, no souvenirs. Yet the image of Welcoming Ireland, I found, by and large, to be true. Irish people, it seemed to me, were genuinely interested in visitors as people rather than as walking chequebooks.

Dark-haired Bríd Maher drove me back to her home, where there was a tray of freshly-baked scones and a pot of hot coffee waiting. There was more talk: late as the hour was, we talked until past midnight. I was all talked-out.

Tired as I was, I was still able to admire the room that Bríd showed me into. It was fresh and white, with white lace quilt covers on the beds and a shower off the room. The radiator was on and she had switched on an electric blanket for me. I ate breakfast next morning looking out over Dungarvan Bay. It was a beautiful morning; clear blue. Bríd gave me a breakfast of the sort that would keep me going all day and then said that she was terribly sorry, but had unexpectedly to go to work for nine o'clock this one morning. If I wanted more of anything, I was to help myself from the kitchen. And just pull the front door out after me when I was leaving.

She bustled about, finding school-books and collecting up children and suddenly they were all gone. I had the house to myself and the trust of the person who owned it. The cost of my stay in Maher's was £8.00, but what price someone telling you "Just pull the door out after you?"

I packed up and left Maher's. In the frosty blue morning, I quickly discovered that I'd left my woollen scarf behind me in Mooney's.

Mooney's was closed and there was nobody answering the door. I wrote a note, wrapped it around a pound coin and dropped it through the letterbox. When I arrived in Kinsale a few days later, my scarf was waiting for me on the poste restante shelf of Kinsale post office.

I spent that day hitching towards Cork, through Grange and Youghal. From Youghal to Carrigtohill, where the turn-off to Cobh is, I had a lift with a lorry-driver, who told me that his two small daughters had just given him a long list of the presents they wanted for Christmas.

"Mountain bikes! Typewriters! Talking dolls!" he groaned. "Turtles! Turtles! And more Turtles! But sure, Christmas is for the kids. We'll manage to give them a good time and we'll try and get them the things they want."

I asked him if he remembered any of the Christmas presents he'd been given as a child.

"Would you go away. That's a long time ago!" Then he considered and said, "Do you know, someone gave me a clockwork drummer boy one year and it was the best present I ever got. I brought it everywhere with me. I loved it. Took it with me to bed and all. And when it broke, I was like an eejit after it."

All the way to Carrigtohill, this man talked to me about

194

the tin drummer boy that had given him so much pleasure as a child. I couldn't help feeling touched, listening to this powerfully-built man recount, without the slightest embarrassment, the bright memory of a childhood toy and its loss.

From Carrigtohill, I hitched across to Cobh. How the generations of Cobh parents had managed to wheel their children in prams and buggies up and down those incredibly steep streets, was a mystery to me. Looked back at from the harbour, the houses of Cobh rose up in brightly-coloured layers, like the steps of some fantastic stairway.

Many of the houses were Edwardian or Victorian; classic seaside resort houses and although they were formally arranged in squares and ovals and crescents, the overall impression I got, wandering about Cobh, was of a rambling extravaganza sort of place that was larger than life.

Cobh was full of surprises: hidden stone steps that tumbled pedestrians down to the bottom of the hill; a huge cathedral that was crammed with Celtic decoration; unusual views of gables, attic windows and chimney pots; sudden vistas of the sea that revealed themselves for a moment in the bright crack of light between houses. There were so many ways of looking at Cobh that I climbed up and down the hill several times, amazed at the way it appeared to change; the tread in the stairway altering each time.

It was late in the afternoon by the time I got into Cork city, where I made my way to Union Chandlery on Merchant's Quay. Toni O'Connell, whose mother Pat I had already stayed with in Connemara, and Laura Bowen, had "known each other since we were embryos" as Toni once put it. I could not claim to have known them that long, but they were both old friends, and Mamie and Michael Bowen had asked me to stay with them when I reached Cork. Laura herself was now living in Dublin, having recently come back from London.

I left my rucksack with Paul Bowen at the Chandlery and took the bus out of the city to Monkstown, some ten miles away. Mamie Bowen opened a bottle of wine and sat me down by the fire, asking me to tell her about the journey so far. This ritual of story-telling went on in every house I stayed where I knew the people. As the weeks progressed, the story-telling sessions became longer from house to house. It was, in a way, the oldest and simplest ritual of travelling and one which had been common in ancient Ireland, where the seanachaí spent their whole lives going from house to house, telling stories to entertain their hosts and receiving in exchange, hospitality and a bed for the night.

After a boisterous evening meal, Mamie went off to play bridge, friends turned up for John, Paul and Gwen, and we all went out to the Eastern Star, known locally as "The Pucks".

The Eastern Star, alias The Pucks, was a small, dim pub a few miles south of Monkstown, with a handful of old men, one of whom declared to me, "All the other pubs in Ireland are only lounge bars!"

I was quite happy to play pool and talk to the Bowens and John Buckley, none of whom I'd seen for some time, but they'd brought me here to get a story for the book and a story they were determined to get. Amused, I watched Gwen tackle the elderly man next to her.

"This girl is hitching around Ireland and she's writing a book about it," she announced. "Would you have a story for her at all?"

"I would, now so," Seán said delighted, reaching across to shake my hand.

"Out with it!" Gwen commanded and grinned over at me triumphantly.

During the Second World War, Seán told us, when petrol was rationed, a Clonakilty man called John Corcoran had four hundred geese that were due to be sold at a market in Cork. He had no way of transporting them the thirty-odd miles to Cork city. Not to be beaten, John rounded up his four hundred geese and marched them all the way to Cork.

"It was known as the Great Clonakilty Goose Run," Seán said. "I heard that story when I was a lad. He didn't lose a single goose and before he took them to market, he washed their feet in paraffin oil, because they were sore. Eight hundred feet!" Seán cried. "*Eight hundred feet!*"

Whether this was a true story that had become blurred over the years or was simply a yarn, I do not know, but everyone in the Eastern Star enjoyed the extravagance of that inspired detail of eight hundred geese feet being washed in paraffin oil by the man who had gone to such trouble to get them within reach of the dinner-plates of Cork.

The following morning dawned clear and blue once again. I didn't know how long more these frosty blue days would last, but I wanted to be sure I spent most of them on the road.

An elderly man driving a white Mazda stopped to give me a lift, when I was hitching out of Monkstown. As I usually did, I opened the back door, tossed my rucksack in, shut the door again and made to open the passenger door.

The elderly man was obviously under the impression that I had clambered into the back with my rucksack, because I had no sooner shut the back door than he put his foot on the accelerator and took off. Aghast at the prospect of losing my rucksack, not to mention my diary, I fled after the car, yelling "Stop! Stop!" and waving my arms frantically.

About a hundred yards down the road, the car pulled in and I sprinted towards it with a speed and energy I had not believed myself capable of.

"I haven't all day to wait for you to be opening and closing doors," the driver said grumpily, when I eventually reached the car.

I sat in the back with my rucksack, in case he should again take off with such alacrity once I got out of the car.

"Are you sure you're in now, with your many pieces of luggage?" he said sarcastically.

At Carrigaline, I got out, taking my many pieces of luggage with me.

It took a long time to get the rest of the way to Kinsale, but by walking and a series of short lifts, I eventually got there in the late afternoon. I had cousins in Kinsale, who ran Boland's Craft Shop and Newsagents at the centre of the town but I had not seen Tony and Colette Boland for years and could not recall ever having met Ray, Liz, Steph or Jackie, my four second cousins. I hesitated about going to see them, but here I was in Kinsale, and there was Boland's shop on the corner.

I went inside to buy a newspaper. If I was recognized, fine. If not, I'd just go on my way. But Colette recognized me straight away, found out what I was doing in Kinsale by a few rapidly-fired questions, told me I must stay with them as long as I liked, and commandeered Jackie to take me up to the spare room and to make me some tea.

I stayed for two lovely nights in Kinsale with the cousins, coming and going as I pleased through the shop. The weather continued to be cold and blue. In such weather, Kinsale Bay looked as if it was composed of clear blue glass; the water perfectly still; the sailing boats moored in the inner harbour for winter, barely moving the surface of the water, as if they were frozen into it. The incredibly cold blue sky had the quality of ice in it and at night, the waxing bone-white moon over the water made everything glitter with a peculiar light.

I could not get over the quality of the light those few bitterly cold days in Kinsale. For a time of year when daylight hours are short and usually dull, there was something strange and wonderful about the clarity with which everything was etched out. Everything looked polished. It was the sort of light you see after a heavy fall of snow; when everything takes on a phosphorescent blue-white colour and gleams with unusual purity and weirdness.

Kinsale, which holds an annual gourmet festival each October, had so many restaurants that I wondered how they could all survive. But Tony assured me they were all quite different and that each did well in its own share of the market. Kinsale also had several craft shops and antique shops, so it obviously had an affluent summer population.

The Kinsale Museum had preserved a rather twee sign which it displayed on its gates.

The Tying of horses to these gates prohibited by order.
Town Clark.

I had to hunt for the museum key with a certain degree of dedication. A passerby told me to ask for the key from Brendan Cantillon in the Spar Supermarket. In the Spar Supermarket, I was told that the key was with Angela Perkins and that she might be in Mother Hubbard's coffee shop. She wasn't, but they assured me I'd find her in Greyhound's Bar, where I did eventually find her.

Apart from a cane deckchair salvaged from the *Lusitania*, which had been torpedoed off the Old Head of Kinsale in 1915, the most interesting items in the chill and cavernous museum space were the shoes of Patrick Cotter, the Kinsale Giant, who lived from 1760 to 1806. He measured eight feet, three inches and his shoes looked like pudding bowls to me, being about eighteen inches long. The little card informed me that Cotter had "worked first as a plasterer in Kinsale, then made a fortune on the English stage."

Also displayed were his knife and fork; crude items of cutlery that resembled gardening implements. Did a man who was, after all, only two feet taller than usual, really require such trowel and saw-like bits of cutlery? What size could his *mouth* possibly have been?

The nearby St Moltrose Anglican Church displayed on its door a long poem which beseeched the visitor to "Enter this door.../As if a choir/In robes of fire/Were singing here/Nor shout, nor rush/But hush/For God is here."

Peace and tranquillity was obviously the last thing on Imran Komanine's mind. He had signed the *Visitor's Book* with the comment, "Get Rushdie!"

The night before I left Kinsale, the cousins and I had tea in the drawing room. I was curled up in an armchair by the fire.

"Where are you going next?" Colette asked.

"I'm going to go to Ballinspittle to look at the statues."

She laughed. "You know, the last person who sat in that chair and told us she was going to Ballinspittle to look at the statues was Edna O'Brien!"

Edna O'Brien, they told me, had turned up in the shop looking for directions to Ballinspittle a couple of years previously and they had invited her upstairs for afternoon tea. "She sat just there, where you're sitting now."

199

I felt as if I was sitting on Edna O'Brien.

Kinsale Harbour narrows and wanders back inland to Inishannon, a distance of some nine miles or so by road. To shorten the journey from Kinsale town across to the Old Head of Kinsale peninsula, a bridge was built across the harbour. When I set off again, the glassy blueness having sadly dissolved to greyness, with rain on the way, I walked out of town and crossed this long bridge.

I waited beyond the bridge, hitching cars and watching a young girl ride cautiously by on a nervous horse, to which passing cars gave a wide and courteous berth.

A silver Fiesta travelling at a low speed pulled over. The driver, an old man who was hunched over the steering-wheel, peering out at the road through thick-lensed spectacles, introduced himself as Joe Dempsey from the Old Head of Kinsale.

"Is it Ballinspittle you want?" Joe asked. "Well, I'll be going there eventually. Hop in and I'll bring you out to the Old Head first."

Time being flexible as usual, I agreed.

As usual, I reached for the seat-belt and as usual, I got a surprised reaction.

"I never bother with those things myself. Sure, by the time they'd get around to summons me, it wouldn't be worth their while at my time of life."

Joe may have run the risk of being summoned for not wearing a seat-belt, but he would never have been pulled up for exceeding the speed limit, since the marker on the speedometer dial never moved beyond twenty miles an hour.

We came in sight of the young girl and the nervous horse about a mile down the road. "A grand animal that!" Joe cried out in admiration. "Would you ever look at that animal now!"

He blasted the horn in noisy salute and waved happily to the outraged rider, who threw him a murderous stare before absorbing herself in trying to control the frightened horse.

"A beast fit to pull a chariot!" Joe enthused, oblivious to all this activity. I looked out the back window, saw the girl frantically reining in the chariot beast and shaking a fist in the direction of the car, and could only laugh.

200

Joe Dempsey had a way with language that I had never heard before. He put words together in a way that made his sentences sing. Joe slapped the steering-wheel. "Tell me," he sang out, "what are the three hardest things to fit?"

"I don't know," I replied. "Tell me."

"A shoe for the foot of the Alps,

"A quilt for the bed of the Ocean,

"And a cap for the Old Head of Kinsale!"

Joe poked me in the ribs and nodded his head in the direction of the glove compartment. "Have a look at the notebook in there," he said, proudly.

I took a fat red notebook out of the glove compartment and looked through it. It was full of names and addresses, all written by different hands. There seemed to be an address from every country in the world. Joe told me that these were the names of people he had given lifts to. "I'm on this bit of a road every day and I've been giving lifts to people for six years now."

He asked me if I had a camera and when I said I did not, he showed that he was disappointed. "You could have taken my photograph, d'you see. People send them back to me from all over the world."

If I couldn't take his picture, then Joe was determined to show me something to remember him by. Another poke in the ribs. "Look at this, now!" "This" was a pioneer pin, of the kind worn by those who abstain from alcohol. "It's real gold," he said. "It cost me eighty pounds," he added with awe. "You can apply for one when you've been a pioneer for fifty years. And where are you from yourself?" he asked.

"The last place I worked was London."

He clucked in sympathy. "I emigrated for years myself," he confessed.

"Was it to England or America?"

"It was to the other side of the bridge at Kinsale!"

Halfway down the peninsula, Joe turned the car into the driveway of an old farmhouse. "You'll come in for a cup of tea before we go another bit of the road?"

It took Joe a long time to get out of the car and walk the few yards to the house. He leaned heavily on a stick and walked only with the greatest difficulty. It occurred to me that he treated his car like a very large wheelchair.

Joe's daughter-in-law was just about to leave the house, and was not at all surprised to be told by Joe that he had given me a lift, obviously used to people coming and going all the time. She made us tea and then went off with her small daughter Valerie.

"She comes in every day," Joe told me. "The daughter wants me to go and live with her in Tallaght. But sure, wouldn't I be lost up there? My daughter-in-law comes and lights the fire every day and everyone knows me here. I've lived here most of my life. Wouldn't I be lost up there?" he repeated.

"You'd be lost up there."

Joe dipped biscuits in his tea and said nothing. Suddenly, he grinned over at me. "My wife's over there in the drawer. Would you like to see her?"

I was greatly taken aback. *Does he mean ashes?* I thought, not at all sure if I wanted to see such small fragments of a life.

Joe was already scrabbling in the drawer. He produced, not a casket of ashes, but a tattered sepia photograph in a cracked frame. The photograph had been taken on Joe and Eileen's wedding day. The two of them stood stiffly together and stared carefully and unblinkingly at the camera.

"I have to put it away, because the grandchildren got a hold of it and broke the glass. Isn't she a lovely woman! And wasn't I a grand man then. Didn't I have a good stand in me!"

He dusted the photograph off with his sleeve. Eileen Dempsey had been dead for fourteen years. "She just said to me one day, 'I have a pain', and we had the priest that evening and she was dead that night. As quick as that," he said sadly and replaced the photograph in the drawer.

Joe asked me to reach up and take down two albums from the top of the dresser. I spread them out on the table. The albums were bulging with photographs, letters and postcards from the people whom Joe had given lifts to on his "bit of road" over the years. The photographs all featured Joe, with a different rucksacked person in each photo. I looked more closely at the photos. The car in these pictures was a red Fiesta. The car in the driveway was a silver Fiesta.

"What happened the red Fiesta?"

He chuckled. "Up in fire! Up in fire!"

He stood in the middle of the floor, leaning on his stick as I replaced the albums. "How old do you think I am?" he asked proudly.

"A fair old age."

"I'm eighty-four years of age! But maybe I shouldn't have told you that until I had you brought to Ballinspittle!"

We drove down to the end of the peninsula, where the land dropped away and the sea consumed the horizon.

Joe pointed out to sea. "Did you ever hear tell of the *Lusitania*?"

"I did," I said, remembering the cane deckchair in the Kinsale Museum with an unpleasant sensation, as I stared out over the stretch of water from where it had been salvaged. "Didn't it go down just here, off the Old Head?"

"It did," he said. "And I remember the day it went down."

I did a rapid bit of mental arithmetic. In 1915, Joe would have been nine years old.

"I had just cycled my bike home from school and there was a whole crowd of people gathered up there on the hill, all looking out to sea. We could all see the ship going down and we knew what was happening to those people.

"And the thing was, the alert for an emergency was put out at Kinsale, and they had blankets and hot water and everything ready for them, but didn't they bring the ones that lived to Cork and the extra bit they went made a whole lot more die of exposure on the way. It was a terrible day. And we could see it all from the hill and there wasn't a thing we could do."

Joe fell silent. We stared out over the deceptively flat and innocuous-looking sea in which almost twelve hundred people perished all those years ago.

We drove the back road to Ballinspittle, Joe blasting the

horn outside every house by way of greeting. Walking along by the side of the road was another old man, leaning on a walking stick. Joe knew him, of course, and stopped to give him a lift. I scrambled into the back seat. The other man's name was also Joe.

"Are you going to Ballinspittle?"

"I'm on my way to that big city!" Joe joked.

"Are you all right, Joe?" the New Joe asked.

"Sure, I'm alive anyway and isn't that something?"

"I suppose it is," the New Joe agreed. "I'm awful bad myself these days in this cold weather."

"Sure, we're two old crocks now, but we had our day!"

"Begod and we did!"

The two of them slapped their thighs and laughed merrily. Sitting in the back seat and listening to those two old men laughing away made me think it might not be at all as bad a thing to be old as I had always casually imagined.

Joe drove me out beyond Ballinspittle village to the grotto, where I said goodbye and assured him I'd send a postcard for his album. He blasted the horn, waved, and then he was gone.

The Ballinspittle grotto was remarkable at once for its amenities. There were loudspeakers on poles, a telephone box, a hastily-constructed toilet block that hadn't yet been plastered, four street-lamps (still burning, although it was now midday), and rows of benches on the grassy embankment opposite the grotto.

The grotto itself was similar to scores of others in Ireland. Bernadette knelt, looking up at the figure of Mary, who stood high up in a stone niche. There was a halo of unlit lights around Mary's head and a rosary between her hands. The grotto railings had the words "I Am The Immaculate Conception" spelled out in tall metal letters. There was also a sign which stated prudently "No responsibility for accidents on these premises". Bunches of plastic flowers mingled with real flowers in the grotto cum rockery; a detail which was both surreal and kitsch.

In the summer of 1985, it was widely reported that the statue of Mary at Ballinspittle grotto was moving. In one of the wettest summers on record, people poured in from all over Ireland, desperate for some colour in those sodden months; incredulous, devout, sceptical, and plain curious to see this moving statue for themselves.

The Kinsale cousins had gone too. I asked Ray if he'd seen the statue move. "It moved all right," he said, and then grinned at me. "But so did the statue in the church here, when I tried staring at it the next week!"

I peered up at the statue. Nothing happened.

A big man who had driven up in a car from the village came over to join me at the railings. "Now, what can I do for you?" he asked, looking up proprietorially at the statue. I resisted the temptation to answer "Make her move!". "I'm just looking," I said, feeling as if this was a conversation with a pushy shop-assistant.

"There was a tourist here the other day and I asked him if he was another atheist from the BBC. We got right sick of them all laughing at us!" He glared at my notebook with deep mistrust.

I set my face in a polite, neutral expression and continued to stare up at the statue, which remained resolutely still.

"Are you a Catholic?" he demanded. "I suppose it doesn't matter whether you're a Catholic or not," he conceded. "The face changed for June Levine and she's a *Jewess*. She was very impressed with our statue. She stayed here watching for two hours and she said it was only like five minutes. She saw what she called the face of a rabbi, but what I would see as the face of the Sacred Heart."

"Have you seen it move yourself?"

"Oh yes, " he answered. "I've seen it trembling. And I have seen the faces of saints in that statue. St Teresa was up there one night. And Padre Pio another night."

"How did you know it was Padre Pio?"

"Ah, you'd know by the beard."

I tried to imagine the bearded face of Padre Pio peering out from under a long white mantle and blue sash and found the image more amusing than inspirational. But this man – who refused to tell me his name – spoke with such conviction that I was in no doubt but that he certainly believed that the statue had moved and that her face had been transformed.

"But she was on the move for twenty years before all this," the man told me. "Children would come home and say that the Ballinspittle statue was moving, but you know how children are. Nobody believed them. But why wouldn't Mary appear to us? Wasn't she the mother of all of us?"

The big man drove me back into Ballinspittle. Of the money that must surely have poured into the village in that miraculous summer, there was absolutely no sign. Ballinspittle was a dismal little place. It was dirty and in serious need of painting.

I struck out along the road towards Timoleague and ate my lunch in the rain while waiting for a lift. This road was running with mud. It smelt, too. I tracked the smell to a very dead cat in the ditch and kept walking.

There were piles of sugar-beet at the side of the road all the way to Timoleague. The man who brought me there told me that farmers left them by the side of the road for collection to the sugar factory in Mallow.

Driving along on the far side of the tongue of Courtmacsherry Bay, I could see what I thought was Timoleague in the distance. But it was Courtmacsherry, playing tricks. As we swung along the road, I could see that Courtmacsherry was not up beyond us, but across the bay.

The driver laughed at my surprise. "It changes places! Courtmacsherry's always on the move."

There was a lovely old abbey down near the water at Timoleague, but I had to hurry on. I was hoping to make it to Rolf's Hostel in Baltimore that evening and it was a dull day that would get dark early.

I climbed the hill out of Timoleague and started hitching towards Clonakilty. Mamie Bowen, speaking of Clonakilty, had automatically said, "Clonakilty, God help us!" When I asked her what the meaning of this suffix was, she told me that during the Famine years, the Clonakilty Workhouse had been a place to where the destitute had gone. "And if you were headed for the workhouse, you weren't likely ever to come out of it alive."

206

The Timoleague woman who brought me to Clonakilty also said "Clonakilty, God help us!" and when I asked her why, she told me the same story that Mamie had told me.

But the man who brought me from Clonakilty to Newmills and who was a Clonakilty man himself, said the same words in a different way. "Clonakilty, God help us," he said quietly. "There was a soup kitchen at the Timoleague end of the town and they fed as many of the Famine victims as they could from there."

Without the exclamation mark and uttered in a different tone, the meaning of the words changed from a cry of despair to a prayer for help. I was fascinated by these two interpretations of the same saying. It was a classic example of the importance of aural history and how some things get lost, or blurred, not in the telling, but in the writing down.

Clonakilty itself, which I regretfully had to hurry through, looked an inviting place with long, narrow streets of bright houses and shops. I got a strong sense of tradition from Clonakilty, which presented itself as an unmistakably Irish place. Many of the shops had their names written in Irish and I was not surprised to hear later than Clonakilty was a great place to hear traditional Irish music.

I had a speedy lift to Skibbereen with a young man who hit the road in spots. At Skibbereen, I did some shopping and went straight out the Baltimore road. It was now almost dark. Luckily, I got a lift straight away that was going right down to Baltimore.

Alan was the manager of the Beacon Park Hotel in Baltimore.

"Have you ever had Helen Lucy Burke down your way?"

"Helen who?"

I was astounded. I had thought Helen Lucy Burke's distinctive and sometimes vicious articles about restaurant meals would be common knowledge to those people in the danger zone of public eating places.

"She writes a food column for the *Sunday Tribune*," I explained lamely. How did you explain Helen Lucy Burke?

He shook his head. "Never heard of her. And whoever

she is, she'll get the same treatment as everyone else if she ever comes down here."

It was fruitless to get into a quagmire of explaining that the whole point was that one never did know exactly when HLB would sit down at one's table.

I was sorry to be travelling down the Baltimore peninsula in near darkness, because I liked what I could see of the many small islands in the bay and the feeling of driving down to land's edge for the second time that day.

9
CROSSING THE WATER
Sherkin Island

Gertrude and Rolf, who were German, had been running Rolf's Hostel in Baltimore for ten years. The kitchen and dining room/common room of Rolf's Hostel were lovely; all wooden furniture and stone walls with a warm and friendly atmosphere but the dormitory was not quite so lovely.

It was a small building across the yard – a building which I called "The Shed"– a converted outhouse of stone. I had no doubt it was a pleasant place to sleep in the summer, but it was less than pleasant in winter.

The Shed smelt strongly of damp and old socks. In the gap between the timber ceiling and the stone walls, a family of mice were having a rowdy time. I slept in the loft area of The Shed, which had a sloped ceiling, and woke several times during the night to small nocturnal scrabblings, just inches from my face. When the mice did not wake me, the cold did. It was cold as a tomb in The Shed and although I nicked extra blankets from unoccupied mattresses, the coldness seeped through like water.

Also staying in Rolf's that night were a Frenchwoman, a Swisswoman and an Englishman; Natalie, Rita and Daniel respectively. Natalie was taking a short break from Dublin, where she had rented a room and was writing her first novel.

"It is about a French girl who comes to live in Ireland and becomes involved in The Troubles," she explained. "I wanted to come and live in Dublin and write it there, because Dublin is where writers live."

"Not all of them."

"Ah, but the best ones all lived there – for a while at least," she said simply.

209

Rita was also on a short break. She told me that she worked in a vegetable co-op in Switzerland and that she never wasted anything. I found her in the women's bathroom that evening, brushing her teeth with black paste from a jar. "It is ashes and juices from vegetable roots mixed together," she explained, as I stared in amazement and wondered how, but how, ashes were meant to clean one's teeth.

Daniel Foley was an actor who had just returned from a six-month tour of Japan. For some reason, he asked me to guess his age and looked absolutely horrified when I guessed him to be in his late forties.

"I'm only thirty-five!"

Daniel told me he had gone out to Sherkin Island some time previously and had promised to go back to the island and perform. Back in Ireland to look for "a cheap house", he was going over to Sherkin next day to give a workshop and perform a one-man Shakespearian show.

"Why don't you come over too?" he asked. "There's supposed to be a boat-load of people coming from Clear Island and the people who invited me over have arranged a house for us to stay in."

Intrigued at the idea of Shakespeare on Sherkin in December, and by Sherkin itself, where I had never been, I agreed.

At two o'clock the next afternoon, Daniel and I took the *Garnish Glory* from Baltimore pier to Sherkin. It was £3.00 for a round trip. Barry, one of the boatmen, told me that he was a Sherkin-born man himself, but that over half the people now living on the island were "strangers".

It was only a fifteen-minute boat-journey to Sherkin, but the distance between Baltimore and Sherkin Island was indefinable. All the Irish islands I had been to, both on this particular journey and at other times, had this sense of absolute containment. Crossing the water, the landscape telescoped down to the area of the island, which became a boundless, separate place; the people who inhabited it became larger than life. I understood why the Tory Islanders called a boat-journey to the mainland "going over to Ireland".

210

The people who had arranged for Daniel to come over to perform were an English couple, Jeff and Mo, who ran The Jolly Roger; the island's only pub. Jeff was a man with many hats. He had once been Props Manager at London's National Theatre; but I was told he was also a draughtsman, a stonemason and a builder. Jeff had built the house where we were to stay the night. As well as running The Jolly with Mo, Jeff was helping to restore the fifteenth-century friary at the mouth of the harbour. Under this particular hat, Jeff was working with the Board of Works and had been loaned a dumper by them to help with the job.

This dumper was waiting at the pier for the boat to berth. The driver, Nick, called out to Daniel. Nick was to chauffeur Daniel up to The Jolly in the dumper.

"Who's this?" Nick asked, looking at me.

"I met Rosita in Rolf's," Daniel said. "She's come over to see the show."

We tossed our rucksacks into the cavity bit of the dumper and then climbed up onto the platform bit and clung on, while Nick manoeuvred the narrow road.

"Poshest transport on the island!" he assured us.

The Jolly, up on a hill overlooking the bay and the small Garrison Hotel, was an intimate little place, with window-seats and a fireplace.

Mo made us coffee and dispatched Nick to transport our luggage over to the house in Horseshoe Bay where we were to stay.

The workshop was supposed to start at three. Just before three, Nick came back to collect myself and Daniel and four children who had turned up in The Jolly. The children scrambled into the cavity of the dumper and peeked out over the edge like baby kangaroos. We rattled past the island telephone box and the Abbey Stores, where we picked up another child and all jumped, tumbled and untangled ourselves from the dumper at the door of the Community Hall.

The Sherkin Islanders are justly proud of their Community Hall. For a population of only one hundred, its creation was a remarkable achievement. Many

211

mainland villages with a considerably larger population than Sherkin have no such amenity. I was told that it had taken a year to raise the money and a year to build it. The islanders had built it themselves, with the ubiquitous Jeff acting as foreman. The hall had been open for seven years.

The islanders had utilized the hall space with a good deal of imagination. There was a small library, open three times a week, which looked well-stocked; a dispensary to which a nurse came every fortnight; toilets; a kitchen; and a large space divided in two by a partition. One side of this partition was where the Sherkin Island Knitting co-op worked, and here there were knitting machines, skeins of bright wool, piles of jerseys and jars of handmade buttons. On the other side of the partition was an empty space, in which Daniel was to give his workshop.

A big, tall American man, George Packer, showed me the library. He told me he'd been living on Sherkin for eleven years.

"How do you manage to make a living?" I asked curiously.

"I'm a writer."

"Are your books here?" I asked, squinting at the shelves.

"Oh no, I write for an American public," he said firmly.

"What sort of books?"

"Fiction," George said, somewhat uncomfortably. "If you take a walk over the island tomorrow, come in for tea and I'll show you some."

We were a motley lot for the workshop. Five children, all English; George and Cordule, a Germanwoman who was his partner; the owner of the Garrison, whom I was told was an ex-Opera singer; Nick, also English; Jo, an Australian. It looked as though I was the only Irish person there.

With five small children, the workshop, no matter how Daniel tried to contain it, kept erupting into noisy boisterousness. In the end, grown-ups and children alike abandoned all inhibitions and tore about the room, miming cutting our way through a jungle, pretending to be giraffes, football players, opera singers; making human sculptures and a tremendous amount of noise.

It was dark by the time we went back to The Jolly. We had toasted sandwiches sitting up at the bar, talking to Jeff and some of the other workshop participants. "Why did you come here to live?" I asked Jeff, knowing even as I asked it that it was one of those questions to which there is no real answer; a bit like "Where are you from?" But Jeff gave a fine answer.

"Well, it's the universal question, isn't it?" He spread his hands out in a wide gesture. "Why are we here? Nobody really knows. You live your life and sometimes you end up in a place without knowing exactly what brought you there, but you feel it's the right place to stay."

Nick, sitting on one side of me, agreed. Jo, the young Australian woman sitting on my other side, echoed Jeff's philosophy. She told me that she had been on Sherkin since August.

"I just found myself wanting to stay on. I didn't even mind losing the return bit of my air-fare."

Jo had lived in the Sherkin Hostel until it closed at the end of the summer, and was now renting a house on the island for ten pounds a week "between two of us. I'm just here. I don't know for how long."

At Larne, I had watched the ferry-boats depart for Cairnryan and Stranraer and felt the pull of the horizon; felt how shockingly easy it would be to just step on the boat and vanish into another country, drifting from place to place, sinking into another way of life. But I had not done it. Jo had done it; had followed her instincts and stayed on in Sherkin, to explore a possibility; a whim that had turned into a way of life.

"Sherkin people don't like leaving the island," Jeff said. "We have everything we need here."

I didn't for a moment think that Jeff meant things like groceries. He was voicing a state of mind; a way of life. It seemed to me that your attitude to living on an island depended on how you viewed the sea. I'd always wondered how I would cope with living on a small island, never able to decide whether I would feel isolated and suffocated by the contained space; or free and boundless, the surrounding sea merely an extension, a stepping stone to the landscape, instead of a barrier at which everything stopped.

Whatever the reasons, I did not think that Sherkin would ever be a place of limited possibilities for Mo, Jeff, Nick, Jo, George, Cordule and all the other non-Irish people who had somehow found themselves choosing to live on an island.

While I had been listening to Jeff and Jo, my eyes had been wandering around the bar. I noticed suddenly that the bar had a curious, miniature population of people and animals in gold and silver. The more I looked, the more traces I could see of these tiny bits of foil. Clinging to ledges, rope-knots, lampshades, the dart-board, shelves and picture-frames, were scorpions, snakes, cats, horses, bats, fish and brilliantly-worked little people who were in various attitudes all over the bar. The little people were to be found dangling by one arm, they could be seen swarming up wires, they peeked out precariously from behind the dart-board. My favourite was the one holding his hands protectively over his face as he sat cheekily under a lampshade.

Jo admitted to being the creator of most of them. "But everyone's into it now," she assured me. "We call it 'Foilology'." She pointed to the scorpion above the bar, which was made of tinfoil.

"That silver foil – tinfoil – is the best to make things with, because it lasts longer. Chris, who lives in a tent near the hall – did you see it?"

I had indeed seen a tent pitched in a field near the hall.

"Well, Chris who lives in the tent sometimes comes in here to bake potatoes on the fire and we all nab his tinfoil."

At this stage, I was less interested in Foilology than by Chris, who was living in a tent in sub-zero temperatures.

"To look at him, you'd never know he lived in a tent," Jo said. "He goes swimming to keep clean."

"Even in *December*?"

"Even in December."

"But why, why does he live in a tent?"

"He's no money. And he wants to live on Sherkin. So he lives in a tent," Jo explained patiently.

Pinned up on the wall inside the door of The Jolly was a theatre poster for Sebastian Barry's new play, *Prayers of Sherkin*, which was currently having a very successful run at Dublin's Peacock Theatre. When I commented on the poster, Mo produced a well-thumbed programme from behind the bar.

Encapsulated, the beautiful, lyrical *Prayers of Sherkin* is concerned with a young Sherkin woman who decides to leave the island forever by marrying a man from the mainland and going to live there. The play is set at the turn of the century. Sebastian Barry had never been to Sherkin.

"When we saw the advance notices in the paper, we were afraid it was a play about contemporary Sherkin," Mo said. "We didn't know if it was a play about us or what. Someone from the island went up for the opening night and came back down with the news that we could relax, it was a period play. It's she who brought down the poster and the programme. We're hoping maybe they'll do it down here in the hall sometime. Oh, the relief when we found out it was a period play!"

Mo laughed. So did everyone else in the bar, except me. It was too late now to explain to the islanders the reason why I was on Sherkin.

"It'll be a grand late night," everyone assured me, but lack of sleep after the night at Rolf's was beginning to swamp me. I decided to give the grand late night a miss. I'd been given directions to get to Jeff and Mo's house in Horseshoe Bay and walked back past the Abbey Stores, climbed over a five-bar gate and went up a grassy lane. "First house on your right," Mo had said. "There's a caravan in the garden."

I found the house without any difficulty and since there was a full moon, continued walking along the path, which looked down over Horseshoe Bay. In the moonlight, the little bay looked magical. I could see how it had got its name: the water lay within the perfect symmetry of a harbour shaped like a stone croissant or pair of crab-claws.

Back at the house, I found myself a bedroom upstairs and slept in until early morning. I got up hurriedly, anxious to look around the island before the afternoon ferry.

George had told me that he lived out the road that went beyond the church, at the western part of the island. As I walked out past the Abbey Stores and the hall, it became clear that many islanders were going the same way I was, on their way to Mass.

One elderly woman on an old black bike cycled a few yards, then got off and pushed for a few yards and so it went. We made the same progress along the road. I asked her where George's house was.

"George? I know who he is all right, but do you know, I don't know his house at all. It's a long way past the church and I haven't been further than the church for years."

Sherkin Island is only three miles wide.

"You'd better ask someone else," she said as we reached the church and she laid her bike in a ditch.

There were rows of bicycles leaning against ditches on either side of the church. The church itself, into which I looked, was bare and simple, with twelve pews a side and a sizable congregation.

"Do you know where George lives?" I asked John, a tall, bearded man who was standing outside the church.

"Oh, George lives a long way away; at the other end of the island. A right long way." He pointed to a white house that was visible on the brow of the next hill. "See that? That's George's house."

Hadn't been further than the church for years? A house on the next hill was a long way away? Continuing on towards the house, I thought again about distances and how, within the three-mile area of Sherkin, there was a space so open and densely-textured that two lives need never entangle and at the same time, a space so physically small that a couple of hours tramp and you could say you had "seen" the island.

It was a sobering thought, when I referred it back to the way I was travelling; covering miles and miles most days. How much was I missing? Looked at that way, the idea of ever managing to capture something about a country and its people when I was travelling in such a hit-and-miss fashion, seemed impossible. It made more sense when I thought of what I was trying to do as a written equivalent

216

of those random images of Ireland selected by the Real
Ireland photographers; those images which Ciarán Carson
had described as depending "not so much on a view as on
a point of view".

I continued walking. Down to my right was an idyllic
little sandy cove, which looked inviting even in December.
The road straggled and narrowed; the hedgerows
wandered; from the top of the small hill, I could see bright
glimpses of sea. Sherkin seemed to have some amazing
coves, harbours and beaches; each one that I had seen so
far was startlingly, unexpectedly beautiful.

George's house was a traditional old farmhouse, long
and low, painted white, with lavender-coloured window
sashes. George was spreading manure in his garden. He
showed me several neat plots where, during the year, he
harvested a dizzying range of vegetables, among them,
kale, leeks, petit-pois and broccoli.

Their cherry tree outside the front door had lost its
leaves, but it was not bare. Cordule had decorated the tree
with old wool. The stark tree against the white walls of the
house looked wonderfully exotic; bright and vibrant
colours of purple, orange, blue and green strands of wool
strung, twisted and draped along its branches.

Eleven years previously, George had seen a two-line ad in
the property pages of the *International Herald Tribune*, for a
farmhouse on Sherkin. "I used to read the property pages
for fun, but here was this little ad one day. It had a contact
number for Paris and I was living there at the time, so I rang
the number out of curiosity. I needed a holiday, so I took the
ferry over and came straight to Sherkin. And when I walked
over that hill back there and saw that little beach, I thought
'I could live here'. I've lived all over the world, but this is
the only place I found that I knew I could settle in."

I asked George if he had seen other parts of Ireland. He
told me he had not. "I'd found the place where I wanted to
live," he explained. George reminded me of my brother
David, who had been living near Caherdaniel on the Ring
of Kerry for several years and who seldom left the place,
considering a day away to be a day wasted. If this was that
elusive place called "home", they'd both found it.

217

George had had quite a life. I got only glimpses of it, but those glimpses were intriguing. He had once been an English professor at Princeton and had taught creative writing.

"Did you have anyone famous go through your classes?"

He laughed. "Christopher Reeve! Superman! Although he didn't turn up very often, he was always off at drama."

George asked if I'd been up at The Jolly, and chuckled. "That's only been there for four years. Before that, we had the shebeen. A few of us got together about six years ago and decided to build a shebeen. We converted an old creamery building and started making homebrew and we sold it for twelvepence a pint. Oh, we had some great nights in there!"

"How big was it?"

George indicated towards the kitchen area. "About that big." The space George was looking at was no more than ten feet by five.

"We could squeeze about twenty people in, and a little stove heater. The wind and the rain'd be howling and blowing outside and we'd be snug as bugs inside. Dolly, one of the islanders, she had her twenty-first birthday party in there."

I wished I'd been on Sherkin six years earlier. "But what happened to it?"

"There were a couple of reasons. One was that we all made perfect five-gallon lots of homebrew, but we never seemed to get it right in larger quantities. And a few people got sick from drinking it."

Privately, I wondered if the twelvepence-a-pint bit had had anything to do with illness.

"And the other thing was that the old lady who lived next to the shebeen, although she was a regular and loved all the crack that went on there, she got mighty tired of people peeing on her doorstep. And then Jeff started running The Jolly and he'd been one of the main people behind the shebeen (Jeff again!), and so it just faded out.

"But a couple of nights ago, Norman – did you meet Norman?" I remembered a man with white hair and a magnificent white beard, telling bawdy jokes. George

218

laughed. "That's Norman! Well, Norman said to me that a pint costs a pound fifty now and that we should think about starting up the shebeen again! But it won't happen," George said, somewhat sadly. "We'd be taking business away from Jeff, and besides you can never have a good thing twice."

I asked to see one of George's books. He went upstairs and came back down with a cloth-bound copy of a novel entitled *That Quail Song, Sam, Say It Again*. It had the address of a Boston publishing company inside, with a publication date of 1969. George had bought the Sherkin house with the film options of *That Quail Song*.

"I write mostly for magazines now," he told me. "But I've just finished a big novel and I'm going to America in the spring with it. At the moment, I'm very interested in writing about coincidence. That's a subject there's a lot to be got out of."

We talked about truth-being-stranger-than-fiction. I told him about statues that moved, postmen who vanished and a place called Boolavogue that a lifetime's search had never revealed.

George had his garden to get back to and I had a ferry to catch, so I said goodbye. "Come back anytime," George called, waving me off from the garden.

Daniel had already left; gone out on the morning ferry with the priest after Mass. I found I'd missed the early afternoon ferry and so adjourned to The Jolly for a couple of hours, where several Sunday papers were being passed around.

The phone rang while I was there. It was Daniel. "He got a lift to Bantry. He's on his way to look at a house on Bere Island," Mo told me. "He said to tell you he was sure your paths would cross again."

10
UNMAPPED COUNTRIES
Skibereen to Valentia

It was too cold to consider having a shower next morning at Rolf's so I just scrambled into my clothes, filled a flask and hit the road. I had a lift to Skibbereen with a German man in a four-wheel drive. He told me he had been in Ireland for fifteen years, running a German company in Skibbereen.

"I could never go back to Germany. This is home now."

That word again.

By this time of the winter, I was wearing almost the entire contents of my rucksack; doubling up on socks and jerseys and sometimes wearing both leggings and jeans when it was really cold. Consequently, whenever I came across a launderette – which was not often; "Everyone has washing-machines now" – I bundled everything into the machine. This is what I did when I found the West Cork Cleaners in Skibbereen. Left with only the Gore-Tex suit to wear, I wandered around Skibbereen, looking like a mobile pillar-box and attracting several curious looks, since it was not actually raining.

Back in the West Cork Cleaners, I looked at the cards pinned to the noticeboard while waiting for my clothes to dry. One card made me laugh out loud.

Con Keane. Painter. Decorator
Interior and Exterior Painting
Paperhanging. Tiling
Make Your Old Headstone Look Like New

Con catered for everyone, it appeared; cradle to grave.

Fully dressed again, I hitched out towards Ballydehob and the Mizen peninsula, and got a lift to the viewing point high up over Roaring Water Bay. Roaring Water Bay was silent; its surface undulating with scores of small islands. Among the islands were several wooden boxes; long and slender and looking like driftwood from that height. They were mussel farms. They were less intrusive on the landscape than the salmon cages I'd seen in Clifden Bay and Killary Fjord, but they still spoilt a magnificent view.

Conor gave me a lift to Ballydehob. "Ballydehob is full of hippies," he told me. "And Germans. Unfriendly Germans. They just sit in pubs and criticize the way we run our country."

Conor proved to be the only person I got a lift from in west Cork who had such sour things to say about the cosmopolitan communities of the area.

There were some interesting, faded murals on gable walls and house-fronts in Ballydehob: owls, fiddlers, angels, cats, and Celtic symbols. I didn't see anyone who looked even vaguely like a hippy. In the post office, the conversation was all about Mary Robinson, who was being inaugurated as President that day.

I walked out of the village and sat on a wall, listening on my pocket radio to the commentary of the inauguration. The sheep in the field behind me looked up in vague bewilderment as, when Mary Robinson ended her speech with the words, "I am of Ireland, come dance with me in Ireland", I took her at her word and danced for joy in the road. For Irishwomen, this day was nothing less than inspirational.

Christine, who brought me to Schull, had been listening to the inauguration on her car radio. "It's a great, great day for Ireland!" she sang out, when I got into the car.

On the hill outside Schull were two large white egg-shaped objects. I asked Christine if she knew what they were.

"Radars for tracking aircraft. One of them was blown up by the IRA about seven years ago. They thought they had something to do with English surveillance – God knows why! Just this terrific bang about two in the morning."

I told Christine that I was trying to hitch out to the Mizen Head.

"If you ring up the lighthouse keeper at the Mizen and tell him you'd like to see around, I'm sure they'd let you in," she said.

So at Schull, I went off to find a phone-box. There was a queue for the phone. Hippies at last. The two people in the phone-box, a man and a woman, wore long, trailing clothes. The man had a superbly unkempt beard and the woman had a nose ring. Rapunzel would have looked bald beside them.

The woman waiting in front of me glared at them. "They came over from England four months ago and decided to stay. Look at them! They don't care if we stand here waiting all day."

"It's a public phone," I said mildly.

She eyed my rucksack. "Well, it's obvious you *do* have all day to waste," she sniffed.

When I got through to the Mizen Head lighthouse, a polite voice told me that unless I had a visiting permit from Irish Lights, I wouldn't be allowed entry to the lighthouse. I was extremely keen to see the lighthouse. I remembered Gwen Bowen's direct approach. For the first and last time, I tried the I'm-writing-a-book line. It didn't work.

"How interesting," the polite voice observed. "Well, if you can get a permit, you'll be very welcome. Otherwise, you're wasting your time."

There were several small groups of people gathered on the streets of Schull. They were all discussing the inauguration, which had been televised live. "It was great to see her, all the same," one old man conceded.

"Sure, a change won't do us a bit of harm," his companion agreed.

At the Bunratty Inn, where I had lunch, there was a spontaneous and impromptu toast to the new President.

"A historic day for Ireland," one man declared, rising to his feet.

I hitched on to Goleen, getting a lift from a Frenchman who told me he was a salmon farmer. I didn't really know where I was going, but Crookhaven seemed to be as far south as I could go down the Mizen peninsula. I wanted to keep going. So I hitched on towards Crookhaven and got a lift from a man who told me he was half-English, half-Italian and was currently renting the old Crookhaven lighthouse as a place to live, while waiting for his new house to be built.

The road that led towards Crookhaven was completely empty of cars. There were small lakes, sudden rock-faces, and a strange sense of lushness in the undergrowth and hedgerows, even though it was the middle of winter. In one of the small lakes we passed, I saw a stone cottage apparently floating on the water, islanded on its own foundations. There were stepping stones out to it from the shore's edge, and glimpsed so briefly from the car window, it looked like something from a landscape of dreams.

I could see Crookhaven long before we actually got there. Crookhaven, was literally, a sheltered harbour in the shape of a crooked arm. The village itself was at the opposite side of the water, at the end of the crooked arm. The slice of water in the harbour looked so incredibly clear that I could almost count the stones in the harbour.

"Have you got friends or relations there?" the man asked who was driving me there.

"No."

"Are you staying there tonight?" he asked doubtfully.

"Yes, I hope so."

Crookhaven looked extraordinary. It also looked very small and was extremely remote. It crossed my mind that I might have difficulty finding somewhere to stay that night, but this was such an unwelcome thought I pushed it away.

Crookhaven proved to be even smaller that it had looked from across the water. There was absolutely nobody about. It was like a ghost village. O'Sullivan's Pub was shut. The post office was shut. The General Store was shut. The Welcome Inn and Crookhaven Inn were shut. There was a shop called "Annie's (and sometimes Toni)" which was shut and so utterly empty, that when I looked in the window, I had no idea what it was that Annie and sometimes Toni sometimes sold.

This was Crookhaven.

True, it was a Monday, but it was only mid-afternoon. How and when did the people of Crookhaven post letters, buy groceries and have a drink?

There was one other building which I had not investigated. It was right by the water; an outsized, ugly and obviously brand-new apartment block coyly masquerading as an outsize, ugly and brand-new house. It was so out of character and out of scale with the rest of Crookhaven that I left it until last to look at, half-hoping it would have vanished by the time I got to it.

I knocked on the door and a woman peeped out at me from behind Venetian blinds. I could hear a dog yapping inside. The woman opened the door to me cautiously and the dog growled at me from behind her skirts. This was the first sign of life I'd seen in Crookhaven.

The block contained sixteen apartments. She showed me one; an antiseptic pine and white-walled box with a shocking lack of natural light. It was clear I needed somewhere to stay for the night and equally clear that all sixteen apartments were empty and would remain empty that night.

"The best I could offer you would be £40.00 for the night – with an £80.00 deposit, of course."

I laughed. "Of course." I asked if there was anywhere else at all to stay.

"You *could* try the Marconi Inn back the road," she said, "but *I* wouldn't pin my hopes on it."

I started walking back the way I had come. So far, I had always been lucky in managing to find a place for the night, just turning up and eventually discovering somewhere that was open. It meant I never had to plan ahead; never had to book; and it allowed me complete freedom. So far, it had worked, but Crookhaven had me beat. It seemed it really did only come to life in the summer.

The Marconi Inn had post on the mat. It was shut. It was my last hope. There was a holiday house on the opposite side of the road and its name was "Journey's End". I laughed hollowly.

There was nothing for it but to strike back the way I'd

come. It was four o'clock by now and the light from the Fastnet lighthouse was already winking across the sea. After I had been walking for about an hour, it was completely dark. Pitch-black. There were no stars and no moon, but there was the comforting, rythmic winking of the Fastnet lighthouse.

I got out my torch. The batteries were running low. I'd meant to get spare ones for several days, but had let it slip, since I hadn't used the torch for some time. It was an eight-mile walk from Crookhaven back to Goleen and no guarantee of anywhere to stay there either. I switched the torch off, thinking I should keep it until I heard cars and needed to be seen.

Suddenly, I heard the distant hum of a car-engine. It was coming from the Crookhaven end of the road. I switched on the torch, put out my arm and stood well in, waiting for the car.

It passed me by without stopping.

I started walking again, after addressing several extremely vulgar words to the tail-lights of the vanishing car.

After another hour, when I guessed myself to be near Goleen, I heard another car. This one stopped. The driver was a Schull man, who told me it was unlikely I'd find anywhere to stay in Goleen at this time of the year and so I found myself travelling back to Schull.

I stayed that night in the Station House B & B in Schull. The back of the house was literally at the side of the road and the front of the house overlooked Roaring Water Bay. It was a satisfyingly appropriate place to stay, sandwiched as it was between the road and the sea.

Mrs McCarthy and her daughter were watching highlights of the inauguration. "I'd have liked if her dress was a bit longer," Mrs McCarthy commented. "I mean, *those knees!*"

My own knees were clamouring for a rest and I found myself climbing into bed soon after nine, meaning to write up my diary in bed, but falling asleep before I'd even uncapped my pen.

In four days in west Cork, almost all of the people whom I met and whom I had lifts from had been foreigners or "blow-ins". The term blow-in seemed to include anyone who had not actually been born in the area, so that the expression covered both Irish citizens and foreigners.

"I'm a blow-in," Jim told me. Jim picked me up outside Ballydehob. He was American and had emigrated to Ireland.

Why?

"The quality of life," he said. "The scenery," he said and then laughed. "When you can see it, through the rubbish!"

In Bantry, there were people stringing Christmas lights across the streets. Out in Bantry Bay, I could see the huge oil tanks on Whiddy Island, scene of the 1979 tragedy in which fifty-nine men died in an explosion.

Beyond Bantry, the landscape seemed to thicken. Lush south-west Ireland, warmed by the Atlantic Drift and simultaneously cooled by the endless soft rain, was damp and verdant, even in winter. The startlingly-green moss clung to every surface, the waterfalls were everywhere, the fuchsia still blazed scarlet in the hedgerows, and the greenness seeped through everything.

It was a chill day, but a day permeated with dampness. Usually, when I walked for some time, I was comfortably warm in my layers of clothing, but a couple of miles out of Bantry and I had stripped down to a t-shirt and jeans, which were soon soaked through with sweat.

I was glad to get a lift. Pat, a Glengariff man, did not believe I was Irish. He would not be convinced. With so many blow-ins in residence in this part of Ireland, I could hardly blame him.

We talked of the fuchsia, which had been introduced from South America.

"At least it doesn't do any harm, not like some things they bring in," Pat said.

"Like what?"

"The mink. The mink is a scourge. About ten years ago, everyone wanted to be into mink farming. And so they brought them in. And then there was all this fuss about fur coats and nobody was buying them any more and there was no money in the mink. And *this eejit* who had a mink farm around here, he just opened the cages six years ago and let them all go. Hundreds of mink. They're killing all round them. They've spread up two peninsulas in six years. They have the food-chain destroyed. And they got into *my* hen-house one night and killed twenty-five of *my* hens."

Pat looked murderous at the memory of his dead hens. He cut the corners of the winding road to Glengariff viciously, as if he hoped he'd run over a mink at every one.

The village at Glengariff looked a neat and faded Victorian place, with ironwork and verandas on the buildings. Islanded among such luxuriant growth and looking out over Bantry Bay, there seemed to be something restrained and prudish about Glengariff. It was a maiden aunt of a place.

I would have liked to have stayed in Glengariff itself for the night, but the nearest hostel was the independent Tooreen Mountain Hostel, a few miles up the mountain pass to Kenmare. The road up to Tooreen wound its way through thick forest. I found it hard to believe that this was the main route to Kenmare. There were hardly any houses and a strange, back-in-time atmosphere to the road. I hoped very much there'd be other people staying at Tooreen, but doubted it.

Tacked to a tree a mile or so out of Glengariff was a fierce little notice.

The Wicked Shall Be Turned Into Hell

Whatever God-fearing person had put the sign up had chosen its location with a good deal of deliberation. The light had drained from the sky and it was a colourless, gloomy afternoon. I walked up and up and on and on, with the trees crowding the horizon, barely allowing the road through, and as I sweated up this road, I found myself unable to stop thinking about Hell.

Tooreen Mountain Hostel had obviously been built originally as a summer house. It was a lovely Fifties-style split-level place, with a flat roof, balconies and a mountain stream tumbling through the wild garden and views out over the Caha mountains.

The wardens lived in a cosy little house a field away. The woman came over to show me where everything was.

227

"You'll have company," she told me. "A young Australian man." There was a peculiar tone in her voice. It sounded something like rage. I wondered why.

Like many houses that are originally built for summer use only, Tooreen's heating system appeared to be non-existent. There was one Super-Ser gas heater in the large common room, with a little warning note stuck to it. The little note warned me that it was dangerous to turn on more than one of the three burners.

It was clammy and freezing in Tooreen. I switched on the heater and the windows steamed up. I switched it off and my fingers became so numb that I couldn't hold my pen. I switched it on again and wrote up my diary for the afternoon, the condensation trickling down the windows and an unpleasant, fuggy smell of gas seeping through the room.

George, the "young Australian man" arrived back at Tooreen very late in the evening, when I was on the point of going to bed. George had been at the hostel for some days, walking in the mountains each day and exploring Glengariff hostelries in the evenings. I had to admire George. He was pissed as a newt, but had managed to manoeuver the steep, twisting, God-fearing road through the forest without a torch and arrive apparently unmoved by the experience.

George looked at the notice on the heater. "You know why it says it's dangerous to put it on full-blast?"

"Yeah," I said off-handedly. "It's so it'll last three times as long and the wardens won't have to buy a new cylinder of gas for ages."

George looked at me with respect. "Imagine you working that out!"

"Nothing to it," I said airily, flicking on the heater to full power, as George wandered off in the direction of the kitchen.

There had been a legitimate reason for the little warning notice. Switched on to three burners, an enormous mauve-coloured flame swooshed out and lunged for my legs with the voracious fury of a starving wild animal that's been kept caged up. Fortunately, I was able to jump out of the way and managed to turn off the gas supply to the cylinder.

George was rattling about in the kitchen. He called to me, asking if I wanted to partake of his "special" – baked beans in a can of soup.

"No thanks, George. And George?"

"Yup?"

"Better leave the heater to one burner. I tried it out on full power just now and it's a *little* bit temperamental."

George had a four-thousand acre sheep station in Jambin, Queensland. He missed it.

"The space of it," George explained, tucking into his special. "You're always running into things here. That's why I've been here for a few days, away from all the towns, just walking in the mountains. I think I'll go to Kenmare tomorrow, though. But it's cold, ain't it? I reckon it's colder inside than it is outside."

This last comment was repeated so many times that it began to sound like a Hare Krishna mantra. I went and stood outside the door for a few minutes.

"George, you're bullshitting. It's cold inside, but it's definitely colder outside."

"I think I'll go to Kenmare tomorrow," was the reply.

I found out why there had been that odd tone in the warden's voice when she'd mentioned George.

"Well, I've been here a few days – I think I'll go to Kenmare tomorrow – and I've been out walking. And the warden, she has this dog, see? Well, she *had* this dog, see? And the mutt followed me on one of my walks and then it just went walkabout and I thought it'd come back here. But it hadn't. It's lost. And she's not too pleased. That was two days ago and it hasn't turned up yet. Hey, don't you think it's colder inside than it is outside?"

"I'm going to bed," I said. "See you in the morning."

"Hey," George said and grinned. "Are we the only two people staying here tonight?"

I stared at him. "Yes, I believe we are."

George laughed. "Well, see you in the morning – if I don't see you sooner!"

What George meant by this remark, I didn't really want to find out. I took the precaution of placing my rucksack in front of the door, having first removed my torch, which I put under the pillow. It may have been colder outside than it was inside, but I began to think the difference in degrees was perhaps not all that much and that maybe George had had a point after all. I ended up piling six blankets on my bed. I woke up several times during the night, not because of possible amorous advances – George was snoring soundly in the next room – but because it was so cold.

I got up early next morning and got ready to leave. George emerged as I was just about to go. We said goodbye to each other.

"Where are you heading today?" he asked.

"I'm not sure. Out the Beara peninsula somewhere."

"Well, I think I'll go to Kenmare today." He shivered. "Hey, don't you think it's colder inside – "

I didn't wait to hear the rest, but struck out into the morning.

Heading out the peninsulas of west Cork and Kerry, to which there were only narrow causeway necks of land, was a bit like setting off to visit islands. Studying the Beara peninsula on the map, the tiny villages and townlands of Derreenacarrin, Trafrask, Adrigole, Derreeny and Curryglass led out like stepping stones to Castletownbere. I thought I'd probably get lifts from village to village and so had made an enormous stack of sandwiches and filled my flask, expecting a long day on the road.

But I'd only been walking out from Glengariff for a few minutes when I got a lift from James, who was driving all the way out to Castletownbere. I should have been pleased, but I felt somehow cheated. It felt wrong to be speeding along the southern side of the Beara peninsula in this way, flicking so swiftly through the townlands and villages. I was passing it all by, travelling smoothly through the wild and rugged scenery, in an air-conditioned car with a car-phone and a smart briefcase on the back seat. It was the hitch-hikers equivalent of flying and I sat helplessly and looked out at the landscape from a great distance.

James was a Corkman. He worked for Unifish, who had a branch in Castletownbere, the second-largest Irish fishing port, after Killybegs.

"In season, Castletownbere is full of Russians, Poles and Spaniards. They land their catches there. But you won't see much activity there just now. The quota has been fished out for the time being."

I told James I'd been hitching around the coast.

"Northern Ireland and all?"

"Northern Ireland and all."

"Now that's a place I never have any inclination to visit at all. But I have been there; I went up for a rugby match once."

I had discovered the Michelin map of Ireland to be sometimes inaccurate in the spelling of placenames. Ennistymon, for instance, was "Ennistimon". Spiddal became "Spiddle"; Renvyle was "Rinvyle". They were minor inaccuracies. I knew that places often have Gaelic names that anglicization has blurred and that subsequently, there can be two versions of the same placename.

You expect modern maps to be accurate. When you look at a map and study the location of places, because they have a name and are in the right location, you assume the cartographer to have a sort of God-like all-seeing eye. Wherever you go, it seems, someone's been there before you, because they've found this place and marked it down. In a way, it almost takes the joy out of exploration.

The typefont in which Castletownbere is recorded on the Michelin map is of a size similar to that of the villages to its east and which I had just come through. But this typographical information is misleading. Castletownbere could not be considered similar in size to villages such as Trafrask and Derreeny: Castletownbere was a fair-sized town and the largest settlement on the Beara peninsula.

I was immensely cheered when I found these small blunders on the Michelin map. They told me that I knew these places more intimately than the cartographer. Looked at like this, the densely-textured map suddenly assumed a fluidity that allowed me to reinterpret it; to discover and chart out my own journey through places that to the Michelin cartographers were just names, but places that became real to me.

Castletownbere, quota fished out, was a very quiet place, overlooking the hump of Bere Island. I wondered if Daniel had found his house there. I'd thought that Castletownbere would probably be as far as I would get that day. But there

I was, and it was still only midday. I wandered up and down the town. I couldn't help feeling I was only seeing part of Castletownbere. The peripheral, floating population of the town, the fishermen who came and went, were missing.

I prowled about the town, the shops of which looked practical and sensible and useful. The shop-fronts were plain. Castletownbere was no Clifden. Wellies and overalls were on sale everywhere, but aran jerseys and linen tablecloths were thin on the ground. There was obviously more money in catering for fishermen than for the tourists, who were such transitory customers.

I found only one craft shop in Castletownbere; a shop that was also a bookshop. By this time, I'd decided to keep going, but I didn't really want to do a Crookhaven on it again and find myself stranded at the tip of the peninsula with nowhere to stay. I asked Gertie O'Sullivan in the craft-and-book-shop – which was nameless, in keeping with the unfussy, no-nonsense feeling of Castletownbere – if she knew of any B & Bs open in Allihies.

"I'm not sure," she told me. "I'm only a blow-in, so I'm still not sure about things like that."

"How long have you been here?"

"Twenty-two years."

Outside Castletownbere, I got a lift along the road a few miles with Geraldine, a dark-haired woman who had two small children in the back seat; Orla and Óisín. She told me they had been living in the area for eight years.

There was something familiar about Geraldine's face and something equally familiar about the names of her two children. But I couldn't puzzle out what it was. It only dawned on me when I had got out of the car and was waving goodbye to Orla, who was waving to me from the back window and then it was too late.

Geraldine Osborne, her husband Danny and three children – Tempy, Orla and Óisín – had only recently returned to Ireland after a year spent living an ethnic life among the Innuit people of Greenland. With their three small children, the Osbornes had journeyed by dog-sled and slept in tents and igloos. The Osbornes were adventurers, travellers, survivors. They had stories to tell. I had seen some in the newspapers that summer. And I had just waved them off down a side-road without asking Geraldine Osborne a single question about such an extraordinary journey.

Cross, I set off walking towards Allihies. Annette, who lived out near Dursey, gave me a lift for another couple of miles. She told me that if I couldn't find a B & B around Allihies, that the warden of the An Óige hostel would probably open up the hostel for me. I hoped I wouldn't have to do this. It was a dead cert the Allihies Hostel would be Arctic, since it had offically shut at the end of September. I'd had lots of see-your-breath and pile-on-the-blankets hostels in the last week and I wanted a break for a night.

Annette let me off a couple of miles outside Allihies and drove on down the road towards Dursey. I walked on, glad to be walking, feeling the place slow down and spread out around me.

It was very, very quiet. It was so quiet that I could hear the movement of the sea, although it was perhaps more than a mile away. Out on the tip of the Beara peninsula, I felt cast far out into the Atlantic. The landscape seemed to be composed almost entirely of sky, with a scrap of land the one narrow road was nicking its way so tenuously through.

Annette had told me I'd reach a gap in the road from where I'd be able to see Allihies, at the other side of the Slieve Miskish mountains.

The view from the gap was stunning. I was looking down over a valley at the village of Allihies – a few scattered houses and a huddled street – and out over a yellow strand, caught by the arm of Cod's Head, and out over the Kenmare River to the Iveragh peninsula; the whole lumpy spine of it, shaded blue and smoke-grey. And there was more, in this generous ocean; there were the tiny islands of the Bull, Cow and Calf, scattered out beyond Dursey and there were the distant islands of Scarrif and Deenish and more distant still, the outlines of the Skellig Rocks looking like thin, sharp ghosts on the horizon.

I was lucky. On a cloudy day or a rainy day, I wouldn't even have seen as far as Allihies. It was glorious. No camera would ever have captured it. It was too sprawling and huge to fit into a photograph; the landscape had so much depth and distance to it. To see it properly, you had to see it yourself. I sat on a ditch at the gap and ate my way through the rest of the sandwich-stack.

When I'd recovered from the visual shock of the view from the gap, I set off again, to walk down towards the huddle that was Allihies.

About a mile from Allihies, a man who had obviously seen me walking down the road, jumped out from over a wall. His black and white sheepdog jumped out after him.

The first thing Padraig – for he later told me his name – said to me was, "What do you think of Mary Robinson?"

I was startled. Mary Robinson, ensconced by now in Áras an Uachtaráin in Dublin's Phoenix Park, seemed a world apart from tiny Allihies, way out the Beara peninsula.

"We all voted for her down here," Padraig told me. "We think she's a grand woman."

"Yes, wasn't it wonderful," I said, finding my tongue.

"And where are you from yourself?" he asked.

"Clare," I said this time.

"Clare." Padraig said the name slowly. "Clare. Is that a nice country now?"

A nice country? Again, I was startled. I hadn't heard properly, I told myself. "It's a grand place."

"This is my farm," Padraig told me. "Up there's my house." He indicated a small farmhouse a few fields away. "Are your people farmers?"

"No."

"That's a pity now. Will you be long in Allihies?"

"I'm not sure."

"Well," he said cheerfully, "I'll probably see you later on in the pub." He whistled to his dog and they both disappeared over the wall again.

Further down the road, a small, bent old man walked steadily in my direction. He was carrying a bundle of driftwood, tied together and slung over his back. He looked straight ahead of him and kept walking on, ignoring me completely. When he had drawn alongside me, he said sharply, "Where are you from?"

"Clare, " I found myself repeating.

"Huh," was the reply. He kept walking on. When I looked around a minute later, he had completely vanished. Swift appearances and disappearances seemed to be an Allihies peculiarity.

Allihies village, on the hump of a small hill, had one grocery cum general store and two pubs. I asked in the shop if there was anywhere to stay for the night. A customer in the shop told me her name was Deirdre and that she'd come down from Dublin three years ago to live here.

"The drop in income is almost crippling, but I have all this," and she waved her hand out towards the ocean.

Deirdre pointed to a house down the end of the village, back the way I had already come and suggested I try there.

Veronica O'Sullivan told me she did not usually do B & B at this time of the year, but wouldn't see me stuck. I left my rucksack in the hall and went out for a walk.

The Allihies area was once rich in copper mines. The mines are all worked out now, but the mine-shafts remain. I followed an old green road up to the mines. On this side of Slieve Miskish, the small fields seemed lusher and greener than on the Castletownbere side of the mountains. Islanded between straggling stone walls, they looked jewel-like. There were signs at intervals along the green road.

Caution
Old Mine Shafts In This Area

I investigated some of the old mine-shafts and instantly regretted it. The deep shafts were full of rubbish. I sat, high up the green road, with my back to the rubbish dump and looked out over the valley. It had been a clear day and the evening sunlight cast a burnished orange glow across the fields. The stone poked up through the fields like bones. It was a strange place. If I had been told there were fairy creatures in this area, I would have believed it. The place was humming with strangeness.

Back in O'Sullivan's, having tea in front of the fire and feeling a bit strange myself, Veronica said, "Wasn't it fantastic about Mary Robinson!"

"Why is everyone talking about Mary Robinson?" I asked, puzzled.

Veronica told me proudly that Mary Robinson had actually started her Presidential campaign in Allihies. "Right down here, in tiny little Allihies. This is where it all began."

Allihies people brought up Mary Robinson in every conversation I had in Allihies. I got the impression that they felt personally responsible for putting her into Áras an Uachtaráin.

"Well, it's a real coincidence," Veronica told me, "but there's someone else staying here tonight as well! This man was actually booked in here a month ago, but my son took the message and I forgot about it until he turned up. He's walking around too, like you."

John Westley and I adjourned to the Lighthouse Pub for the evening. John was the tallest, thinnest person I had ever seen. He looked like he might break if you hit him, but he was much, much tougher than he looked. John was English. He had set off walking from London on 5 August and was going to walk the entire coastline of the British Isles to raise money for Multiple Sclerosis. He reckoned it would take him until October of 1991. At Holyhead, he had taken the boat across to Dublin and when he'd walked the Irish coastline, he would cross the Irish Sea again and continue on up through Wales. It would be a nine-thousand mile walk.

I was dazzled. It was an extraordinary undertaking. John had got coverage from the British Press, sponsorship from Royal Mail and had a back-up team in England, who kept in touch with him and phoned ahead to book him places to stay.

"Mostly, when they hear why I'm doing it, they let me stay for free."

He hoped to raise a quarter of a million pounds by journey's end. In the four months since he'd been walking, he had worn out three pairs of boots. John's boots were Scarpa walking boots, the same boots I was wearing. I'd had mine for two years. I tucked them under the bench, feeling positively lazy.

I was keen to know what sort of rain gear he was using.

"I tried out all sorts of things and all of them let in water after a while. So I went back to what I'd had originally. I used to work for Royal Mail, so I have a Royal Mail jacket and it's the business."

John never stayed anywhere longer than a night. He was walking the most isolated roads; all the tiny roads that trickled out to the furthest reaches of the land – this was John's route. He often slept out, since such a route did not always mean he could make it to a settlement.

"People are always stopping and offering me lifts, but I'd never accept a lift. I'd feel awful if I cheated."

"What on earth are you going to do when you finish?"

He laughed. "Well, it's only been four months, but I can see already it'd be a bit difficult to go back to Royal Mail! I'll have to write a book about it."

"But what made you want to do this?"

"One of my relations has Multiple Sclerosis. I wanted to try and do something to help and I'd always wanted to see a bit of the country and the two things just merged."

"Did you do lots of training?"

He laughed again. "Well, no. I just set off. My knees get pretty sore every now and then, but my feet are fine."

John made it all sound like falling off a wall. He was genuinely embarrassed when I expressed my admiration for what he was doing.

"You can do anything if you want to do it enough," he said simply.

Someone tapped me on the shoulder. It was Padraig, who introduced me to Timmy, his friend. I hardly recognized Padraig. He was all dressed up in a suit.

John left to go off and write up his diary. I stayed on, talking to Padraig and Timmy.

"Where are all the Allihies women?" I joked, since I was the only woman in the bar, as was usual.

"Oh, the ladies only come out at the weekends," I was told.

In the course of the conversation, Padraig told me that he wasn't married. I remembered the proud way he had said to me, "This is my farm" and "Up there's my house". I tried to be as tactful as possible, but there was no tactful way to ask this question.

"What will you do with your farm?"

Padraig looked stricken. "I have a nephew in England," he told me. "I'll hand the farm on to him and he'll come home."

I felt bleak. I couldn't believe the English nephew would want to run a farm on the edge of the Beara peninsula. Maybe I was wrong. I hoped I was.

Padraig and Timmy asked where I'd come from. I told them I was hitching around the coast. They both nodded their heads.

"Travel is a grand thing for some," Timmy said.

"And do you do any bit of travelling yourself?" I asked.

"I was never in Dublin, but I was in Cork once," Timmy answered.

I looked at him in disbelief. But he looked back at me solemnly, obviously puzzled by the expression on my face.

"Sure what would I be wanting in Dublin?" he said. "Isn't this where I live?"

It was such a sensible and honest answer that I suddenly felt immensely clumsy, asking these two men such silly questions.

Padraig looked at Timmy with interest. "You were in Cork once? I was never further than Bantry myself."

Never further than Bantry? I knew then that I had not misheard Padraig's remark earlier that day, "Clare? Is that a nice country?"

That detailed Michelin map, spread out on the floor of my London flat, may have made me feel that Ireland looked enormous but that night in Allihies, I felt a whole lifetime of exploration could never reveal the many unmapped countries hidden within Ireland.

Over breakfast next morning, I asked John if he'd seen anything unusual so far while he'd been walking around Ireland.

"Well, the most recent thing I saw was a few days ago, on the other side of the Beara peninsula. I was a couple of miles out of Trafrask and it was beginning to get dark.

And up beyond me, I could see all these sparks on the road and hear the sounds of voices.

"When I eventually caught up with it, I found a group of men on the road. Two of them were bowling and the rest of them were following. I asked one of them what was going on and he said they'd set off to bowl from Trafrask to Adrigole and that a man from each village was taking it in turns to bowl. Whoever could make it to Adrigole in the least number of throws was the winner.

"They told me that the steel bowl weighed twenty-eight pounds and that there was three grand riding on the game. And afterwards, I remembered I'd seen all these peculiar chalk marks on the road that day. Apparently, after each throw, they chalked the man's initial on the place in the road where the bowl had hit it."

I'd never heard such a story before. Afterwards, I was told that Cork was famous for such bowling games.

I set out walking along the road that wound its way along by the shores of Ballydonegan Bay. It was beautiful, empty, silent. The road was at the edge of steep land and literally a few yards from the sea itself. I soon lost sight of the Allihies valley. There were sheep sleeping peacefully in the road. Again, I felt a peculiar sense of timelessness about this area.

When I had long lost sight of Allihies, I heard a car coming out of the distance. It was a pick-up truck, driven by a young man whom I recognized from the Lighthouse the night before. I threw my rucksack into the back and climbed in to share the front seat with Aram's whippet, Layla.

"Christ, my head," Aram groaned. "You left last night when it was only starting."

There was a Buddha on the dashboard and a bottle of Lucozade in an old hot water urn from a Stanley cooker. Aram swigged away at the the Lucozade and his whippet whimpered, head on his knee.

Aram still felt ill. I left him in peace and looked out the window. He was taking a side road down to Kilcatherine Point, a couple of miles beyond Eyeries and so I got out at the turn off and walked on towards Ardgroom.

On the village street of Ardgroom, there was a tiny mint-green shop-front, with a little sign saying "Teas". The door was open. The only other sign of commercial activity in Ardgroom was Harrington's Grocery and Post Office combined. I continued down the street, bought a newspaper in Harrington's and then went back up to the little place that said "Teas".

Inside, it was dim and quiet, with a low ceiling. On the left of the shop was an old wooden counter with shelves on the wall behind it, neatly stacked with jars and tins. To the right, there were two tables, both with oilcloths. The table in front of the window was stacked with cardboard boxes of eggs and loaves of bread. The other table, the one I sat down at, was bare.

After a while, an elderly woman, with grey hair and glasses, put her head around the door that connected the shop with the house. She seemed surprised to see me sitting there.

"Are you all right, dear?" she said.

"I was wondering if I could have some tea?"

"Tea?" She looked baffled.

"The sign outside says 'Teas'," I explained.

"Oh that!" She laughed. "I forgot to take that down after the summer! But I'll make you a pot of tea anyway, and I have a fruit cake freshly baked, will that be all right?"

"That'd be lovely."

Mary O'Sullivan brought out the tea and then went back to having her lunch in the kitchen beyond. She left the door open and we called across to each other at intervals.

"Have you enough of everything out there?"

"Yes, it's lovely, thank you."

The walls of the little shop were covered in religious pictures. Most of them were of the Sacred Heart. But there was one secular picture. It was a photograph of a woman who looked like Mary and she was holding a lace-making frame.

"Is this of yourself?" I called.

Mary came out to see what I was talking about. "No,

that's not me, that's my sister Sheila. She's a great one for the lace-making. She's in hospital for tests at the moment and it's lonely here without her. But if you're interested, I could show you her frame?"

Mary went upstairs and came back down with a home-made wooden frame, in which a piece of net was being worked on.

"She does it for a hobby and sells them in the summer," Mary told me. "It's a pity she's not here to tell you about it herself. Would you like to see some of her little bits?"

I said I'd love to.

Sheila's little bits of hand-worked lace were kept in an old cardboard chocolate box. There were glass mats and collars and cuffs and handkerchiefs. I picked out one piece; a circular piece about six inches in diameter. It had a fuchsia pattern worked onto it.

"How much is this piece?" I asked longingly.

"Four pounds."

"*Four pounds?*" I was incredulous.

"Is that too dear?" she said anxiously.

"Well, I don't know too much about it, but it seems half-nothing to me," I said frankly. "If you really mean four pounds, I'd love to buy it, but you should put your prices up for next summer."

"Well, it's not really fair to make people pay too much for them," she said. "The Kenmare Lace Shop in Kenmare now, I find their prices high!"

"But it's hand-work," I said. "It takes time, doesn't it?"

She looked down at the piece still in the wooden frame. "I suppose it does, but she enjoys doing it and it's only a hobby."

Sheila O'Sullivan had been taught the craft of lace-making as a girl by her grand aunt. Her grand aunt in turn had learned it from the nuns in her convent school. So far, Sheila herself had not passed the craft on to anyone, because, Mary told me, nobody was really interested in learning in the area.

The piece of fuchsia lace was wrapped up in greaseproof paper and put into a brown paper bag. Mary wrote their address on the back of the bag.

"That's in case there's anything you'd like made. People sometimes ask her to make special things for them."

I continued walking along the road that would take me to Kenmare. A few miles beyond Ardgroom, the county boundary for Cork ends. The Beara peninsula is divided between Kerry and Cork; a division formed by the natural boundary of the Caha mountains. The landscape gradually became somehow less extravagantly peculiar. The closer I walked towards Kenmare, the more the day lost that odd sense of timelessness.

Roger, a Corkman, brought me the rest of the way to Kenmare, stopping off along the way at factories and hotels to pick up dirty overalls, sheets and towels and to deliver fresh ones.

I spent two nights in Kenmare, in the lovely independent Fáilte Hostel. Outside, it was snowing. Inside, I wrote up my diary in a kitchen that was beautifully warm from an old Aga cooker that was kept going all the time. I had a room to myself. It was clean. It was warm. I slept for uninterrupted hours while the mountains disappeared under heavy falls of snow.

I knew the semicircle of towns and villages from Killorglin to Kenmare well. This was old holiday stomping ground for me. Kenmare was where we went from Bunavalla, near Caherdaniel, for a day out; to investigate the craft shops and bookshops; to stop for coffee in Mickey Ned's; to buy a new jersey every year in the labyrinthine Quill's Woollen Mills. Both the jerseys I was wearing were Quill's jerseys from Kenmare; one my own, one I had pinched from my eldest brother, Arthur.

In early years, at the end of the day out to Kenmare, we had all got into the car and driven back to the holiday chalet at Bunavalla. More recently still, I had hitched in and out to Kenmare for the day from the cottage I had rented at the foot of Eagle's Hill near Staigue Fort. It was peculiar to be in Kenmare at this time of the year. I wandered about for those two days, not driving or hitching anywhere at the end of the day and feeling like a left-over tourist from the summer.

When I started hitching out of Kenmare, although the icy

roads and white mountain backdrop was a new dimension to this landscape long-familiar to me, I could feel the sense of journeying abandon me, mile by mile.

The stretch of road from Kenmare, through Blackwater Bridge and Tahilla, shadowed by the Macgillycuddy Reeks and dense forest, was trecherous. The black ice on the roads gleamed dully. The snow-level was creeping ever further down the mountain slopes and even the lowest levels were now almost entirely blanked out by white. The landscape shone. Even on the finest summer day, I had never seen this part of Kerry so clearly defined. The blue and grey coloured mountains, the lush hedgerows, the small fields, had all disappeared under snow, leaving only their shapes behind.

Sneem in winter looked even more picture-book like. The little salmon fish weather vane on the Protestant church swam against a background of white mountains. The white marble panda bear in South Square had grown another skin of snow. The abstract sculpture on the green looked like a piece of origami; the steel forms cold with snow. In North Square, the steel cypress tree shone bright as an icicle. And between the bridge and the church, the stone and stained glass pyramids created that summer looked like strange Celtic igloos.

I kept going. I was headed for Bunavalla, halfway down the Coomakista Pass. My nephew, whom I had not yet seen, was to be christened the next day in Caherdaniel Church and the entire family would be arriving that day.

I got a lift as far as the top of the Pass. The scenery here was incredibly beautiful. The slope of the mountain overlooked Derrynane Bay, the peninsula of Lamb's Head, the Kenmare River and the long limb of the Beara peninsula. It was a view I had first seen when I was a year old so that I could never remember not knowing what the view from Coomakista Pass looked like. When I looked down from the top of the Coomakista Pass, I did not only see a view, I saw a succession of childhood holidays. I knew this winding two-mile road to Bealtrá Harbour like the lines in the palms of my hand.

Here was the house I'd walked to each day to collect

243

milk. There was the rocky outcrop from which I'd fallen into a sea of nettles. This was where the shortcuts across the fields were. Here was the stream I tried jumping year after year until the magical time came when I was big enough to do it. There was where the collie dog had lived whom I'd pretended was mine each holidays. Down there was the stone we'd called the "Waiting Stone" where half the family waited for the other half to trail up from the beach. In that field had been a gate made from two pieces of crossed wood. I'd run into it one day and still had a two-inch scar on my right thigh from a nail that had been sticking out of the wood.

The landscape was thick with memories.

My brother David had loved this place so much he had come back to live. Now he was married and had his own family. Their door was open. I walked in and had my first glimpse of my nephew asleep in a Moses basket and the journey was left behind on the doorstep.

In such familiar territory, the Michelin map was redundant. I hid it in my rucksack and left off the second skin of Gore-Tex for the weekend. For the christening, I borrowed a dress from Anne, my sister-in-law, tights from my sister Caitríona and a coat from my mother.

The star of the weekend and the reason for us all being together was baby Cian, who smiled and laughed and gurgled through the christening and the party afterwards, as if he knew all this was in his honour.

The next day, with two carloads of family heading west around the Ring, I didn't even hitch out of Bunavalla. I sat into my father's car and got a lift beyond Waterville to the turn-off for Ballinskelligs.

I walked for most of that day; walked towards the bridge at Portmagee, along by Ballinskelligs and St Finian's Bay and Ballynahow. The hours of rhythmic walking mantraed me back into a feeling of journeying again.

At Knightstown next morning, emerging from the rambling Royal Pier hotel-turned-hostel, I went across the road to the little post office in search of pre-stamped envelopes.

The man who was standing behind the counter was

looking across at the Portmagee Channel through a telescope.

"Pre-stamped envelopes?" he echoed. "What on earth are they? You're the first customer I've had all morning," he said, hunting through drawers. "My wife, who's the postmistress, has gone to Cahersiveen to do some shopping and I'm in charge. Pre-stamped envelopes?"

He ended up tearing open a packet of Christmas cards, taking some of the envelopes out and stamping them.

While I wrote addresses and licked envelope flaps, he asked me the usual questions. "Last-place-I-worked-was-London," I rattled off, in between mouthfuls of gum.

"Worked there every winter for years myself," he said, going back to look through the telescope. "But at least I'm still here. My kids now, we have seven kids and four out of those seven are in Canada and the States. Isn't that a cruel lot from one family?

"And I have a friend who said to me one day, 'At least when we export our bullock, we get paid their freight and for the price of their meat, but when it comes to exporting our young people, they have to *pay* to leave the country.' And what are we left with? Airmail letters. That's all we're left with from our young people."

The letters I was posting were to friends across England, all of whom were coming back to Ireland for Christmas. The only times we all seemed to get together now were at Christmas parties, which went on for days in different locations around the country, as everyone tore about, trying to see as many people as possible.

The comment about emigrants having to pay to leave the country was only half the story. I knew from experience that for Christmas, it was almost impossible to get a reasonably-priced flight out of London to Ireland, even if you booked early in the year. It was always the same. With a captive Irish population in London, the airlines knew they could charge on average twice the price of an Apex flight – and get it, time and time again – because people wanted to come back for Christmas. You paid to leave the country, but you paid twice as much to come back to it.

Map 3   Dundalk to Waterford

246

11
DRIFTING
Dingle

I felt at home in Dingle. I had only intended to stay for a couple of nights, but I found myself staying on, day after day.

My first night, I stayed in the independent Seacrest Hostel at Lispole, because it was the only hostel on the peninsula with a washing machine and I'd heard on the grapevine that the launderette in Dingle town was closed for the winter.

I spent that night at Seacrest reading through the *Visitor's Journal*. It was the most interesting such journal I'd come across. Reading my way through all the different handwriting in the *Journal* was like reading a whole series of short stories; fragments of poetry and romanticism and confession. Dingle seemed to have charmed some extraordinary emotional reactions from people.

"The hills are magnificent and the animals meek."
Rob, USA
7 June 1990

"I arrived here several days ago... It was evening and the mist was at its thickest. I really thought I'd come to the end of the earth."
Kirsten, Berkeley, California
10 July 1990

"I'm quite sure that the hardest piece of work of putting down our thoughts has been to be sure of today's date... We are both just starting our lives after being imprisoned for 13 years in Germany. This country is a great deal further on our way home,

even if we haven't reached it yet. But maybe we may reach it never. Perhaps our home is the road itself."
Chris
11 July 1990

"here, even the rocks are magic."
Unsigned and undated.

"Went up to the mountain and cried. Don't go up there. You might find my sorrow."
S.H.
5 August 1990

"I have come to Ireland on a whim.
I had been in Asia for 18 months and wondered if I could ever find anything to match it.
I have sat in dirt-floored huts of stone in the Himalayas, eating boiled potatoes with Tibetan monks; felt the amazing power of the Dali Lama as he held my hand; travelled on the wind, lost in the swirling borderless realm of the Dreamtime with an Aboriginal Elder during a ritual of initiation; tracked tigers in the oldest rainforests of the world, looked them in the eyes.
Not only did I see my reflection, I saw life.
To Derek and Pauline (the hostel owners) I truly believe my stay here has allowed me an opportunity to break back into the mainstream at a safe pace."
Colin
14 November 1990

I waited for my washing to dry in the tumble-drier and found myself wondering about all these people. It was dark outside and I was alone in the hostel. Had Chris really been in prison, or did he mean he'd been a prisoner of Germany itself? What had S.H. been crying about? What sort of landscape lay beyond the darkened windows, where even the rocks were magic? Was Colin spinning yarns? I couldn't believe he had managed to intrude upon the sacred, secret Aboriginal ritual of initiation.

I looked in my diary. While I'd been watching the football match in Warrenpoint, Colin had been at Seacrest, writing this strange entry in loose, straggly letters with red biro. I hoped he was all right and that the mainstream had not proved too shocking and that he would have a good Christmas, but perhaps he had just been bored and whiled away the time by inventing a past. I'd never know. At any rate, the *Visitor's Journal* at Seacrest was an intriguing introduction to Dingle.

Dingle seemed to coax stories out of people. When I hitched from Lispole into Dingle town itself, I was given a lift by a man from "the other side of Anascaul". It was only a few miles into Dingle, but in the time it took to travel the distance, he told me that in 1941 he had gone to England and stayed there for forty-seven years, returning in 1988 with his wife.

"We wanted to come back home. And after all those years in England and eventually coming home, my wife has gone into Dingle hospital with cancer. I'm on my way to visit her now. Wasn't that a sad way for our retirement to end up?"

I'd been in Dingle for two days before I realised there was more than one street in the town. It was a place I discovered slowly; a place that allowed one to drift within it; a place that was constantly being redefined by the sea-mists. Sometimes, I could glimpse the mountains beyond the town, but for most of the time I was there, they remained mysterious; shawled in mist and blurred from view. There was a liquidity and a generosity to Dingle that kept me there for days, while a soft rain seeped through the town, feeling peaceful and absolutely happy.

The streets of Dingle were built on small hills and the shops on them undulated with bright blocks of colour. There were simple strings of coloured lights in the streets and one stone-faced gable wall had sprigs of holly stuck into its crevices of stone.

The Dingle shops were deceiving sort of shops. They looked as if they should be selling something particular, but turned out to be selling something that was completely at odds with what you had been led to believe from the outside.

John Currane's Drapery sold clothes, but also had rack

upon rack of magazines squirreled away inside. T. Galvin's Travel Agency on the Main Street looked as if it should be a pub. When I looked more closely, I saw that part of the building *was* a pub and that the travel agency carried out their business in the side that the old grocery had been on. Dick Mack's proved to be half pub, half shoeshop. A place that looked like a typical take-away turned out to be the post office, in which I counted a record-breaking sixteen mission boxes and one stuffed white hare. From outside, The Islandman looked like a smart resturant, with Venetian blinds and lots of dark-green paint, but inside, I found it to be a bookshop, cum coffee shop, with a bar at one side.

Even the Westlodge Hostel where I stayed was not what it seemed. Painted a dark red, with sloping walls and little windows, it looked a bit like a small barn from the outside.

John, Dan and Mike, three local men, were running the hostel for the winter. They were carrying out repairs and kept up a running commentary of good-natured banter to each other and to the hostellers.

"Rosita, d'you know what you're really sleeping in in this here *hostel*?"

"No?"

"A piggery! A piggery! This place used to be a piggery!"

The common room had an old coal stove which was kept going from midday on and which made the place beautifully warm and cosy. There was a specially-built round table, which was a natual gathering point.

John, Dan and Mike cursed extravagantly. They were putting up Christmas decorations the day I arrived and I laughed with them as lights resolutely failed to illuminate, the Christmas tree kept falling over and holly berries would not stay on their branches.

"Holly and tinsel!" they groaned. "Holly and tinsel!"

There were several people staying at the Westlodge. I know that we often went out together in the evenings and that almost every night after the pub we told our stories around the table and that someone played a tin whistle, someone else played a bodhrán, that one night they persuaded me to dance a wildly-impoverished Irish jig, and that we all sang, but when I look at the names in my notebook now, I cannot even recall what half of them looked like.

"Bev", "Monique", "Fabio". These names now stir no memory, although I know with certainty that I had long conversations with all three. Beside the name "Clarence", I had written "science fiction". *Science fiction?* I puzzled over my own scrappy notes, baffled. Then it came back to me.

Clarence was a German of indeterminate age, with a magnificent mane of long hair and a beard, whom I don't think was staying in the hostel, but who dropped by most nights. He told the stories that made us laugh the most and all of which have completely vanished from the sieve of memory. But I remembered why I wrote that note beside Clarence's name.

"Science fiction, Rosita! Life is science fiction!"

The lights flickered off one night and we were left with the red embers of the fire and Clarence's voice booming through the darkness, saying, "Science fiction! This is science fiction!"

There was an Australian called Rodney whom I went walking with and often shored up with in Dick Mack's, inhaling the smell of new leather and Guinness. Rodney had left behind a way of life.

"My girlfriend and I had been living together for two years and it was at the stage where we either married or separated." He told me that he was a scientist but that when he went back, he wanted to train as a cabinet-maker. "I want to use my hands. I want to make physical things."

When I asked him his age, he glared at me in deep distress and said, "That's one question I'll never answer!" and sank into such gloom that it took me the rest of the night to make him forget my unconscious blunder.

I couldn't help wondering why he was so upset. He couldn't have been very much older than me.

I remember that we all shared our food with Jenette, a French girl, who was waiting in Dingle for money to come through to a bank. There was an American called Chris, with a beard, who told me he'd been travelling "forever". There was a Canadian named Edward, who told me he lived on Moose Island in Lake Manitoba in Canada, from where he edited the local newspaper and had to constantly take to his boat to bring the copy to the mainland.

Curious, I later looked up Moose Island in the *Times Atlas*. It was the tiniest slit of yellow, even on the large-scale maps of the *Times Atlas*, and was lapped round by fictional-sounding places – Dancing Point, Drunken Point, Grindstone Point. *I know someone who lives there*, I thought, and wondered if Edward was back there by then, plying his boat from island to mainland and writing articles about a fictional-sounding place called "Dingle".

I was the only Irish person staying in the Westlodge. "Early Christmas holidays," I lied firmly by way of explanation. It was too long a story for the easy camaraderie around the table.

There were several craft shops in Dingle. I spent some time looking around one called Commodum. The woman who was running it told me that everything for sale in the shop, except the silver jewellery, was made locally. There was an entire range of craft-work in Commodum; hand-turned bowls, silk printed scarves, jerseys, paintings, pottery, carvings, etchings, lace, hanks of wool, stuffed toys, shawls. As well as these items, other shops sold hand-made furniture, leather goods, lamps and rugs – all also locally made.

The further distant the settlement, the more craft shops there seemed to be. When I thought about it, it suddenly made sense. It was another way of making a living; a modern-day return to the old cottage industries of the west of Ireland, where women had brought in extra money by knitting jerseys at home. It was a practical way of making a living; using hands and imagination to adapt to a financial survival in the remotest areas of Ireland. Such shops needed customers, of course, but I could see that in the summer, there would be enough tourists to buy up the work of the winter and then another cycle of industry would begin.

I spent my days in a curious sort of busy idleness, unable somehow to write a single line in my diary. Three of my favourite haunts – The Islandman, An Cafe Liteártha, Eirí na Gréine – all supplied newspapers. It was possible to let whole afternoons slip by, reading newspapers and browsing through books, drinking coffee and engaging in conversation with whoever happened to be sitting beside me.

In the evenings, there always seemed to be a session of traditional Irish music going on in at least two pubs. The vibrant beat of the bodhrán, the haunting lilt of the tin whistle and the strange soughing of the uilleann pipes seeped out into the streets and I found myself being charmed inside by the music. The musicians moved about from pub to pub and played different instruments each night. Sometimes, I found them in O'Flaherty's, sometimes in An Droichead. Sometimes they ended up in the hostel.

It was my first time to hear the uilleann pipes being played, reputedly the most difficult Irish instrument to master. Eoin Duignean, the piper, always stopped conversation while he played his strange music that seemed to shiver into it something of the dreeping mist and the vague mountains outside.

One evening, I went with Chris and Lawson, an Australian, to a disco at the Hillgrove Hotel, the floor almost collapsing under the combined weight of our thumping walking boots. Another evening, I went with Edward and David, an American, to a Christmas concert given by the local schoolchildren.

There was high excitement in the halla na mbraithe, where the concert was being held. Small children chased about, parents chased after them; there was a constant rustling of papers and squeals of recognition from the audience as the evening progressed.

"I'm sure it'll be great crack," I had assured Edward and David, who were dubious about the entertainment level of a school concert. "There's sure to be lots of traditional Irish music and dancing." That sold it for them.

The curtain went up to the strains of the senior choir singing *Wandering Star* and going on to sing, with great gusto, *Springtime in the Rockies* and *The Black Hills of Dakota*.

"Irish music?" they teased, greatly entertained.

One afternoon in The Islandman, when I'd been in

Dingle for perhaps three days, I struck up conversation with a local man about Fungi.

"Have you seen him?"

"Ah, I've seen him the odd time from a distance. They've made him into a real old racket. You'll probably see him yourself, but don't be expecting him to go jumping out of the water or anything like that."

Fungi the Dingle Dolphin, had been familiar to me as a name for some years. I knew vaguely that he seemed to have adopted Dingle as a place to live and that he had somehow turned into a tourist attraction.

On the Tourist Information stand outside Dingle's Super Valu Supermarket, I read some Fungi-facts.

He is an adult male Atlantic Bottlenosed dolphin, about 10 years old. He is totally wild and free; he catches his own fish and is self-sufficent in every way. He took up residence at the mouth of Dingle harbour as a young dolphin, possibly orphaned, in 1984. Since about 1986, he has actively sought the company of human beings.

There have been several other cases of solitary bottlenosed dolphins befriending human beings in recent years; most have moved on or been killed after a year or two. Fungi in Dingle is unique both for the length of time he has been here and for the variety and complexity of his interactions with people.

Fungi's presence permeated Dingle in all sorts of ways. There was an entire range of Fungi merchandise in the shops; t-shirts, notebooks, mugs, button badges, postcards, stickers and tea-towels. Long's Restaurant, down the road from the hostel, displayed a hanging sign with the name of the restaurant painted over a leaping dolphin. In the An Droichead, I saw a large painting of Fungi. I was told that in the Scellig Hotel, there was a mural of Fungi on one of the swimming pool walls. In the bookshops, I looked through whole books inspired by Fungi; Heathcote Williams' long illustrated poem, *Falling for a Dolphin*; and Ronnie Fitzgibbon's *The Dingle Dolphin*.

The Dingle people themselves, from what I could make out, treated the whole Fungi phenomenon with an offhand mixture of casual possession and bewilderment. Some people told me they'd never seen him. Others spoke of sighting him from their fishing boats, "but we have a job to do. We don't take any notice of him."

John or Dan or Mike told me why he had the awful name of Fungi.

"There's this man called Chris Courtney and he's the first one who really took notice of the dolphin. At the time the dolphin came into the harbour, Chris was trying to grow a beard. It was a scraggy old thing and his mates gave him the nickname "Fungi" because it was like his face was growing some sort of old fungus. And the name got passed onto the dolphin, because it was originally associated with Chris."

The morning after the exchange in The Islandman, I went to try and see Fungi for myself. There were fishing boats that would take you out into the harbour. Apparently, the dolphin often surfaced when he heard the sound of the engines. I didn't want to be brought out in a boat. I wanted to walk out along the harbour myself and see what I could see. I'd been told he was sometimes seen near the harbour mouth in the mornings and so I set off walking along the muddy track that led out of the town towards the harbour.

I walked along the wide scoop of Dingle Harbour, out past the Scellig Hotel, along the wet beach and slippery stones and glistening seaweed for a mile or so. All the time I was walking, I kept glancing over the water, but nothing disturbed its smooth surface, other than seagulls and the odd cormorant.

I reached the square Gothic tower of Hussey's Folly. The harbour narrowed beyond the ruined tower. I climbed the hill beyond the tower and looked out over the neck of water that funnelled out to sea. It was flat calm and absolutely empty-looking.

I stood there for some time, watching and waiting. I'd often heard it said that Fungi was half-tame; that he liked human company. *Perhaps*, I thought, staring out over the smooth water, *perhaps he knows the sound of the name he has been given*. There was nobody else in sight. I stood on the

255

hill in the soft mist and called out over the water.

"Fungi! Where are you?"

My voice was small and thin. I cupped my hands over my mouth and tried again.

"FUN–GI! WHERE ARE YOU?"

This time, the cry rang out clearly and as I lowered my hands, I saw, from the corner of my eye, a dorsal fin slicing quietly up out of the still water.

It was the closest thing to magic I've ever experienced, standing on that small green hill with a soft mist falling and calling up a dolphin from the sea. Possibly it had nothing at all to do with my voice, but that's the way it happened.

I don't know how long I sat at the end of a little pier that ran out into the water and watched as the dolphin played with a seal, an armspan away from me. The two sea creatures rolled underwater, poking up their heads at intervals to check that I was still there. They rolled and slooshed and arched their way through the clear water as I found myself unconsciously applauding and calling and crooning to them, completely oblivious by now to whether anyone could see me or not.

There was more. The dolphin swam as far up to me as he could, fixed me with an intent stare as if to say, "You mind you keep watching me," then swam several feet out to deeper water. The seal poked its glistening head out of the water, whiskers trembling, and watched the dolphin too.

The dolphin disappeared. Then he suddenly exploded out of the water in a perfect, flying arc, was gone, and then soared out of the water again and again, jumping higher and higher each time. I found myself laughing like someone gone mad. I was mad. I was delirious with joy.

When he had finished jumping, he glided back to the pier, rolled over on his back and looked up at me. I could almost hear him thinking, "Wasn't I great!" Outclassed, the seal had disappeared. I laughed again; the dolphin flicked his tail and went arching out steadily towards the open sea, until he disappeared from sight.

I did not return to the mouth of the harbour a second time. It was too joyous and extraordinary an experience to attempt to recreate.

Some days later, I was still wandering contentedly through the streets, putting sentences together in my head. The mist had risen off the small hills behind the hostel. That was a major event.

I came out of the post office one afternoon and saw a familiar figure standing on the opposite corner. *Caught.* It was my uncle, Art O'Beoláin, who lived in Ard na Caithne near Smerwick Harbour, further west out the peninsula. I knew then it must be Friday, because it was on Fridays that my uncle and aunt made the weekly journey into Dingle town to buy provisions. My aunt Maura drove up the street to collect Art, but by then, he had already seen me.

They were amazed I'd been in Dingle so long and had not contacted them. They wanted me to come out with them to Ard na Caithne there and then. I agreed to come out the next day and waved them off. I hardly ever saw these relations and it would have seemed incomprehensibly rude of me if I had said that this one time, I would prefer to stay all the time in the Dingle hostel.

Dingle suddenly stopped being a fluid place without fixed boundaries. Ireland shrank in size once more; a tiny place populated entirely by friends, relations and mutual acquaintances.

I heard a lot of talk about new marinas in Dingle and a planned interpretative centre to be built out near Dunquin and a new road and new hotels and lots, lots more beds for tourists. Interpretative centre? To interpret what? All you had to do was open your eyes and look at the landscape for yourself. Surely no one else could interpret it for you.

I closed my ears to the sounds of the planned invasion of extra tourists, of interpretative centres and new marinas. Where did you draw the line between tourism and greed? I hoped Dingle wouldn't reinterpret itself in the process of creating all these things. To me, that winter, it seemed perfect the way it was.

On the Saturday, I hitched a lift through Ventry and over Mount Eagle. The Blasket Islands lay off Slea Head; curiously diverse islands, oddly shaped, swelling up from the surface of the water.

"See that one?" the driver said to me, pointing to the most easterly island. "They call that one 'The Sleeping Giant'."

"Yes, I see!" It was amazing. The island looked exactly like a floating sea-giantess.

Tiny Dunquin Harbour, with its steep, winding road down to the sea, sea-stacks, clear green water and upturned curraghs, was beautiful and terrifying. I wound my way down to the sea at the bottom of the steep road and looked across at the Great Blasket, trying to imagine generations of islanders rowing their curraghs back and forth.

It was a rough day out at sea and the stern shelter of the harbour was almost forbidding; warning of the danger of the capricious whims of the sea. The sea in the Blasket Sound was like an animal, prowling bad-temperedly in and out, the waves growling and spitting up surf. There was an incredible power about the strength of the water sucking in and out of the tiny harbour. I found myself keeping well back from the water's edge.

This was the most westerly point in Europe. Beyond the sleeping giantess, at the other side of the Atlantic Ocean lay the landmass of North America; the horizon of which so many of the emigrants from this area had sank into, bringing with them a memory of this exact bit of coastline. How had the men and women who had emigrated described the place of their birth to their children in a time when there had been no cameras to record it? The landscape would have lived on inside their heads, but how could words alone pass it on?

I walked the rest of the way to Ard na Caithne, around by Clogher Head and through Ballyferriter. The power of the sea is inexhaustible. The variety of the harbours and inlets, cliffs, headlands, bays and beaches that the sea can create is astounding. The landscape kept changing every few yards; the light from the great, rushing clouds shone and faded, illuminated and darkened sea and land by turns. The land seemed to race towards the sea, sweeping high up against the sky in immense green waves.

I'd been out of London for months by then, but it was

still a shock to wake up in the morning, look out the window and be able to see so far. Cities make their own complicated patterns; intricate networks of roads, streets, canals, tubes, railways and bus-routes are tributaries it can take a lifetime to explore, so that you are continually extending the boundaries of your own particular city, but the *landscape* of a city slams to a stop at the house across the street.

My aunt Maura and I went out walking together the afternoon after I'd arrived. She wanted to get fresh eggs from Anne, their neighbour. Jimmy, another neighbour, came out to his front door to greet us. He was all dressed up.

"He's off to the Old Folks Party at the Dun an Óir Hotel," Maura whispered to me. "We went last year but we're not going this year."

At Anne's house, we collected the eggs and lingered on the doorstep a long time, talking.

"If you'd come by in an hour's time, you could have had fresh spring water too," Anne said. "The lads are up the fields."

"Oh, is the well going now?" Maura asked.

Anne told me that on their farm, they used vast quantities of water, which meant paying a hefty water-rates bill each year. "So we decided to get the diviners in to look for water on our own land. Three diviners from Glin. They were here for a week and then they found it, way down. We're going to keep on the main system for another year, till we see if our own water will hold out and then we'll go independent. It's beautiful clear water."

The diviners had left only the week before. I was wild with disappointment. I would have loved to watch them; to see the forked hazel suddenly tug itself towards the ground, responding to the presence of the water deep within the earth.

The next morning, my aunt and I again went walking. She came with me as far as the beach beyond Smerwick Harbour. The wide bay of the beach was a natural short cut across to Murreagh, from where I intended to hitch back into Dingle and then out over the Connor Pass. She gave me a bag that bulged with sandwiches, slabs of fruit cake and oranges and waved me off from the Smerwick end of the beach, shivering in the chill wind that had whipped up since we'd left the house. She stood there waving for a long time and then suddenly she was gone.

It was a long walk to a road of any sort and a longer walk still to the road that went into Dingle. The Brandon Mountain is a natural barrier between the eastern and western parts of the peninsula and once you go west of Dingle, it's back through Dingle you have to go once more, unless you hike the 951 metre Brandon Mountain.

I reached Dingle in the late afternoon. The person I'd got a lift from was going across the Connor Pass. The car whipped briskly past the Westlodge.

"I've changed my mind," I said suddenly. "I'm going to get out here after all."

When I walked into the hostel, Dan or John or Mike looked up and said, matter-of-factly, "Well Rosita, you're back to us so?"

In Dingle, I'd found a place I felt so at home in and so in tune with that I could have happily abandoned the idea of exploring the rest of the coastline, and just shored up there for the remainder of my time. But I was running out of time.

I stayed two more nights in Dingle and then I knew I would have to leave. I had a long-standing arrangement to meet someone in Dublin at the end of that week, a commitment to spend Christmas with my family, and an airline ticket paid for to Scotland for the New Year.

Perhaps it was just as well. It would have been entirely possible to stay on and stay on, in a sort of Rip van Winkle way, and then to wake up one day and wonder like Chris, how to "break back into the mainstream at a safe pace".

I walked out of Dingle, feeling unexpectedly bereft. *But I can always come back*, I thought. *I can always come back.*

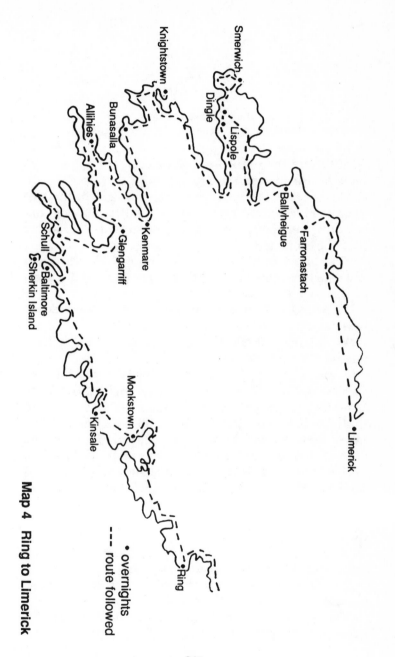

Smerwich

Knightstown

Dingle

Lispole

Allihies
Bunasalla

Kenmare

Ballyheigue

Farronastach

Schull
Baltimore
Sherkin Island

Glengarriff

Monkstown

Kinsale

Limerick

Ring

• overnights
--- route followed

Map 4   Ring to Limerick

261

12
A BOAT
Ballyheigue to Ennis

It was almost the end of my journeying. I stayed in Ballyheigue the night I left Dingle, in the Villa Nova guesthouse, where the Stack family were busy with Christmas preparations. Áine, the younger of the two daughters, sat concentratedly by the fire, making and colouring in paper cutouts of angels and Santa Clauses for their Christmas tree.

"Give an angel to the lady," Kathleen Stack urged and Áine shyly presented me with a paper angel and a short time later, a Santa Claus.

The Stacks were making an early start to Limerick the next morning, to do some Christmas shopping.

"We'll bring you to Limerick if you like," Brendan Stack offered. "It's a terrible day."

It was raining with the same ferocity of the rain the day on Árainn. The offer of a dry, swift passage to Limerick was tempting. I could even have been back in Ennis by nightfall. But the Michelin map tempted me more. Between Ballybunion and Ballylongford, on one of the "other roads" was marked the village of Lisselton and I knew that a mile or so from Lisselton, and unrecorded by the Michelin map, lay the townland of Farnastack.

"Could you take me part of the way?" I asked. "As far as the bridge over the Cashen?"

"And surely. It's on our way. But you won't come on into Limerick with us?" Brendan Stack asked, puzzled.

The village of Lisselton was hardly more than a couple of pubs and shops at a crossroads.

"Can you tell me which direction Farnastack is in?" I asked someone on the wet street.

"Up there, a couple of miles!" he shouted, pointing and running for shelter.

Farnastack was no more than a name to me. I had often heard my father mention it. I knew that there was land there which my great, great grandfather had bought and where the subsequent generations had built a house in which they'd lived. Shadowy relations about whom I knew almost nothing.

My grandfather had died of pneumonia two weeks before my father's birth. My grandparents had honeymooned in Cornwall; travelling around on an old motorbike which he drove, while my grandmother bounced along in the sidecar. I loved that story of their whacky honeymoon. Besides that, all I knew of my grandfather was one sepia photograph on the highest shelf in my father's study.

I'd often climbed up and taken down the photograph to stare at it in an attempt at some sort of recognition. But the photograph was of a very young man; his face still blank. He looked slightly puzzled; was looking sideways, beyond me to something else. By now, I'd grown to be older than the face of my grandfather; the photograph still on the highest shelf.

None of my grandparents were alive when I'd been born. I hadn't noticed for a long time that I was missing out on a generation. But now I was curious. I wanted to see Farnastack; to see at least the landscape my grandparents and great grandparents and great great grandparents would have had imprinted in their consciousness; to see the house whose name I'd somehow always known.

"You can't deny the history," Pat O'Brien had said to me on Inishbofin. "The desire to see where you came from." Pat had been Irish-American, travelling a long distance to see where his grandmother had come from. Thomas Keneally the Australian had travelled even further to explore something of the people and the country from where his grandparents had come. But Kerry was only the next county away from Clare. It was strange to have waited so long to seek out what was so near.

Tony Boland in Kinsale had told me the old house had

been empty for a couple of years, but I knew there were still Bolands living in the townland, although I had no recollection of ever meeting any of them.

"I'm looking for the Bolands," I bluffed at a house, when I judged myself to be about a mile out of Lisselton.

"Is it Dan Boland or Joe Boland you want?" the elderly woman asked.

"Dan Boland," I said wildly, grabbing at the first name I heard.

"Up that road. The bungalow on your left." She stood at the door and watched me go back down the path. "Where do you come from?" she called after me.

"From here," I called back to her. "I came from here."

It was wide, flat, wet country with scattered farms and high ditches and narrow roads that were hardly more than tracks.

I stood outside the door of Dan Boland's house and felt unsure suddenly. I hadn't a clue who any of these people inside were. It was still only ten o'clock in the morning. What was I going to say?

A man with a wry smile and sharp eyes opened the door while I was still wondering what I would say.

"I'm Joe Boland's daughter," I blurted out. "I was just passing and I thought I'd come and see the house at Farnastack."

It was Dan, my father's first cousin. He didn't seem at all surprised to see me. He brought me in, sat me down by the range and put a bottle of whiskey on the table.

"You'll have a drop of that before we go anywhere?" he asked, fetching glasses.

"It's a bit early," I hedged. "Tea's grand," I said, looking at the kettle on the range.

"Ah, you'll have a drop?"

"I only drink draught Guinness," I lied, thinking that was the one drink you could only get in a pub.

Dan ducked into another room and brought out some bottles of draught Guinness. "Now!" he said triumphantly.

Josephine, his daughter, came to my rescue with a cup of tea. Bernie, his son home from Chicago for six weeks, sat at the table and ate breakfast. None of them were the least fazed by my arrival. I told them what I'd been doing.

"Writing a book, is it?" Dan said. "You know my father, your great uncle Robert was a poet? He'd be up at the old house and he used to do more writing than farming. It was always full of people, the old house. They were all the time coming and going and telling stories and having dances. Ah, it's a pity he's gone. You'd have liked each other."

I'd read my great uncle's poems. He'd been a sort of Kavanaghesque bard, writing irreverent ballads and sonnets, with such titles as "Sonnet to a Lavatory", "Ode to a Cow Dung" and "Ode to a Spud", and letters in verse that he sent to Castleisland Court whenever he received a summons. He'd kept a diary in verse, recording local events, the doings of neighbours, the changing weather.

This morning, cobwebs hang around my brain;
Chunks, snow and ice, opaque each window pane.
The Arctic spreads her circle lower and lower.
With frozen teeth, she's biting to the core.
29 January 1954

"Bernie'll take you around Farnastack," Dan said. "He'll show you the old house and where Browne and Mageen's shop used to be, that Bob wrote a ballad about."

It was still pouring outside. I couldn't see a car anywhere. Bernie pointed to a tractor. "If I put a bale of straw in the trailer for you to sit on, will that be all right?"

"That'll be great." I climbed into the trailer carefully and settled down on the bale, holding tightly to the sides. Bernie started the tractor and we belted off down the lanes. Within minutes, I was soaked through, between the rain falling down and the puddles spraying up from the muddy track. The bale loosened a little under my weight and bits of straw lodged in my hair, in my mouth, in my clothes.

As the tractor rumbled on, I screeched with laughter at the absurdity of it all.

On the corner of a road in the wide, flat, wet townland of Farnastack, Bernie stopped the tractor. We climbed over a gate and stood looking at the stub of a gable wall near the corner of a field. This was all there was left of Browne and

265

Mageen's shop, where locals had gathered to gossip and talk, and of which my great uncle had written in 1934:

> *A neat little kitchen, with a shop there as cute,*
> *Hugged close in a corner like a telephone booth,*
> *Where she sold fags and matches, a choice of blend of teas,*
> *Soap, candles and pepper, and other sundries.*
>
> *In here was the Tryst where the long winter night*
> *Flew swift with the gusts of argument bright;*
> *Here conventions were flouted, as well might have been*
> *In this humble old cabin with Browne and Mageen.*

I paced about the space between the gable and drystone wall. It had been *here*. The shop had been *here*, the talk had been *here* and if I hadn't been told this and shown this ballad, it would have been no more to me than a heap of old stones in a field. Every family surely knew such places; these spaces in countless wet fields that were layered in stories like aural palimpsests; stories only families passed onto each other; unpublished poems that circulated only between family members.

"We'll go up to the old house now," Bernie shouted, above the noise of the tractor when I was back on the straw-bale once more.

We turned through an old gateway and clattered up a long, straight avenue. I couldn't see the house until we were actually in the yard, because it was protected by a wind-belt of trees. Farnastack House had been built in 1872. It was a long, one-storied house, with a slate roof and the original window sashes. The rooms, of which there were many, all had high ceilings and big windows. There was nothing left inside the house, except a few chairs and the fireplaces. It had a damp, dilapidated smell to it now, but I could see it must have been a fine house once.

I prowled about the house, opening doors of rooms that concertinaed into each other; rooms where my relations had been born and where they died. The place smelt of damp and ghosts. I peeled off some scraps of wallpaper and folded them carefully into my notebook.

"Come and look at the loft," Bernie said. We went out into the yard, where there were outbuildings and one huge stone barn-like building. I saw two pint glasses balancing on a wall at the side of the yard, with two bottles of Guinness beside them. The glasses were already swirling with rainwater.

"In here!" Dan shouted. He was in one of the outbuildings, plucking the Christmas turkey. The place was thick with feathers. He waved the turkey in my face. "Are you seeing things? Take her up now and show her the loft, Bernie, and I'll go and light a fire in the house. I brought down the Guinness you wouldn't drink earlier!" He laughed. I laughed. Bernie shifted uncomfortably from foot to foot. "Go on now!" Dan commanded and turned back to the turkey.

The barn – or stalls, with a loft above – had been built in 1874. Bernie told me that a hundred and fifty cattle had been housed beneath the loft. It seemed that hay had been stored in the loft early on in its history, but the gregarious nature of my Boland ancestors had dreamed up a more social use for the vast loft.

"They had dances here at weekends," Bernie said. "They had a licence to sell drink and all. The loft could hold five hundred people and they came from all over north Kerry. There were dances here off and on for nearly fifty years; until the late 1920s. This place was famous in its time."

We'd climbed the rickety wooden stairs to the loft, which was immense and empty; only a few hay-bales drifted up against the walls. Five hundred people dancing here! One hundred and fifty cows trying to sleep beneath! The floor of the loft – still original, Bernie assured me – now sagged. It looked threadbare. I wouldn't have entrusted even one dancing couple to it now, let alone five hundred people. We lingered close to the stairs, away from the sagging bits of floor. Dust and more dampness; more ghosts, more memories and more stories.

Will you dance with me? I wanted to ask Bernie. *Let's have Bolands dancing in this loft one more time.* But Bernie turned to go downstairs and the moment was lost.

There was smoke rising from one of the chimneys of the

267

house when we went outside again. Dan had lit a turf fire in the open hearth of the kitchen. He sat me down in a chair and handed me a bottle-opener, a glass and a bottle of Guinness.

"Stories!" he said. "This is the right place to be for stories. This kitchen here – this was where all the nights of story-telling went on. And you're here at last! So tell us what brings you here."

I opened the Guinness and tried to dry out in the thin, warm smoke of the fire. I told them stories of the things I'd seen and heard on my journey. I told them of my time in Allihies and about looking for Fungi in Dingle. Dan and Bernie laughed. The sound echoed peculiarly through the empty house.

Then Dan told me stories about the people who'd lived in the house. He'd lived in Farnastack all his life. He knew the house and landscape like the lines in his hands. The fire died down, the bottle was empty, I felt I should go.

There was one more story. "Travelling around the coast?" Dan mused. "Did you know that your grandfather built a boat; that he started building it out in that loft you've just seen and that it's still sailing on the Shannon Estuary to this day?"

"A boat?" I said, hardly able to believe it. "A boat?"

"A boat," he repeated firmly. "You mean you didn't know that?"

A boat, I thought. *He must have known the sea, then.* He must have loved water; been good with his hands. Perhaps he'd dreamed of sailing it around Ireland, never knowing he'd die so young. My grandfather built a boat and he started building it out in that loft. A boat built over seventy years ago, still sailing today.

Bernie drove me back to their own house. Dan had thrown the turkey to me and we drove back the muddy track, me holding onto the plucked turkey with one hand and clinging onto the side of the trailer with the other. *A boat*, I thought. *A boat.*

I collected my rucksack at the house and Bernie drove me down to Lisselton Cross. "Enjoy America," I said. "Thanks for driving me around." I gave him a hug; he smiled awkwardly, waved and rattled away in the direction of Farnastack.

I reached Limerick after dark. After the simple strings of coloured lights in the streets of Dingle, the clotted bulbs of colour, of endless tinsel, illuminated stars, bells, holly wreaths and Christmas stockings suspended above the streets of Limerick, looked clumsy and top-heavy.

Dazedly, I wandered through the shops. Piped Christmas carols were playing everywhere. *The Little Drummer Boy* blared through Penneys. O'Mahony's resounded to *Away in a Manger*. Roches Stores blasted out *Good King Wenceslas*. Outside Todds, there were carol singers singing *Feed the World*. Inside, *Jingle Bells* played cease-lessly.

I wandered around Todds, with *Jingle Bells* blaring through my head; a newly-purchased newspaper stuck under my jacket to protect it from the rain. The endless carols and lack of food made me feel light-headed and dull, but I gradually became aware of something peculiar.

A store detective was trailing me through the shop, muttering something into a walkie-talkie and eyeing the bulge beneath my jacket. I caught a glimpse of myself in a mirror and laughed. No wonder the store detective was following me. I was covered in Farnastack mud and the traces of Kerry rain. There was still straw in my hair, which stuck out wildly in a great, wind-tossed mess.

"Merry Christmas," I said to the store detective on my way out, waving the newspaper at him.

In the An Óige hostel in Pery Square, I threw half my clothes into the dustbin. Old when I'd started out, the constant wear and the ruthless briskness of various tumble-driers had finished them off. I was so distracted I'd forgotten to do any shopping for dinner. It was still drumming down rain outside and I didn't feel like going out again.

I emptied the contents of my rucksack onto the floor. There, among the flotsam and jetsam of objects at the bottom of my rucksack, was the packet of wholegrain Mixed Veg Savoury Rice I'd bought months ago in Ballyvaughan. Pleased by the symmetry of this, I ate the rice for supper.

I had originally thought I would try and hitch across south-west Clare, but to do this from Limerick would have meant branching off west from Clarecastle, which was only a couple of miles from Ennis; meant pretending base was still hours away. My heart wasn't in it. I didn't want to lengthen the journey for the sake of lengthening it.

Ennis it was. Next morning, I left all my cooking paraphernalia in the "Food for Everybody" shelf in the kitchen and struck out through Limerick. I quickly got a lift in a truck from Jim, on his way to Shannon to repair motor engines.

I stood at the side of the road for Ennis and wondered about my last lift. It was raining and I felt peculiarly at home by now at the side of the road, in the rain.

An old Renault pulled in up ahead. *This is it,* I thought. *The last lift of the journey.* I went to open the passenger door.

"Rosita! It *is* you!" The driver was about my age, with long, dark hair. She grinned at me. "Don't you remember me?"

I didn't. I hadn't a clue who she was.

"Rachel! Rachel MacDonald. And I knew who *you* were straight away."

Rachel and I had gone to preschool together, gone to each other's birthday parties as children and then gone our separate ways as we grew up and moved away. I tried to remember the last time I'd seen her, but could only come up with my ninth birthday party. I felt a bit aggrieved to be recognized so easily; it was not very flattering to think you hadn't changed your appearance since the age of nine.

Casting vanity into the back seat with my rucksack, I climbed in. I explained the reason for my rucksack.

"And you?" I asked. "Where are you these days?" A memory twanged as I asked this question. I hadn't seen some of my old schoolfriends for years, since we'd all left Ennis, but our parents were still there and so I had been kept more or less up to date on the movements of friends I'd long lost touch with.

Rachel, my mother had told me about the time of our Leaving Cert, wanted to be an undertaker. She assured me she'd heard it from Mrs MacDonald.

"Was it true?" I said, "that you wanted to be an undertaker?"

"Yes, of course," Rachel said, matter-of-factly. "But it's a family-run business. It's almost impossible to get in if you're an outsider and being a woman makes it even more difficult. I still want to be an undertaker."

"What did you do instead?"

"I did an embalming course at Manchester University. Now I'm working in the Friederich Alexander University in Erlangen, dissecting bodies. I'm working with this man on a book. He's writing it, I'm dissecting the bodies and he's taking the photographs. But I'm getting fed up of Germany. I might be going to Japan next year. Dissect Japanese bodies. I'm just back for Christmas, but I'd love to come back home for good – except there aren't a lot of jobs here."

"Will I put in the book that you'd like a job back in Ireland, dissecting or undertaking?"

She was immensely pleased. "Please do," she said, as Ennis came into view.

Rachel left me to the front gate. "Happy Christmas!" she called.

It was the twenty-first of December; the shortest day and the longest night of the year. At Newgrange, the morning light of the winter solstice would have illuminated the five-thousand-year-old burial chamber. It was the apex of winter.

From today on, the days would start to get longer.